Hartly Hou[se]

Sophia Goldborne

MANCHESTER
1824
Manchester University Press

Hartly House, Calcutta

Phebe Gibbes

Edited and with an Introduction by
Michael J. Franklin

Manchester University Press

Published by Manchester University Press
Altrincham Street, Manchester M1 7JA

www.manchesteruniversitypress.co.uk

British Library Cataloguing-in-Publication Data
A catalogue record for this book is available from the British Library

ISBN 978 1 5261 3437 0 paperback

First published by Oxford University Press, New Delhi 2006

This edition first published 2019

Typeset by
Servis Filmsetting Ltd, Stockport, Cheshire
Printed by Lightning Source

For Caroline

Contents

Acknowledgements

In preparing this edition I have used the printed materials and manuscript resources of the British Library; the National Library of Wales, Aberystwyth; the New York Public Library; the Beinecke Library at New Haven; and the library of Swansea University. I am pleased to acknowledge my gratitude to the helpful efficiency of the library staff at all these institutions. Lastly I must record my thanks to Jennie Batchelor, Isobel Grundy, Andrew Ashfield and David Hopkinson for communicating the fruits of their valuable research with kindness and good humour.

Note on the text

In the absence of any extant manuscript, the text of this edition is based upon the first edition of *Hartly House, Calcutta*, published by J. Dodsley, Pall-Mall, London in 1789 in three volumes octavo (BL 1425.b.16). A further edition, apparently pirated, appeared in Dublin in the same year, printed for William Jones, in a single volume, duodecimo. A German translation, entitled *Hartly haus, oder Schilderungen des häuslichen und gesellschaftlichen Lebens in Ostindien*, appeared in Leipzig in 1791. *Hartly House, Calcutta*, subtitled '*A Novel of the Days of Warren Hastings*' and edited by John Macfarlane, was reprinted in Calcutta by Thacker, Spink and Co. in 1908. It has also received three modern reprints, one in Calcutta (Gupta Press) in 1984; the second, edited by Monica Clough, from Pluto Press of London and Winchester, Mass., in the bicentennial year of 1989; and my own edition from OUP India in 2007.

The long 's' has been modernized, and a few running quotation marks in the left-hand margin have been eliminated. Obvious misprints and errors of spelling, many of which were possibly the result of the printer's difficulties with the author's handwriting, have been silently corrected, but contemporary spellings (such as 'chuse' or 'controul') and idiosyncrasies of grammar and punctuation have been retained for the sake of authenticity. Original spellings capable of confusing the modern reader have been noted. The variant spellings of the surname ('Goldborne', 'Goldborn', 'Goldsborne') present something of a problem. 'Goldsborne' appears most frequently and might thus be thought to represent the authorial intention. I have, however, preferred 'Goldborne' and used it throughout for two reasons: firstly this spelling appears first in the novel and in capitals (arguably, if similarly capitalized in the MS., least likely to be misread by a printer) in the subscriptions of the first and second letters; secondly, this spelling more clearly reveals the onomastic significance of the heroine's maiden name which the author develops.

Introduction

Phebe Gibbes: Life and writing

[T]his is the age of liberality, and my pencil shall bring its industry decent rewards; tambour, netting, embroidery I am perfectly mistress of; and, O insult me not so far as to call it degrading, to make use of the weapons with which God and nature has furnished me, to defend myself against the dæmon poverty.[1]

Thus the eponymous heroine Elfrida, in the face of her husband's having gambled away the family fortune, declares her proud but patient self-reliance. While it is obviously fruitless to speculate whether this heroine's creator suffered a similar reversal, it would seem undeniable that what amazed Elfrida's acquaintances: '"You work for your living and not for amusement!"', was for Phebe Gibbes, despite the 'liberality' of the age, a continuing and necessary reality. The products of her work can be charted across a period of more than three decades of novel-writing. The year 1764 saw her promising and in many respects remarkable debut; extraordinary industry led to the publication of two novels: *The Life and Adventures of Mr. Francis Clive* (for which she received five guineas),[2] and the epistolary *History of Lady Louisa Stroud, and the Honourable Miss Caroline Stretton*. Three years later two more of her novels appeared: *The Woman of Fashion: or, the History of Lady Diana Dormer* (1767); and *The History of Miss Pittborough* (1767), a 'virtuous novel, which chastity may read without a blush, and the most intelligent may peruse with improvement'.[3] Exceptionally, in 1769 Gibbs produced three novels: *The History of Miss Sommerville* (1769); *The Fruitless Repentance; or, the History of Miss Kitty Le Fever* (1769); and *The History of Miss Eliza Musgrove* (1769). The second of these Richardsonian works, she informs the Royal Literary Fund, was 'approved by Dr Goldsmith', and the third received a most sympathetic account from the *Critical Review*. Its reviewer detected a female hand which, if not 'equal in genius to [Charlotte] *Lennox*, [Frances Brooke] *Brookes* [sic] and [Sarah] *Scott*', had produced a novel 'which is upon the whole interesting and affecting'.[4] An intriguing range of novels follows, appearing at fairly regular intervals (there are gaps between 1770–1776 and 1779–1785), and *Hartly House, Calcutta* (1789), may well have been followed by two others in the 1790s.[5]

The last five years have seen a substantial increase in our knowledge of Phebe Gibbes and her family, thanks to the extensive archival research of David Hopkinson and Andrew Ashfield. The latter's labours in the London Metropolitan Archives confirmed that in all probability our author was the Phebe French born on 18 March 1736 to Martha and Anthony French of Peartree Lane, Shoreditch.[6] Hopkinson has established that Phebe French married Charles Gibbes of Towcester (1736-81) on 21 May 1761 at St Peter's, Kineton in south Warwickshire. The couple moved to London where four children were born in quick succession: Anthony, baptized in St George's Bloomsbury on 12 April 1762; Lucy, baptized at St James, Westminster on 24 June 1763; Alexander, also baptized at St James on 27 November 1764, who seems to have died as an infant; and Frances (born about 1766).[7] Her husband had inherited land in Warwickshire and Buckingham, but Phebe's claim that the family's fortunes had been adversely affected 'in consequence of the bad management of my Husband's father'[8] is substantiated by Hopkinson's discovery that her father-in-law, an attorney and money-lender Charles (1699–1779), was declared bankrupt (*London Gazette*, 21 July and 29 December 1759, 30 May and 22 August 1761).

Had Phebe Gibbes not applied to the Royal Literary Fund for financial support in the May of 1799 and the October of 1804, we should have known even less than the slender amount of biographical detail we currently possess. She claimed that she had published no fewer than 'twenty-two sets' of novels, some books for children, translations from the French, and articles for that powerful rival of *The Gentleman's Magazine, The London Magazine, or, Gentleman's Monthly Intelligencer*.[9]

Gibbes was doubtlessly proud of contributing to this major London monthly magazine, published by an influential and powerful syndicate of booksellers. In her letter of 19 October 1804 to the RLF she enclosed both an account 'of the Chief books I have written (Children Excepted)' and a list of 'Fugitive Pieces', amongst which appears: 'London Magazine three years the Benevolent Society'.[10] She was as good as her word; I have discovered that 'The Benevolent Society' was no figment of her imagination. In the April 1769 number of *The London Magazine; or, Gentleman's Intelligencer* she announced its formation, a society 'of feminine manufacture and feminine population', the indispensable qualification for membership being '*amiable sensibility of heart*'. Owing a little to 'Mrs Phoebe Crackenthorpe' of the *Female Tatler* (8 July 1709–31 March 1710) and more to Eliza Haywood's eponymous *Female Spectator* (April 1744–March 1746), 'The Benevolent Society', something of a feminist invasion of the augustly male *London Magazine*, ran for the best part of three years (April 1769–December 1771), introducing a greater authenticity to readers' 'genuine' letters and the Society's responses.[11] It is likely that Gibbes's sentimental magazine initiative was prompted by comparatively generous and regular payments at a time when tight margins and temporary slumps in book publishing made life difficult for even a prolific novelist.

Phebe Gibbes died at some time between 1805 and 8 May 1822[12] after having made a final attempt to lay to rest the spectre of 'the demon poverty' by 'writing a substantial study of the orders of the poor'.[13] Thus even the death of our author lacks explicit detail, but from the postmodern perspective summoned up by those words, the literary career of Phebe Gibbes presents a fascinating example of anonymous authorship.

In all her fourteen (or is it indeed 22?) novels, the author identifies herself once only, as 'Mrs. P. Gibbes', on the title-page of *The Niece; or, The History of Sukey Thornby* (1788). This situation was not exactly uncommon, for in that very year no fewer than 66 of the 80 novels listed in a recent bibliographical survey were published, like hers, anonymously.[14]

The reasons for such anonymity were many and various but, in her submission to the Royal Literary Fund, Gibbes claimed that her family rejected 'every species of Literature, except devotional'; such pressures, added to the fact that she was 'a domestic woman, and of a withdrawing Temper I never would be prevailed upon to put my name to any of my productions'.[15] In this way she presents a perfect example of the ways in which a female novelist's anonymity internalizes patriarchal demands for propriety and effacement.[16] The absence—in all but one instance—of her name from the title-pages of her works mirrors her effacement, and her authorship must be proved; with one letter she encloses an authenticating note from the publisher Joseph Johnson to verify that she had written *Elfrida; or, Paternal Ambition*.[17]

Her scrawled petitioning letters reveal that she was a widow with two daughters. She writes of her 'distress of losing an only son at Calcutta, for the advancement of whose flattering prospects, I narrowed my originally limited widow's provision, for he died, poor creature, before he was enabled to make me one transmittance'. The painstaking research of David Hopkinson at the India Office of the British Library has recently revealed that Phebe's eldest son, her key source of information, if not emolument, was in all probability an East India Company writer, named Anthony, who died on 1 May 1786.[18] This personal tragedy, amongst the few concrete facts about her life, resonates in the repeated concerns of her fiction. The theme of parental incompetence, marked by acquisitiveness, personal vanity, addiction to gambling, or inattention to female education, is frequently developed. While mercenary motives are invariably repudiated, the pursuit of property and wealth and a somewhat understandable desire for upward mobility complicate her novels of sensibility, grounding them in the realisms of materiality.[19]

India, in several novels, unsurprisingly represents a land of opportunity to make or recover fortunes. There one might 'gain a competency', acquire Nabob-like wealth, or at the very least, make some sound investments.[20] Looking poverty squarely in the face, the admirable Elfrida sells her finery and asks the upstanding young Wilmot (who has been commissioned to retrieve immense subcontinental treasure), to invest a hundred pounds of the proceeds from her silk gowns and jewels 'in such ventures as promise the best emoluments in India'.[21] But, as Sophia Goldborne, the heroine of *Hartly House*,

Calcutta, informs both her correspondent Arabella, and the intrud-
ing reader on the opening page—India, that 'mine of exhaustless
wealth' is also 'the grave of thousands'. It was the land from which the
author's son had never returned.

Despite their intrinsic interest, only three of Phebe Gibbes's novels
[*The Life and Adventures of Mr. Francis Clive* (1764); *The Fruitless
Repentance; or, the History of Miss Kitty Le Fever* (1769); and *Hartly
House, Calcutta* (1789)] have received any modern critical attention
whatsoever, purely on account of the fact that these are the only novels
which have received modern reprints. Isobel Grundy takes our author
as an exemplary case of scholarly neglect: 'Gibbes is creeping into
critical notice, but she is not likely to be rediscovered in the foreseea-
ble future except by those with access to a very good research library
indeed'.[22]

The Life and Adventures of Mr. Francis Clive has been the subject of an
intelligent reading by April London, who examines gender, genre, and
the pursuit of property by entrepreneurial females in this under-rated
novel, in which the reformation of both her husband and his virago
seducer is effected by a cross-dressing wife.[23] Addressing the same
text, Isobel Grundy herself has focused upon Gibbes's empathetic
treatment of the seduced maid, Hannah, who dies a long and ago-
nizing death from an apothecary's crude abortifacient. Gibbes 'uses
an episode of illicit pregnancy to protest the unequal condition of the
sexes [...] more than forty years before Wollstonecraft', anticipating the
social protest of novelists such as Mary Hays, Mary Robinson, Anna
Maria Bennett, and Mary Wollstonecraft herself.[24]

Such appreciation of Phebe Gibbes as ahead of her time was sadly
lacking when her novels appeared. The *Critical Review* characterized
The Life and Adventures of Mr. Francis Clive as 'judged by every reader
of sense or taste, to be execrable'.[25] Contemporary reviews were not all
so full of bile, and interestingly, the account of her other novel of 1764,
*The History of Lady Louisa Stroud, and the Honourable Miss Caroline
Stretton*, which immediately follows, and was most likely from the pen
of the same reviewer, grudgingly condescended that it possessed: 'a
recommendation, which is very uncommon in modern novels, we
mean, that the most cautious parent may trust it in the hands of a

child of either sex'.[26] The reviews were generally and predictably mixed, and few approached the largely enthusiastic response which Mary Wollstonecraft was to give to *Hartly House, Calcutta* in the *Analytical Review* twenty-five years later.[27] Throughout a quarter of a century of Gibbes's output, the majority of the reviewers faulted her grammar and damned her with faint praise. This account of *Elfrida* from the *English Review* may stand as a typical example:

> Though there are several interesting situations in this novel, and some very noble sentiments interspersed, it is altogether but an indifferent piece, being improbable in many places, unnatural in some, puerile in others and incorrect throughout. The first volume consists chiefly of the conversation of children; but as the situations between Elfrida and her two husbands is new, and prettily worked up, some little imperfections may be overlooked.[28]

If this reviewer found novelty in the author's handling of Elfrida's unintentional bigamy, we may also discern a keen sense of the topical as Gibbes strives to earn her living from her novel-writing. In a book published in the year Earl Cornwallis sailed for Calcutta as the new Governor-General, the plot—enlivened with native American ambushes and poisoned arrows—is concerned with both America, the empire he helped to lose, and India, the empire he helped to secure.[29] Eight years earlier, her *Friendship in a Nunnery; or, The American Fugitive* (1778) had reflected Gibbes's enthusiasm for the newly-independent America: land not only of the free, but of companionate marriage, uncorrupted manners, and boundless opportunity.[30] Whereas some readers might have praised such topicality, others poured scorn on her republican sympathies. While applauding its style and language, the *Critical Review* found its politics too inflammatory, declaring that the novel:

> would make a capital figure in the most conspicuous column of a republican print. The misfortune of it is, in our political novel, all this learning comes from a young lady who is 'turned of fourteen.' What may not be expected from the old men and sages of that happy continent, when its maidens, its babes and sucklings talk, and write, and reason thus![31]

William Enfield, the humane Unitarian minister and Warrington Academy tutor, whose historical and philosophical works were respected on both sides of the Atlantic, reacted differently in the *Monthly Review*, praising the topical relevance of the novel's stance on female education:

> The picture here exhibited of convent-manners is perhaps too deeply shaded; it is, however, marked with such peculiar traits as to shew the Author to have drawn from the life; and there is so much truth, as well as execution in the piece, that it merits some attention in an age, in which it is become too fashionable for females to receive the last finishing of their education in a convent.[32]

Apart from her concerns with education and the growth of sensibility, with gender politics and, what April London terms, 'confederacies of women', Gibbes maintained a life-long and sometimes experimental interest in the politics of genre. In this context, Enfield's remarks concerning her 'draw[ing] from the life' and the presence of 'so much truth [...] in the piece', highlight her efforts to balance elements of realism and romance in the novels produced by her well-practised pen. She began her career with two novels, one of which was written as a third-person narrative, conventionally associated with authorial authority, and the other in the epistolary form, developing a Richardsonian model, which facilitated the impression of immediacy in terms of inter-personal relationships. She continued to produce both more 'masculine' third-person narratives and novels in the epistolary form which was increasingly considered a 'feminine' genre, but her work in each is characterized by a concern for authenticity and a focus upon interiority. As early as 1764, the *Critical Review*'s critic was led by Gibbes's contrasting characterization of the two female correspondents to conjecture that the epistolary novel, *The History of Lady Louisa Stroud, and the Honourable Miss Caroline Stretton*, was 'the product of different pens'.[33] Her narratives of incident and narratives of character continued to complicate the generic mix of the novel. In 1788 *The Niece; or, The History of Sukey Thornby* demonstrated a streak of originality; Gibbes declared that her novel was 'written on a Plan *entirely new*, (to avoid the many repetitions of "*Said he*," or "*Said she*," which so frequently grate the ear) I have thrown the several incidents by way of Dialogue, and it would not be any impropriety if it were called

"*A Dramatic Novel.*'" Furthermore she claims that she is using the immediacy of this dramatic emphasis to further the novel's educative role; her preface continues:

> The chief business of Novel writing (the English, as likewise the French) has been for many years, with some few exceptions, to set *gallantry*, *dissimulation* and *amour* in a pleasing point of view, but the publication of the following sheets arises from a different motive. It is in order, immediately, to teach the innocent and unwary, to shun the toils of the designing, and give them a faithful picture of the fatal consequences of being ensnared; a motive which cannot fail to secure the work the candour of the public, however its imperfections may exclude it from approbation.[34]

Gibbes herself was well and truly 'ensnared', not like Elfrida in netting and the labours of the tambour, but in earning a meagre living by her pen. But, as she directed her heroes and heroines towards the safe havens of financial competence or prosperity, she retained, in the face of critical rebuffs, a certain ironizing humour about her 'spinning', a trait she had displayed from the outset:

> Thus have I conducted my hero through a variety of genuine scenes, to the summit of human felicity, and were I to spin this work to a longer continuance, I must have recourse to fiction.[35]

Representing India: Metahistory and the reception of *Hartly House, Calcutta*

Hartly House, Calcutta introduces further ironies to its author's jest concerning the necessity of having 'recourse to fiction'. As we have seen, although she must have gained a modest reward from the articles she submitted to the *London Magazine*, the periodical had proved of little assistance in her long and diurnal quest to earn an honest crust. Now, within weeks of the appearance of *Hartly House, Calcutta*, virtually the whole of the novel's lengthy Letter VI was reprinted, under the heading '*Picture of the Mode of living at* Calcutta. *In a letter from a* Lady *to her friend in* England', in *The Aberdeen Magazine* of 2 July 1789.[36] No mention was made of its being extracted from a novel, and it is highly unlikely that Phebe Gibbes ever received any remuneration for it.

This plagiarized use of a fictional epistolary chapter as a genuine letter from Bengal says much for the perceived authenticity of her account, not to mention the credibility of her heroine as a reliable 'Indian correspondent'. The fact that this epistolary novel, unlike those of Richardson or Rousseau, avoids the dialogic diversity of multiple voices, featuring only a single correspondent, lends the impression that these are 'genuine' letters from a monologic and authoritative source. An even more remarkable plagiarism of her representation of India was to follow.

The prestigious and widely read *The New Annual Register* (founded by the respected Dr Andrew Kippis, by whom William Godwin, the eminent philosopher and novelist, had been employed since 1784 to write the British and foreign history section), had 'recourse to fiction', and that fiction was Phebe Gibbes's. In the 'Principal Occurrences' section of *The New Annual Register*, under the most specific sub-heading of '7 June 1790', and following news items concerning the safe arrival of two of lieutenant Bligh's officers of the Bounty, and new military regulations of parity for 'king's and company officers in India', is to be found the following description of the retinue of Mubarak ud-Daula (1757/8–1793), Nawab Nazim of Bengal, Bihar, and Orissa:

> The procession of the nabob from Chitpore to Calcutta, in order to pay his compliments to earl Cornwallis, on his arrival in India, is worthy of description, as it gives an idea of the style of magnificence of eastern princes.
>
> Seven elephants of the first magnitude were led by their keepers, in like manner as our sumpter horses; seated on the back of one of which, on a throne of indescribable splendour, was the nabob, with a man behind him holding a superb fan, in the very act of collecting the breezes in his service.
>
> The throne was composed of gold, pearls, and brilliants; and the nabob's dress was worthy a sovereign: nor was ever animal more grandly caparisoned than the no less honoured than exulting animal on which he rode.
>
> His state palanquin followed. Four pillars of massy silver supported the top, which was actually encrusted with pearls and diamonds; and, instead of verandas, fine glass plates on every side, as well as the back and front, to shew his mightiness's person to the greatest advantage.
>
> Arrived at the entrance of the governor's house, down knelt the half-reasoning animal for his illustrious master to alight, who proceeded with an

immense retinue dressed all in new turbans and uniforms, to a breakfast that had been prepared for this princely guest.[37]

Such a princely plagiarism within the pages of such an august publication must be extremely rare, and one can only imagine the mixture of feelings with which Phebe Gibbes, after a quarter of a century of being accused of implausible fictions, must have reacted to her elevation to the news section of *The New Annual Register*. This incident raises many questions, all of which have a pronounced bearing upon our novel. The first must reflect the simple law of supply and demand—India information was comparatively hard to come by, and there was substantial public interest in such colourful intelligence. Readers were familiar with satirical descriptions of returned 'nabobs', but such a splendid picture of a real nawab, complete with elephants and resplendent in sparkling prose and plate-glass, was welcome indeed, contrasting as it did with the comparatively dry and monochrome news items which surrounded it.[38]

In larger terms we are led to think about hierarchies of discourses, and especially to consider the fictionality of the historical archive and the historicity of the fictional archive within the context of representations of India. In this way *Hartly House, Calcutta* can be seen as a species of eighteenth-century metahistory.[39] This fictive/historical epistolary novel, like others of Gibbes's narratives, was also extremely topical. But first, having considered this 1791 example of journalistic plagiarism, let us go back two years to consider the immediate reception of Gibbes's novel in 1789.

Hartly House, Calcutta was published as a three-decker novel by the most respectable firm of Dodsley of Pall Mall in foolscap octavo, priced at seven shillings and sixpence, and we know that it earned Gibbes twenty pounds from James Dodsley, and an appreciative review from Joseph Johnson's *Analytical Review*.[40] She had published her *Elfrida* with Johnson three years earlier, and it is probable that both he, and the critic assigned to review *Hartly House, Calcutta*, knew much more about Mrs Gibbes than we do. In fact, the reviewer, who was none other than Mary Wollstonecraft, might well have seen the career of this professional writer as casting something of a shadow over her own aspirations to earn her living by her pen.[41] Be that as it may, Wollstonecraft was an exacting and frequently severe critic, and the fact that she was pleased with the novel must have proved extremely encouraging to Gibbes. The review opened on a most positive note:

> An entertaining account of Calcutta, and the different inhabitants of the country, apparently sketched by a person who had been forcibly impressed by the scenes described. Probably the ground-work of the correspondence was actually written on the spot, in various humours, that naturally sink or raise the spirits; but afterwards touched up, and stretched out by introducing quotations from our English poets—a little too often perhaps.[42]

Wollstonecraft's recognition that these volumes might well contain eye-witness material and 'on the spot' reportage goes some way to explain why *The New Annual Register* journalist had chosen to plagiarize a key description. It is doubtful that Gibbes herself ever made the passage to India, and it is possible that Wollstonecraft knew that this novel drew upon eagerly-awaited letters from Calcutta, written by a son who was 'forcibly impressed' by what he had seen, but was fated never to return. Letters, of course, provided a link between the genre of travel-writing and that of the epistolary novel, between the comparative objectivity of the transmission of information and the construction of (what was often) female subjectivities. Wollstonecraft, like Gibbes, was interested in both.

Wollstonecraft, having made a small attack upon the language of the novel which cast a certain 'aspersion upon [Gibbes's] parts of speech' ('A few words and expressions, have an air of ignorance or affectation; indeed they are not English'), she continues to praise its handling of realistic and reflective moments:

> [T]he style is easy, and the reflections pertinent: particularly those which contrast an uninterrupted round of gaudy pleasures,—pleasures which are most apt to fascinate thoughtless minds, with the swift stroke of death, that sweeps without distinction all ages to the tomb, nor warns them by previous decay.

From Wollstonecraft, whose recent publications: *Thoughts on the Education of Daughters* (1787), the book of stories for children, *Original Stories from Real Life* (1788), and her anthology for women, *The Female*

Reader (1789), had embodied a sternly didactic note, praise for the educative and instructive aspects of these Calcutta letters would have delighted Gibbes. Furthermore, Wollstonecraft's review focuses upon Gibbes's success in achieving exactly what she had been attempting over many years—to mingle the imaginative and the informative in the sugaring of the educative pill:

> These letters indeed are written with a degree of vivacity which renders them very amusing, even when they are merely descriptive, and the young reader will see, rather than listen to the instruction they contain. A short story ties the series together, and gives life to the animated account of Eastern manners, by awakening private interest, and displaying the affections of individuals, whose characters are distinguished, though not nicely discriminated.[43]

It was not only youthful readers who required information from Bengal and, in this respect, the critical reception of *Hartly House, Calcutta* reflected a large degree of unanimity. Its documentary accuracy was lauded by the *Critical Review*:

> We have been much pleased with these volumes; for, in the guise of a novel, they will convey much information. They contain a pleasing, and, we think, an accurate description of Bengal and its capital, Calcutta.[44]

William Enfield, who had praised Gibbes's attack upon convent education in *Friendship in a Nunnery; or, The American Fugitive*, found her representation of colonial life a reliable one: 'These volumes contain a lively and elegant, and, as far as we are informed, a just picture of the manners of the Europeans residing in the East Indies'.[45] In the same way, the critic of the *European Magazine* declared that Sophia's letters 'appear to represent a true picture of the municipal manners and customs which at present prevail among the European inhabitants of that great emporium of English emigration'.[46] Such an apparently mercantile and slighting description of the Fort William Presidency says much regarding the political stance of this review-writer. It also provides a stark contrast with the opinion of the *English Review*'s critic, who found her picture of metropolitan Calcutta a 'second-hand' and unreliable imposition upon the public:

> The work, indeed, seems to have no other object than that of representing our countrymen in that part of the world as mere triflers and insignificants,

the female sex as so many wax dolls, as prim as brittle, and imported for exposure in a market just as capricious; and life as an endless rotation of the same insipid, gaiety, satiety, and delirium, without business, and without decorum.[47]

This question of the accuracy or otherwise of Gibbes's representations of life in Calcutta is a most important one, touching as it does upon central and topical issues of fact, fiction, and faction concerning what exactly had been going on in Bengal. The *English Review*'s critic may be seen to be adopting the political line of a periodical founded and edited by John Murray whose twice-yearly shipments of books to Calcutta represented 'a substantial part of his retail business', and in whose interest it lay not to trivialize or impugn the servants of the East India Company.[48] On its launch in 1783, the very first article in the *English Review* had been a substantial review of Nathaniel Brassey Halhed's *Grammar of the Bengal Language* where the partisan reviewer praised the unappreciated labours of the Calcutta Orientalists.[49]

If we feel that this critic is being rather heavy-handed in his treatment of a novel of sensibility, it should be remembered that political sensitivities were running high and any publication bearing Calcutta in its title might be subject to unusually detailed scrutiny. While it may have suited critics of Hastings' regime to endorse even fictional representations as accurately reflecting the trifling hedonism of colonial fortune-hunters, such reductive treatment of colonial life would have greatly irritated the politicians, intellectuals, and lobbyists who formed the pro-Hastings 'Bengal Squad'.

Edward Said has argued that representations are necessarily subjective, politically and ideologically 'implicated', and certainly the reception of *Hartly House, Calcutta* was problematized by the ongoing debate concerning representations of British behaviour in India.[50] The supreme irony involved in the over-reaction of the *English Review*'s critic is that Phebe Gibbes was self-evidently on the same side. Her representation of India, set in the period from the last months of Hastings' government to the establishment of Cornwallis's, and published in the second year of his impeachment, was very much a political intervention on behalf of the former Governor-General. It is true that it failed to detail the research activities of the Asiatic Society of Bengal, as no doubt would have pleased the critic of the *English Review*, but that was not the business of a novel of sensibility. On the level of a more popular readership, Gibbes's novel did more than that: it clearly demonstrated that Hastings' Orientalist regime was characterized by an atmosphere of intellectual sympathy and racial tolerance.

'A Novel of the Days of Warren Hastings'

Of Warren Hastings, Governor and Governor-General of Bengal from 1772 to 1785, Dr Johnson had declared: 'It is new for a Governour of Bengal to patronise Learning'.[51] As we have seen, the paucity of reliable Indian intelligence might lead to periodical plagiarism, but in Bengal Hastings had realised that it was information, rather than military superiority, that enabled a comparative handful of Europeans to subdue and administer an entire subcontinent. Hastings introduced rigorously Orientalist government policies to ensure that British sovereignty was exercised in Indian ways, and to facilitate these policies he tapped all available sources of information. A wide spectrum of native experts and informants was patronized; pandits and *maulavis* were commissioned to compile law codes for use in the Supreme Court, and his patronage of works such as Francis Gladwin's translation of the *Ā'īn-i Akbarī* ['Institutes of Akbar'] (1783–86) provided valuable insights into Mughal statecraft and political theory.

Beyond the immediate exigencies of power, Hastings appreciated that the production and distribution of knowledge about India was inextricably connected with political patronage, he defined the role of the Orientalist state as mediator between the worlds of politics and scholarship. In his admiration for the *Bhagavadgītā*, which he viewed as 'almost unequalled in its sublimity of conception, reasoning, and diction; a work of wonderful fancy', and in his encouragement of Sir William Jones's foundation of the Asiatic Society (1784), Hastings demonstrated an openness towards Indian culture which was to prove groundbreaking.[52] He was concerned with reconciliation between 'the People of England' and 'the Natives of Hindostan' and what he was attempting to encompass at a level of political policy, Gibbes was illustrating at the level of the sentimental novel.[53]

Just three years before the publication of *Hartly House, Calcutta*, Sir William Jones's 'Third Anniversary Discourse to the Asiatick Society' (1786), with its epoch-making remarks on the refined nature of Sanskrit and its close familial relationship with the classical languages of Europe had radically adjusted pre-conceptions of Western cultural superiority, introducing disconcerting notions of relationship between the rulers and their 'black' subjects.[54] The openness of Gibbes's young heroine, Sophia Goldborne to Hindu culture, her fascination with Hinduism's apparent vindication of sensibility, and her determination to learn its fundamental tenets from a young Brahman pandit, are predicated upon the pluralism and enlightened tolerance of this brief Jonesian period of sympathetic and syncretic admiration for India.

Sir William Jones and the circle of Orientalists inspired by Hastings were maintaining that Hindu civilization had much to teach the West. Hastings was also one of the first Europeans to persuade members of the Brahmanical caste to act as interpreters and informants of their sacred laws. Gibbes capitalizes upon this situation by demonstrating that even a young and rather giddy novelistic heroine might prove anxious to pursue this educative light from the Orient. This, however, represents something more revolutionary than the creation of a female Orientalist manqué, or than a Christian being taught by a Hindu, for Gibbes daringly disturbs the ideologies of both race and gender by displaying a European woman cultivated by an Indian man. In this subversive manner the insights of early Indology are translated into an easily accessible discourse, that of the sentimental epistolary narrative, which could appeal to a larger novel-reading public.

From the time he arrived in Bengal in late September 1783, Jones had been communicating the revelation that was India at a variety of levels of discourse, from the official Anniversary Discourses to the Asiatic Society, research articles, and letters to influential friends at home, including Burke, Hastings, Joseph Banks, and his former pupil, Earl Spencer. Between 1784 and 1789 he had also been attempting to introduce the Hindu pantheon to a wider audience by writing a series of 'Hymns to Hindu Deities', published in both Calcutta and London. Driven by a desire to dignify and classicize a religion which many Western writers continued to condemn as a monstrous mythology,

Jones's hymns, utilizing the form of the Pindaric ode, Miltonic reso-
nances, and replete with unfamiliar names, were demanding reading.
By contrast, Gibbes's novel of sensibility introduces some of
the tenets of Hinduism in an easily assimilable form to the circulating library member through the infectious enthusiasm of Sophia
Goldborne, newly-taught by 'my Bramin', as she affectionately—if
appropriatingly—terms her pandit. This has a directness of effect
which is largely absent from the metaphysical magnificence of Jones's
hymns, and which is intensified through its being communicated via
the medium of 'private' correspondence. In some respects it closely
resembles Jones's own genuinely private communications in letters
written home to his former pupil, or to colleagues in Bengal. To his
friend Richard Johnson, for example, he enthused about Sanskrit literature with all the *bhakti* (loving devotion) of a devout Hindu:

> I am in love with the *Gopia*, charmed with *Crishen*, an enthusiastick admirer
> of *Râm*, and a devout adorer of *Brimha-bishen-mehais*: not to mention that
> *Jûdishteir*, *Arjen*, *Corno*, and the other warriours of the M'hab'harat appear
> greater in my eyes than Agamemnon, Ajax, and Achilles appeared, when I
> first read the Iliad.[55]

Sophia does not know the term *bhakti*, but her feelings, directed
by her Brahman preceptor, for this 'alien' religion, approach such
enthusiasm. Where Jones and many of his colleagues have been frequently seen as viewing Hinduism through the spectacles of European
deism, Sophia's young eyes clearly see that Hinduism is the religion
of sensibility:

> They live, Arabella, (except from the austerities, in some instances, in their
> religion) the most inoffensively and happily of all created beings—their
> Pythagorean tenets teaching them, from their earliest infancy, the lesson of
> kindness and benevolence; nor do they intentionally hurt any living thing:—
> from their temperance they derive health, and from the regulation of the
> passions, contentment; (p. 51)

While the romance-readers of the circulating libraries are learning of
the moral effects of metempsychosis, and indeed the positive benefits
of 'the regulation of the passions', such lessons are validated by the
spritualizing effect of Sophia's Orientalizing education. As we have

seen, Gibbes had little time for convent education; now she seems to share her heroine's belief in the superiority of Hindu precepts to those of Christianity, and *Hartly House, Calcutta* becomes a species of Orientalist *Erziehungsroman* (novel of education).[56] Sophia's desire 'to converse with beings of so superior an order, and to become an humble copy of their exemplary and beautiful simplicity' involves her in a somewhat unusual ambition for a novelistic heroine—for her soul to be admired:

> to please a Bramin I must have perfections of the mental sort, little inferior to the purity and benignity of angels:—in a word, my good dispositions would be cultivated and brought forward by such an acquaintance and my bad ones corrected; and, as celibacy is their engagement, the soul would be the only object of attachment and admiration. (p. 51)

I have stressed elsewhere the remarkable aspects of this Anglo-Indian encounter, fraught as it is with inter-cultural ramifications—in terms of gender, race, and indeed class—between this subcontinental Sophie and her Vedantic St. Preux.[57] Western stereotyping had feminized the 'Hindoo', in contrast with the perceived potential threat represented by the more potent masculinism of the (imperial Mughal) Muslim, but Gibbes artfully feminizes Hinduism to allow its attractions for her impressionable heroine almost imperceptibly to mingle with her emergent sexuality. This text subtly problematizes the conventional binaries of colonialist discourses, establishing a pro-to-Foucauldian triad of knowledge, power, and sexuality in the sexual politics of the relationship with her Brahman.[58] For Sophia, schooled in the precepts of Sensibility, Hinduism is 'the religion of humanity', 'delightful doctrine', the ultimate sentimental religion; its emphases upon the imaginative and the submissive fuel her intuitive under-standing that the 'sweet' religion of the Gentoos intertwines sexuality and divinity. In Letter XXIV Sophia reveals to her friend Arabella what she had learned of a love that transcends all divisions: 'For love, this young priest affirms, refines the sentiment, softens the sensibility, expands our natural virtues, [...] and unites all created beings in one great chain of affection and friendship' (p. 107). Her Brahman's linking of submission to the will of heaven with pious acknowledgement that

Sophia is 'the loveliest of women', causes him to retire 'with more emotion than quite accorded with his corrected temper, as if he felt he had said too much.' Within a very few epistolary pages she announces: 'I am become a convert to the Gentoo faith, and have my Bramin to instruct me *per diem*' (p. 115).

Gibbes can be seen to be playing with fire as Eastern male and Western female seem to be reversing the accustomed polarities of race and gender. Late eighteenth-century India saw many Company employees 'going native', and even such a morally 'upright', evangelical, and married figure as Sir John Shore, future governor-general of Bengal and founder of the British and Foreign Bible Society, took an Indian mistress. On another level, interracial companionate marriages such as those between Jones's friend, Colonel William Palmer, the Resident at Pune, and his Mughal wife Begum Faizh Baksh, or between Colonel James Kirkpatrick, Resident at Hyderabad, and Khair un-Nissa reflected a considerable degree of racial integration which would prove increasingly rare in the nineteenth century.[59] Any form of sexual relationship between a European woman and Indian man would have been unthinkable, even in the comparatively tolerant period ushered in by Hastings. And this fact demonstrates exactly how daring Gibbes was being, for at this juncture in the novel it would seem that only Sophia's (mistaken) belief that Brahmans were necessarily celibate avoided raising the spectre of miscegenation.

'So many wax dolls, as prim as brittle, and imported for exposure in a market just as capricious'

The critic of the *English Review*, as we have seen, impugned the accuracy of Gibbes's portrayal of colonial life in Calcutta, but perhaps we should consider the accuracy of his representation of the novel. Sophia Goldborne's determination to accompany her recently widowed father, the captain of an East Indiaman, on a passage to India is prompted by a mixture of filial devotion and romantic desire for adventure wholly appropriate for the heroine of a novel of Sensibility.[60] She is certainly not 'imported' into the Calcutta marriage-market, and her vow 'never to marry in Indostan' is made firmly to disassociate herself from with what was later to be termed 'the fishing fleet' (marriageable young women travelling to Bengal in search of wealthy husbands). The reviewer's use of the passive voice is somewhat at odds with Sophia's active energetic preparations for the voyage, occasioned by the opening of her father's pocket-book.

The idea of India was so closely associated with the making of fortunes that a certain mingling of mercenary with more imaginative motives would seem inevitable. It is foreshadowed in the onomastics of her surname, and, as if to clinch the point, she asks rhetorically: 'who has not heard of the all-creative power of gold, and the rapid movement of the wings of inclination?' Goldborne will prove a heroine who, if not born to wealth, will be borne in its pursuit by 'the wings of inclination'.[61] The novel fairly chinks with mohurs (the main gold coin of British India), and the bright alluring power of gold is certainly 'all-creative' of the heroine's more elaborate sexual fantasies.

Heroines, of course, were not heroes; double standards kept them on a shorter leash. It is, however, instructive to see how universally India was seen as a land of opportunity for spirited and well-connected young men. To become a writer, as the clerks of the East India Company were termed, did certainly not limit them to epistolary correspondence. In a letter of November 1790 to the editor of *The Western County Magazine*, entitled 'Asiatic Fortunes', which outlines the advice given to 'every youth of spirit, who has interest', and is thus capable of aspiring to a Company writership. Thus the youth's relations advise him:

> "See what a fortune Hastings has made; he only learnt ciphering and writing, like you, beside some Latin at Westminster school.—Look at Major Scott!— he hardly knew the multiplication table when he left Shrewsbury—now he is a Parliament man, and can speak about what he does not understand for a month together! Get money, my boy in the East, and you may be a Lord in the West." [...]
>
> He [the young EIC writer] arrives in India, and walking out into the streets of Calcutta, he cannot afford to ride; there he sees youths not much older than himself riding in state on fine horses, or carried about in sumptuous palanquins.

Home he comes to his banyan, and tells him what a figure his old acquaintances make.

"And what hinders you," replies his banyan, "from equaling them in splendour: I have money, here, take it."

Money is advanced—the youth has his horses, his coach, his palanquin, his haram; and while in pursuit of one fortune, spends three.

How is the banyan indemnified? Under the sanction of the young man, who is rising in the state, he rises likewise, as he is protected by him, in committing every oppression with impunity, the practice being so general as to afford him perfect security.

The youth, after a few years, less or more, accumulating a fortune in India, by every method of rapacity, returns to England, buys a borough seat, lives in splendour, and votes in favour of the oppressor and the peculator, because in doing that, he prudently imagines he is securing his own wealth.

This is the outline of the manner in which fortunes have been made in India for the last thirty years.[62]

It is interesting to note how this key relationship between a young writer and his 'banian' (an Indian broker, or indeed agent) is parodied, sentimentalized, intellectualized, sexualized, and spritualized by Sophia's relationship with her Brahman.[63] Although such paths to commercial success were hardly open to young women, Sophia, who has both youth and spirit, reveals that life in Bengal might be seen as liberating; on the streets of Calcutta it was not only young men who might be viewed 'riding in state on fine horses, or carried about in sumptuous palanquins'. Pointedly we are informed that 'stays are wholly unworn in the East' (p. 21), and that 'controul is not an article of matrimonial rule at Calcutta' (p. 31). According to Sophia, women in Calcutta are far from being 'wax dolls, as prim as brittle'; on the contrary they prove versatile heroines of Sensibility in their own self-representation:

The manners of the ladies at Calcutta are somewhat contradictory—now all softness and femininity, and now all courage and resolution. [...] They take a particular pleasure, on the one hand, in obliging and informing strangers— melt into tears at every tale of sorrow—and sweetly sympathize with those whose spirits are depressed; on the other hand, you behold them so little attentive to female decorum, and so fearless of danger, that a scarlet riding dress, which gives them most the appearance of the other sex, enraptures them—and, to drive a phaeton and pair with a vivacity, a *dégagement*, or whatever may be the proper epithet, to mark their skill and unconcern, in the midst of numberless spectators, is their delight; [...] I must add, that the ladies of gaiety and *ton* always make a point on these occasions, of having a gentleman companion, who lolls at his ease; the office of managing the reins, etc., etc., being wholly assumed by the lady (p. 41.)[64]

This apparent fearlessness, aided by scarlet cross-dressing, is partly predicated upon the subjection of others; as Felicity A. Nussbaum had convincingly argued: 'Indian men are the feminized binary against which Englishwomen can experiment with unorthodox femininity'.[65] The imaginative geographies of 'self' and 'other', like the binaries of race and gender, become more complex in a colonial context. The celebrated painter, William Hodges, had been struck by the apparent effeminacy of the costume of Indian men, but Phebe Gibbes demonstrates how the intercultural effects of such gender confusion might prove liberating for colonialist English ladies.[66] Furthermore, while elegant female drivers theatrically display their equipages and their cross-dressed selves along the Esplanade, in the Calcutta theatre, as Sophia is delighted to discover, the female roles are played by handsome male actors. Thus gender representation in the colony is confused and complicated by both feminized natives and the cross-dressing of 'the smart young fellows of Calcutta', who play 'the Patty and Miss Sycamore of the *Maid of the Mill*, the Rosetta and Lucinda of *Love in a Village*' (p. 69). The comparative rarity of unattached young ladies in Bengal focuses both their attractiveness and their empowerment. Even more importantly, the colonial space of Calcutta was in itself a stage upon which the performance of Sophia's gender and identity might be played:

You can have no notion of the *nonchalance* and *dégagement* with which I conducted myself through the day; but you will recollect, that women, who are accustomed to live with a multitude of men acquire a *modest* assurance (let me call it) private education cannot bestow. (p. 47)

India was seen by ambitious young men as a site of transformational social mobility, but Gibbes subtly suggests its potential to serve as a transgressive space for bourgeois young women. Sophia's favourite

term '*dégagement*' nicely encapsulates the sense of liberation attendant upon a perceived ability to transgress the confines of domestic
femininity if not traditional European gender boundaries.[67]

Economic factors also enhance the power of women in the colonial bazaar that was Calcutta. Sophia describes the lavish outlay of
Company wives at the 'Europe shops', where thirty or forty thousand
rupees (£3,600 or £4,800) might be spent in a morning's shopping
'for the decoration of their persons' (p. 31).[68] At the same time, the
extremely low costs of labour and of building both facilitated scores
of servants, and allowed the wives of handsomely salaried Company
employees to farm out their children to the superintendence of a
well-paid European governess in the rural retreat of a Garden Reach
bungalow (pp. 38–9).

Such opportunities for comparative independence and for liberation from the discourses of domesticity form an obvious contrast
not only with the condition of native women perceived as immured,
and prematurely aged by repeated pregnancies, but also with the
differing circumstances of *memsahibs* during the later period of the
Raj. Their condition has been described by Kumari Jayawardena as
a 'doubly-refined bondage—isolated in the home as a *woman* and
alienated in the colony as a *foreigner*'.[69] Sophia's bondage, 'being a
kind of state-prisoner, enfeebled and fettered by vertical suns', is not
gender-specific, and phaeton and palanquin continue to enhance her
performative *mobilité* for readers who detect little of the prim brittle-
ness of the wax doll.

'But I am getting upon political ground'

Our heroine's stated reluctance to enter into politics was clearly
not shared by Phebe Gibbes, and in itself may be seen to represent
something of a disingenuous pose. Sophia writes these words within
the context of a substantial plaudit to Warren Hastings, for by his
departure the Company will 'be deprived of a faithful and able servant;
the poor of a compassionate and generous friend; the genteel circles
of their best ornament; and Hartly House of a revered guest'. She
continues:

A more uniform good man, or so competent a judge of the advantages of the people, he will not leave behind him; nor possibly can a successor be transmitted of equal information and abilities. For, Arabella, he has made himself master of the Persian language, that key to the knowledge that ought to constitute the British conduct in India, or can truly advance the British interests. (p. 109)[70]

Such a powerful and indeed knowledgeable testimonial would do no harm to Hastings' cause, appearing as it did in the spring of 1789, in the second year of the impeachment proceedings. In the understanding it reveals of the connections between knowledge and power, the centrality of Persian as the language of diplomacy, and in its balancing of the personal and the political, of 'British conduct' and 'British interest' it could stand alongside the hundreds of testimonials which Hastings received from Company and government officials, from native merchants and Indian rulers. These were, of course, directed to Hastings' defence team and subsequently published only in weighty legal tomes such as the eleven volumes of *Minutes of the Evidence taken at the Trial of Warren Hastings Esquire* (1788–95); Gibbes's blazon of the former governor-general was fully accessible to circulating-library subscribers.

Hartly House, Calcutta was published in the spring of 1789 which had seen the bringing forward of the sixth article of impeachment concerning the presents received by Hastings. On the 21 April 1789, Burke nimbly dismissed the testimonials from India as either the forgeries of European or a species of 'mouth honour' for so wretched were the natives that 'they even bestowed *praises* upon their *undoers*'.[71] Passing from the revolutionary aspects of Hastings' 'merciless pillage and total subversion of the first houses of Asia', Burke warms to his theme of the pollutant and corruptive effect of bribery and peculation, 'vices which gender and spawn in dirt and are nursed in dunghills'. Hastings' appointment of Munni Begam as guardian to the young Nawab of Bengal, Mubarak ud-Daula, is excoriated as an egregious example of such corruption:

Here is such an arrangement as I believe never was heard of, a secluded woman in the place of a man of the world, a fantastic dancing girl in the place of a great magistrate, a Slave in the place of a woman of quality, a

Common prostitute made to superintend the education of a young prince, and a stepmother, a name of horror in all countries, made to supersede the natural mother from whose body the nabob had sprung.[72]

Such a representation, even before Burke furnishes the additional information that she 'kept the greatest gin-shop in all Asia', might have rendered Munni Begam a suitable candidate for fictional characterization.[73] Burke's narrative, in which he feared their 'Lordships might perhaps not find the same degree of entertainment' they had found in the proceedings of 1788, certainly demonstrates that impeachment, like novel-writing, utilized the discourses of high sentimentalism and the Gothic.[74] The ward of this 'slave, common prostitute, and dancing-girl', Mubarak ud-Daula, was actually to become, in Gibbes's narrative, Sophia's 'Nabob of Nabobs', and those readers with tastes sufficiently catholic to encompass both the novel of Sensibility and reports of the Hastings trial might compare the 'fictional' evocation of his magnificent retinue (either in the novel or *The New Annual Register*) with Burke's allegations that the Nawab had been impoverished by Hastings.[75]

It is an amusing fact that in many respects Mubarak ud-Daula is represented in contemporary Indian texts as a young prince who seems very much the Mughal man of feeling. In the *Sëir Mutaqharin* [*View of Modern Times*] (1789) of Ghulam Husain Khan Tabatabai (1727–1806), we are presented with a picture of the young nawab which almost provides an Asiatic and suitably sentimental counterpart to Sophia's sensibility. In this Persian history of India from the time of Aurangzeb down to 1781, which was translated and published in Calcutta in the same year as Gibbes's novel appeared in London, Ghulam Husain stresses the Nawab's civility and compassion, but his sensuality is censured:

Naturally tender-hearted, he listens with patience to those that are unfortunate or oppressed, and he is always disposed to relieve them. But his time is not well distributed; and he is always dissolved in all kinds of effeminating delices [voluptuous delights], and always immersed in the pleasures of the table, or in the company of dance-women.[76]

Ghulam Husain's own political agenda makes him anxious to point to a decline in the standards of Mughal kingship, a decline which has led to the *inqilab* (reversal of fortune, revolution) effected by the East India Company as they consolidated colonial hegemony in Eastern India. Sophia, of course, does not see things in quite this fashion. But another contemporary *nawabi* representation of her 'Nabob of Nabobs' strikes a remarkably similar note. This portrayal of Mubarak ud-Daula is to be found in the epistolary narrative, *The Travels of Dean Mahomet* (1794), the work of a former subaltern officer in the Bengal Army who emigrated to Ireland in 1784, embraced Protestantism, and married into the Anglo-Irish gentry. The narrative of this second-generation Company soldier reveals both the self-division of hybridity and a certain blend of fictionality and historicity as he attempts to elude his own subaltern status (in both Gramscian and Company terms) by representing his family as distantly related to the Nawabs of Bengal. Din Muhammad's portrayal of his near contemporary, Mubarak ud-Daula, is compounded of splendour and magnificence; like the fictional Sophia Goldborne, he is a dazzled onlooker of the Nawab's procession:

> They formed in the splendor and richness of their attire one of the most brilliant processions I ever beheld. The Nabob was carried on a beautiful pavillion, or meanah, by sixteen men, alternately, called by the natives, Baharas, who wore a red uniform: the refulgent canopy covered with tissue, and lined with embroidered scarlet velvet, trimmed with silver fringe, was supported by four pillars of massy silver, and resembled the form of a beautiful elbow chair, constructed in oval elegance; in which he sat cross-legged, leaning his back against a fine cushion, and his elbows on two more covered with scarlet velvet, wrought with flowers of gold (XI).[77]

A head-to-toe description of his personal adornments and sumptuous clothing follows which outshines Sophia's portrayal in its loving and sensual attention to elegance of style and minute detail of fabric, embellishment, and embroidery. This representation, in Saidian terms, is 'entwined' and 'interwoven' with the personal politics of Din Muhammad's self-representational agenda in desiring to borrow some of the reflected magnificence, apparent power, and 'unrivalled elegance' of this distant relation. Where Sophia experiences sensual 'throbs' in seeing 'the Nabob's eyes, sparkling with admiration, fixed on my face!', Muhammad's loving gaze is fixed on the Nawab's lips as they suck aromatic smoke from the diamond-studded golden mouth-piece of his hookah snake. For both observers there is an obvious sexual charge in their wide-eyed proximity to the appurtenances of power. Sophia is mesmerized by the attractions of the 'Other', experiencing an additional intertextual thrill at becoming, like Lady Mary Wortley Montagu in Constantinople, the object of an Eastern potentate's attention. The 'infinite pleasure' which this spectacle affords Muhammad has more to do with the mirroring attractions of similitude and the empowering self-identification of homoeroticism. As the English heroine or the Bengali subaltern are similarly capti-vated they stand alike 'upon political ground', the (sexual) political ground of their own self-representation. For this reason it matters little that Mubarak ud-Daula was described by the Company as 'Nominal' Nawab of Bengal, or that Hastings described him as 'a mere Pageant without the Shadow of Authority'.[78]

In the preface to his *Travels in India* (1793) William Hodges appears thoroughly confident of British public interest in the affairs of India: 'The intimate connexion which has so long subsisted between this country and the continent of India, naturally renders every Englishman deeply interested in all that relates to a quarter of the globe which has been the theatre of scenes highly important to this country'.[79] However, despite the parliamentary attention, successive India bills (the defeat of Fox's East India Bill in December 1783 precipitated a change of government and resulted in the premiership of William Pitt who produced an act to regulate the affairs of the Company in 1784), the recall of Warren Hastings, and the compulsive drama of the ongoing impeachment proceedings, India itself was a 'mere Pageant' for many in the metropolis.

Lacking detailed information concerning what Constantin-François Volney was to term 'the too famous peninsula of India', they might be influenced by the rhetoric of Burke or Sheridan, the economic reports of the East India Company, the self-justification of the 'Bengal Squad', or the plagiarism of *The New Annual Register*.[80] Where representa-tion necessarily involves mis-representation, fiction and history inevitably blur; representations of India were both extremely topical and highly contentious, and in this context the publication of *Hartly*

House, Calcutta may be seen as a timely political and commercial intervention.

'[I] became *orientalised* at all points'

Gibbes was no Orientalist, but she appears to have been the first writer to use the term 'orientalised', preceding the first cited *OED* usage by more than twenty years.[81] This fact is illustrative of the strong vein of topicality that can be identified in her writing. As we have seen, *Hartly House, Calcutta* reveals a considerable awareness both of Indian detail, and of the rationale behind Hastings' Orientalist regime. It certainly provides what is in many ways an accurate sociological picture of colonialist life in the Bengal of the 1780s which usefully complements the travel writing of Jemima Kindersley, the *Original Letters* of Eliza Fay, the *Memoirs* of William Hickey, and William Hodges' *Travels in India*.[82] Though her researches were not as detailed or intensive as those of Sydney Owenson (Lady Morgan) for her novel *The Missionary: An Indian Tale* (1811), it is clear that she used other sources than the treasured letters of her son.

There is an interesting relationship with plagiarism in the work of both these novelists of Sensibility. Owenson had earnestly worked her way through what must have been a most valuable 'Oriental Library' of her former lover, the Dublin barrister Sir Charles Ormsby.[83] Her scholarly fondness for footnotes ensured that many of her respected sources are partially acknowledged, but Owenson's plagiarism is particularly sophisticated. Unacknowledged borrowing, particularly from the writings of Sir William Jones, is used not simply to provide authentic 'costume' for her Kashmiri setting, but is expertly selected to provide her Brahman priestess heroine or the Kashmiri pandit with convincing Vedantic dialogue.[84] Gibbes's procedure is more straight-forward and less subtle. At first she declares that 'historical anecdotes are not compatible with either the taste or leisure of a fine lady at Bengal' (p. 17), but soon relents, arguing that 'it will cost me less labour to write the little it is necessary for you to read, than to refer you to the chapter and verse of those authors who have treated of this world of wonders' (p. 17). Her sources are much less varied and frequently much less expert than those of Owenson. She uses no scholarly footnotes, but to forestall any potential criticism, she cleverly writes this cautionary advice with the pen of her heroine:

> But my dear Arabella, I have one caution to give you, which is, not to set me down for a plagiarist, though you should even stumble upon the likeness, verbatim, of my descriptions of the Eastern world in print; or, at once presume to consider such printed accounts as other than honourable testimonies of my faithful relations: and certain it is, that true and genuine relations of objects and events admit of very little variation of language. This premised, I shall not doubt of informing or entertaining you (and perhaps both the one and the other) in repeated instances. (p. 78)

It is a bold stroke—to regard any verbatim 'printed accounts' as plagiarism of her letters; and, of course, there are rich ironies in the fact that this cunning excusatory tactic is actually validated, as we have seen, on at least two occasions when Gibbes herself was plagiarized.

In detecting the sources of Gibbes's Orientalist information a chain of plagiarism emerges. For Sophia's reflections upon the nature of 'Brumma', for example, Gibbes was drawing practically verbatim upon William Guthrie's extremely popular *A New Geographical, Historical, and Commercial Grammar* (1770), who himself had heavily plagiarized a much more authoritative source, namely *Reflections on the Government of Indostan* (1763), by Luke Scrafton, an Orientalist colleague of Clive.[85] Whatever this might reveal about the shortcomings of both scholarly (and predominantly male) historians and sentimental (and largely female) novelists, it is evident that such plagiarism was a symptom of the paucity of authentic information and a dependance upon relatively few reliable sources.

In the twenty-two years between the publication dates of Gibbes's and Owenson's novels, the researches of Jones and his Asiatic Society colleagues were to transform Western perceptions of the subcontinent and orientalize European Romanticism 'at all points'. In the summer of 1790, exactly a year after she had favourably noticed Gibbes's novel, Mary Wollstonecraft was enthusiastically reviewing another anonymous publication: the London edition of Sir William Jones's revolutionary contribution to Orientalism, his translation of *Kālidāsa's Śakuntalā*, which received only a Calcutta publication in 1789.[86] In the event, Wollstonecraft's praise proved only a faint anticipation of the rapturous response with which the text was to be greeted in continental drawing-rooms: the whole of Europe fell under its spell. Novalis lovingly addressed his fiancée as 'Sakontala', and Goethe, Schiller, and Herder rhapsodized about Sacontalá as the ideal of feminine beauty. The literature of Sensibility endorsed such male reactions to an Indian maiden,[87] but the priority and originality of Gibbes's contribution to cultural realignment must be recognized. It was with a doubly disturbing reversal both of gender and racial polarities that she allowed her sentimental heroine, bored with comparatively dull and callow young Company employees, first to fall in love with her 'black' Bengali Brahman tutor, and subsequently to overcome a certain prejudice against Islam, in becoming enamoured of the Nawab of Bengal.[88] Indeed Sophia's refreshing freedom from colour prejudice seems unassailable from the start. When, earlier in the novel, Sophia had generously thought of the Nawab as a suitable beau for Arabella, she wrote: 'He has, it is true, several wives already; but you shall be his wife of wives; and as for his copper complexion, you are too wise to make that an objection' (p. 40).

Sophia here may be seen as anticipating the epistolary reaction to 'sentimental' polygyny of the accomplished poet and essayist Anna Lætitia Barbauld. Writing to Mrs Beercroft, in September 1790, of her delight in reading Jones's translation of the *Śakuntalā*, Barbauld declares that 'the language of nature and the passions is of all countries', but, unlike the many male reviewers writing in the public sphere, this private female correspondence focuses firmly upon Dushmanta the hero, rather than the heroine Sacontalá:

> The hero of the piece is as delicate and tender a lover as any that can be met with in the pages of a modern romance; for I hope you can pardon him a little circumstance relative to the *costume* of the country, which is just hinted at in the poem: I mean the having a hundred wives besides the mistress of his heart.[89]

There are delightful ironies here, not least in that Jones's success as cultural translator seems predicated on the fact that a Hindu king is favourably judged by the measure of a popular sentimental novel. The playful emphasis in the letters of both fictional heroine and established woman of letters is marked by a comparable openness to the relativity of manners and sexual customs, whether those of a Mughal Nawab or a *Mahābhārata* King. Even more importantly the language of sentiment is seen to possess a certain universality available to both popular novelist and acclaimed Orientalist in their cultural translation.

It might well be that such a novel as *Hartly House, Calcutta*, with its revolutionary revision of the relationships of gender, race, and culture, could perhaps only have been contemplated in the brief Jonesian period of sympathetic and syncretic admiration for India termed by Raymond Schwab 'the Sacontala age', but it must be remembered that Gibbes's novel was no *Sacontalá* 'spin-off'.[90]

The education of Sophia is not complete, however. Her sexual fantasies of abduction and rape, colourfully featuring the Nawab's 'plans for carrying me off', may be indulged in the security that hedges a white English female in Fort William 'where an army would stand forth in her protection and defence'. The colonized female has no such defence, and the disturbing reality of imperial power is borne in upon Miss Goldborne with the brutal rape of a young Indian girl by a Company army officer who has shot her father dead before her eyes. Delighting in the attentions of red-coated officers, she had formerly believed that 'Mars in the East, like Hercules at the court of Omphale, has more gallantry than hostility about him' (p. 46). Now, as Felicity Nussbaum points out, 'The very army she expects to defend her against the nabob's abduction is [...] also the agent of sexual violence against an Indian woman'.[91] The colonial imagination gendered both territory and peoples as feminine spaces to be violated, controlled, and plundered, and the reader is sharply reminded of this fact through the steep learning curve to which Sophia's sentimentalism is subjected. The actualization of imperial subjugation and colonial rapaciousness in this horrific crime forces our heroine to view 'British India' in a different light, as 'a country where fiend-like acts are, I fear, much oftener perpetrated than detected' (p. 163).

Sympathy for the plight of this Indian girl introduces Sophia to the heights and depths of a more genuinely empathetic sensibility—'I am all indignation, terror, compassion, and agitation'—and perhaps a clearer apprehension of the tensions involved in any European woman's collusion with empire, 'colonised by gender but colonisers by race', in the words of Indira Ghose.[92] Felicity Nussbaum's emphasis upon Sophia's 'hasty retreat from the monstrous seductive Orient' involves something of a torrid distortion of the events of the novel. The rape does not involve Sophia in plumbing the dark depths of the Indian sublime, but rather prompts her acknowledgment of the guilty and unacceptable face of British colonialism.[93] The monstrosity and the monster are wholly Occidental. '[T]he Eastern world,' as Sophia laments, 'is the scene of tragedies that dishonour mankind' (p. 157), but the dishonour is upon British manhood, and Sophia has witnessed the wretch being conveyed to prison. She has learned the corruptive power of the precious metal that formed the first syllable of her maiden name and exercised her youthful attentions: 'gold can unnerve the arm of justice', but ultimately she feels confident that the murdering rapist will be subjected to exemplary punishment: 'Lord C[ornwallis] will not stain his noble deeds, by suffering such a villain to escape' (p. 163).

Her sexual attraction towards both Hindu Brahman and Muslim Nawab had been the focus of her receptivity towards both the stereotyped Indias of passive, feminized spirituality, or of magnificent martial masculinity. Now Gibbes effectively uses the reality of sexual violence to expunge all adolescent Orientalizing fantasies from Sophia's mind, simultaneously striking a resonant Burkean note concerning the rape of Bengal.

It is in this connection that I would suggest that Betty Joseph's reading of *Hartly House, Calcutta*, 'as a zone of interference that ultimately threatens the role of the official archive as a repository of fact', is a little too reliant upon the erection of binaries.[94] The brutal 'fact' of the village violation of a girl on a floor stained with her father's blood is in many respects no fiction. And as representation is inevitably politically 'embedded' where are we to locate fact in the archive? Searching through the colourful impeaching rhetoric of Burke we might see Hastings as an envious and despoiling Satan, 'the devil hovered for a while in the Garden of Eden', authorizing the horrific sexual atrocities of Devi Singh, Ganga Govind Singh, and their minions.[95] Perhaps we should credit the genuine letters of Captain Charles Madan, an aide-de-camp of Governor-General Cornwallis, to his father the Bishop of Peterborough, which depict Company control as productive of a pastoral paradise: 'What a glorious comparison the English traveller may make on revisiting the Company's provinces, after observing the state of those belonging to other powers!'[96] The 'Company's provinces' constitute the real 'zone of interference' and, as we have seen, through its being plagiarized both as fact and as news, *Hartly House, Calcutta* and the 'official archive' are, in one sense, indivisible.

The novel's juxtaposition of imperial splendour (both Mughal and British) and village rape takes us beyond the mere problematizing of the hierarchies of colonial power, race, and gender, enabling both reader and heroine to extend their sensibilities to confront the sordid truth of the rights/rites and wrongs of colonial conquest. Isobel Grundy's uncertainty as whether to award the author/correspondent/ heroine 'political-correctness points' for radicalism in raising the topic of interracial rape, or to subtract them for representing the rape in phallocentric patriarchal terms, demonstrates the multi-faceted ambivalence of the epistolary technique.

> This part of Gibbes's narrative might be read as literary realism (a predictable response for a young, idealistic, inexperienced white girl) or political realism (rhetorical appeal to readers to repudiate the commonest form of sexual racist violence), or else an outcropping of orthodox gender ideology, which might stem from Gibbes herself or from her presumed informant, her son.[97]

By means of her sentimental epistolary narrative, Phebe Gibbes translated the insights of Orientalist philology and early Indology into an easily accessible discourse, which could (and still does) appeal to a larger novel-reading public. In the subtlety of its resistance to the binaries of race and gender, of public and private, and of centre and margin, the novel demonstrated exactly how gender and genre might prove validating and authorizing elements in the representation of the subcontinent. If the implications of her plot were to constitute something of a shock to circulating-library sensibilities, it is important not to underestimate Phebe Gibbes's contribution to the metropolitan domestication of Hinduism. Even more significantly the novel mirrors, if on a sentimental plane and in a minor key, the concern of the

Orientalists whose researches were patronized by Hastings to adjust stereotyped metropolitan constructions of India as irrational, static, female, passive, and backward, illustrating that the intellectual traffic between dominant and subject cultures is not exclusively in one direction.[98] Thus *Hartly House, Calcutta*, though subject to a certain cultural negotiation with the tastes of a novel-reading public, enhanced the socio-political aspects of epistolary fiction by providing a faithful and authoritative representation of India.

Notes

1 Phebe Gibbes, *Elfrida; or, Paternal Ambition. A Novel. By a Lady*, 3 vols (London: J. Johnson, 1786), 2: 134

2 This payment was made by the publisher, Thomas Lowndes, on 14 April 1763; see *The Gentleman's Magazine*, 94.1 (1824), 136, cited in Cheryl Turner, *Living by the Pen: Women Writers in the Eighteenth Century* (London: Routledge, 1992), p. 114.

3 *Critical Review*, 25 (1767), pp. 132–5, p. 135.

4 *Critical Review*, 27 (1769), pp. 452–9, p. 452.

5 In a letter to the Royal Literary Fund she claimed authorship of *Zoriada: or, Village Annals* (London: Printed for T. Axtell, 1786) which had been attributed to Anne Hughes, but as *Jemima. A Novel* (London: Printed for William Lane, at the Minerva-Press, Leadenhall-Street, 1795) bears on its title-page 'By the author of *Zoriada: or, Village Annals*', it is possible that she wrote this also. Gibbes also claims to have written 'for the credit and emolument of another hand' [Mrs Lucius Phillips'] *Heaven's Best Gifts*, 4 vols (London: printed for the author, and sold by W. Miller, n.d. [1798]); see BL MSS: Royal Literary Fund 2: 74, letter of 19 October 1804.

6 She was baptized on 3 April at St Leonard's Shoreditch in the temporary 'tabernacle' erected in the churchyard and used while the old church was demolished and George Dance's elegant Palladian replacement was built (completed in 1740). Phebe must have wryly recalled the peal of the Shoreditch bells: 'When I grow rich', responding to the Bailey's 'When will you pay me?'

7 David Hopkinson, personal communication.

8 BL MSS: Royal Literary Fund 2: 74, letter of 14 October 1804.

9 *Ibid.* See also Virginia Blain, Patricia Clements, and Isobel Grundy, ed., *The Feminist Companion to Literature in English: Women Writers from the Middle Ages to the Present* (London: Batsford, 1990), p. 420.

10   BL MSS: Royal Literary Fund 2: 74, letter of 19 October 1804.

11   'The Benevolent Society' was praised by the editor as one of the *Magazine*'s important publications, an 'entirely original' piece (October 1771, p. 526), only to vanish completely from the 1772 volume; its discontinuation belatedly announced in the July 1773 number's 'To our Correspondents' p. 312: *'The Benevolent Society was discontinued by the desire of a numerous majority of our subscribers. Equestrius and his friends are the only subscribers who ever applied to revive it; and we are sorry for it, because it will not be in our interest to gratify their wishes'*. The Society's success with the horsey community, despite its abhorrence of hunting, sheds an interesting light upon its male readership.

12   At this date, 8 May 1822, a marginal note on her husband's will explicitly mentions her as deceased; David Hopkinson, personal communication of 29 October 2012.

13   BL MSS Royal Literary Fund 2: p. 74, letter of 18 April 1805.

14   In the following year, *Hartly House, Calcutta* was one of the 59 out of 71 novels listed to receive anonymous publication; see Peter Garside, James Raven, and Rainer Schöwerling, eds, *The English Novel, 1770–1829: a Bibliographical Survey of Prose Fiction Published in the British Isles*, 2 Vols [Volume I: 1770–1799, James Raven and Antonia Foster, eds] (Oxford: Oxford University Press, 2000).

15   See, for example, the 1690 list of Adrien Baillet: 'the *love* of Antiquity', '*prudence*', 'the *fear* of disgrace and penalties', 'the *shame* at producing or publishing something which would be unworthy of one's rank or profession', 'the *intention* to sound the minds on a subject which might seem new', 'the *fantasy* of hiding one's low birth or rank', and 'the *desire*' to hide a name which might not ring well', cited in Maurice Couturier, *Textual Communication A Print-based Theory of the Novel* (London: Routledge, 1991), p. 61. See also James Raven, 'The Anonymous Novel in Britain and Ireland, 1750–1830', in *The Faces of Anonymity: Anonymous and Pseudonymous Publication from the Sixteenth to the Twentieth Century*, Robert J. Griffin ed., (London: Palgrave, 2003), pp. 141–66; BL MSS: Royal Literary Fund 2: 74, letter of 14 October 1804.

16   Cf. Virginia Woolf, *A Room of One's Own* (Harmondsworth: Penguin, 1967), pp. 51–2.

17   BL MSS: Royal Literary Fund 2: 74, letter of 15 October 1804.

18   David Hopkinson discovered that an Anthony Gibbles (*sic*: a writerly error) died on 1 May 1786, aged 24, and was buried in the Calcutta Mission cemetery. David had earlier revealed that 'Anthony Gibbes began five years as a law clerk in the Mount Street, Grosvenor Square office of the London attor-

ney Christopher Wardell in 1777': personal communication of 18 January 2006. Such training would have fitted the twenty-four-year-old Anthony for a post as an East India Company writer, but he would probably have had need of a letter of recommendation from an influential individual such as Robert Jennings (1750–1805), 'Chief Clerk of the Exchequer', whom she mentions in her letter to the RLF of 17 October 1804.

19 See, for example, *The Woman of Fashion: or, the History of Lady Diana Dormer* (London: J. Wilkie, 1767), 2: pp. 30–31. The eponymous heroine of *The History of Miss Eliza Musgrove* (1769) is actually given in marriage to the aged Lord Hindley to cancel her father's gambling debts of £5,000. The title of *Elfrida; or, Paternal Ambition* (1786) reflects the fact that her father not only farms Elfrida out to a rich relation, but obliges her to marry for fortune and against her inclination. Another and more extensively revealing title: *Friendship in a Nunnery; or, The American Fugitive. Containing a Full Description of the Mode of Education and Living in Convent Schools, both on the Low and High Pension: the Manners and Characters of the Nuns; the Arts Practised on Young Minds: and their Baneful Effects on Society at Large* (1778), anticipates the artistry with which Gibbes combines the Gothic, the educative, and the political in this novel which begins: 'Parents have flinty hearts,—no tears can move them,—children must be wretched'.

20 Phebe Gibbes, *The Life and Adventures of Mr Francis Clive*, 2 vols (London: Lowndes, 1764), 1: p. 10.

21 Cf. *Elfrida*, 2: 36, 136–7.

22 *The Fruitless Repentance; or, the History of Miss Kitty Le Fever* (New York: Garland, 1974); *The Life and Adventures of Mr Francis Clive* (New York: Garland, 1975); *Hartly House, Calcutta*, ed. Monica Clough (Pluto: London, 1989). Grundy adds that these reprints: 'are unsatisfactory. In this situation she is not likely to cross the threshold of a classroom and that is a pity', '(Re)discovering women's texts', in *Women and Literature in Britain, 1700–1800*, Vivien Jones, ed. (Cambridge: Cambridge University Press, 2000), pp. 179–96; pp. 190–91. I ought to add that mine is by no means the only classroom whose threshold Gibbes has crossed. Access to at least ten of Gibbes's novels is now provided by that most valuable resource 'Eighteenth-Century Collections Online'.

23 April London, *Women and Property in the Eighteenth-Century English Novel* (Cambridge: Cambridge University Press, 1999), pp. 124–8.

24 Gibbes imagines the mind of the pregnant girl in a manner quite foreign to the matter-of-factness of Ann Gomersall, who writes of working people in general around Leeds: "not above one wedding in ten that the bride was not in a state of pregnancy before the arrival of the wedding day" (*Eleonora* (London: The

Logographic Press, 1789), 1: 258)', Isobel Grundy, with Patricia Clements (Director), Sharon Balasz, Susan Brown, Rebecca Cameron, Kathryn Carter, Renee Elio, and Dave Gomboc, 'Delivering Childbirth', 'Orlando Project Encoding', http://www.ualberta.ca/ORLANDO/Childbirth.htm.

25   *Critical Review*, 17 (1764), p. 307.

26   *Critical Review*, 19 (1764), 307–8. Gibbes remembered this praise and applied it in her petition, forty years later, to her whole oeuvre which was: 'of moral tendency & said by the reviewers that the most cautious parent might trust them in the hands of a child of either sex', BL MSS: Royal Literary Fund 2: 74, letter of 19 October 1804.

27   *Analytical Review*, 4 (1789), pp. 147–8.

28   *English Review*, 8 (December 1786), pp. 448–9.

29   Gibbes's choice of a title for this novel might well reflect her desire to capitalize upon the success of a 1785 revival of Colman's version of William Mason's *Elfrida*, featuring Sarah Siddons as the heroine; see *The Times*, Thursday, 14 April 1785, p. 1. Interestingly, the title role in the original production (21 November 1772) was played by Elizabeth Hartley.

30   Phebe Gibbes, *Friendship in a Nunnery; or, The American Fugitive*, 2 vols (London: J. Bew, 1778), 1: 15–18.

31   *Critical Review*, 46 (October 1778), pp. 300–301; p. 301.

32   *Monthly Review*, 60 (April 1779), p. 324.

33   *Critical Review*, 17 (1764), p. 308.

34   *The Niece; or, The History of Sukey Thornby. A Novel. In Three Volumes. By Mrs. P. Gibbes. Author of The History of Lady Louisa Stroud* (London: Printed for F. Noble, at his Circulating Library, No. 324, Holborn, 1788), unpaginated Preface. Andrew Becket liked her 'plan': 'the design is undoubtedly good; but we can say little in praise of its execution', *Monthly Review*, 78 (Dec. 1787), p. 441. The *Critical's* reviewer took the accustomed superior moral ground: 'Another attempt at a new plan; but [...] weak and abortive. We are not sufficiently behind the curtain to see the necessity of a novelty of plan: the circulating libraries are still crouded; and each new novel, whether the plan be new or not, is eagerly sought after. The present work is chiefly of a dramatic kind: the conversations are long and numerous; and we at least perceive one advantage in the mode—an advantage beyond that of tedious repetitions in the form of letters, viz. that, by its assistance, a story which could not be expanded to one volume, now requires three', *Critical Review*, 64 (1787), p. 481.

35   Gibbes, *The Life and Adventures of Mr Francis Clive*, 2: p. 136.

36   *Aberdeen Magazine, Literary Chronicle, and Review*, XXIX (Thursday, July 2 1789), pp. 416–21.

37   *The New Annual Register, or General Repository of History, Politics, and Literature, for the Year 1790,* 1791, pp. 21–22. Cf. pp. 153–4 below. Godwin relinquished this duty in the summer of 1791, after completing his contribution to this very number of *The New Annual Register,* though Godwin's responsibility does not seem to have extended to the 'Principal Occurrences' listings. See Jack W. Marken, 'William Godwin's Writing for the *New Annual Register', Modern Language Notes,* 68: 7 (1953), pp. 477–79.

38   Cornwallis had arrived in Calcutta in the September of 1786. News from India took five or six months to arrive in London, but exactly why the Nawab should have taken almost four years (until 7 June 1790 according to the *The New Annual Register*) to welcome the new governor-general might have puzzled some readers.

39   Hayden White, *Metahistory: The Historical Imagination in Nineteenth-Century Europe* (Baltimore and London: Johns Hopkins University Press, 1973); see also his *Tropics of Discourse: Essays in Cultural Criticism* (Baltimore: Johns Hopkins University Press, 1978), where he stresses 'the essentially provisional and contingent nature of historical representations', and 'the fictive nature of historical narrative'.

40   'On 24 February 1789, JD paid G. 20 pounds for *Hartly House, Calcutta'*, James E. Tierney, ed., *The Correspondence of Robert Dodsley: 1733–64* (Cambridge: Cambridge University Press, 2004), p. 561. A single volume 12mo edition, apparently pirated, of *Hartly House, Calcutta* appeared in Dublin (Printed for William Jones) in the same year, and a German edition appeared at Leipzig in 1791. The 1908 Calcutta reprint was subtitled *A Novel of the Days of Warren Hastings,* with notes by John Macfarlane, a prefatory note by H. E. A. Cotton, and an introduction by G. F. Barwick, published by Thacker, Spink and Co. has itself been the basis for two modern reprints, one in Calcutta (Gupta Press) in 1984 and the other by a small London press (Pluto) in 1989.

41   It would seem that Gibbes had the priority in terms of being 'the first of a new genus': see Janet Todd, ed., *The Collected Letters of Mary Wollstonecraft* (London: Allen Lane, 2003), p. 164.

42   *Analytical Review,* IV (June 1789), pp. 145–7; reprinted in *The Works of Mary Wollstonecraft* Janet Todd and Marilyn Butler, eds, 7 vols (London: Pickering, 1989), 7: pp. 111–12.

43   *Analytical Review,* IV (June 1789), pp. 145–7.

44   *Critical Review,* 68 (August 1789), p. 164. In her diary entry for 8 May 1790, Anna Margaretta Larpent, daughter of Sir James Porter, former ambassador at Constantinople, and wife of the Examiner of Plays, John Larpent, records: 'Red [*sic*] the 1st Volume of *Hartly House* A pretty lively Novel the scene at Calcutta, giving descriptions in Letters, & interwoven into a Love story of ye

Manners of ye East. Disgusting Enough & yet Seemingly a genuine picture',
HM 31201, Huntington Library, California. I owe this information to the
kind attention of David Worrall.

45 *Monthly Review*, n.s. 1 (March 1790), p. 332.

46 The review concludes: 'Faithful and lively descriptions of places and
persons, of modes of life and rules of behaviour, of private entertainments
and public ceremonies, form the principal merit of the work; and to those
individuals whose destiny may hereafter lead them to seek their fortunes
in that distant and luxurious region of the globe, it may afford not only
transient pleasure, but solid and useful information', *European Magazine
and London Review*, 17 (1790), p. 118.

47 The reviewer contrasts more reliable accounts: 'For if any credit be due to
those who have lived many years on the spot, and want not capacity for
appreciating men and manners, who are in the habit of observation, and
from their fortune and rank accustomed to associate familiarity with people
of the first distinction; the descriptions which our author gives of society,
of pleasurable parties, of domestic etiquet, and of local peculiarities, in
the vicinity of Calcutta, and the fashionable places of Bengal, are totally
unfounded', *English Review*, 14 (1789), p. 386. His choice of the epithet
'brittle' might well have been influenced by a presumably pseudonymous
satire entitled *The India Guide; or Journal of a Voyage, to the East Indies, in
the year MDCCLXXX, in a Poetical Epistle to her Mother, by Miss Emilly Brittle*
(Calcutta: George Gordon, 1785), in which the sentimental heroine makes
the passage to India, accompanied by her friend Flirtetta, and subject to the
adoring addresses of Captain Trifle.

48 William Zachs, *The First John Murray and the late Eighteenth-Century London
Book Trade* (Oxford: The British Academy, 1998), p. 37. See also my '"The
Hastings Circle": Writers and Writing in Calcutta in the Last Quarter of
the Eighteenth Century', in *Authorship, Commerce and the Public: Scenes of
Writing, 1750–1850*, Emma Clery, Caroline Franklin, and Peter Garside, ed.,
(Basingstoke: Palgrave, 2002), pp.186–202.

49 'There have been times when the labours of a Jones, a Richardson and a
Halhed, would, as well as on account of their political utility, as of their
literary merit, have engaged the notice of men in power. But this is not the
age. The genius of a Hastings does not shine in the councils of St. James's
or Leadenhall-street. The consciousness of having laboured to promote
the interests of Britain in Bengal may of course prove Mr. Halhed's sole
reward', *English Review*, 1 (January 1783), pp. 13–14.

50 'We must be prepared to accept the fact that a representation is *eo ipso*
implicated, entwined, embedded, interwoven with a great many other things

beside the 'truth', which is itself a representation. What this must lead us to methodologically is to view representations (or misrepresentations—the distinction is at best only a matter of degree) as inhabiting a common field of play defined [...] not by some inherent subject matter alone, but by some common history, tradition, universe of discourse', Edward W. Said, *Orientalism* (Harmondsworth: Penguin, [1978] 1995), pp. 272–3.

51   Johnson to Hastings, 29 January 1781; see Bruce Redford, ed., *The Letters of Samuel Johnson*, 5 vols (Oxford: Clarendon Press, 1992–4), 3: 324. Despite his impatience with Empire, the elderly Dr Johnson, embodying the global perspective of Enlightenment Europe, still thought of emigrating to India and learning Sanskrit. Earlier he had written to Hastings: 'I can only wish for information; and hope, that a mind comprehensive like yours will find leisure, amidst the cares of your important station, to inquire into many subjects of which the European world thinks not at all, or thinks with deficient intelligence and uncertain conjecture. I shall hope that he who once intended to increase the learning of his country by the introduction of the Persian language, will examine nicely the traditions and histories of the East; that he will survey the remains of its ancient edifices, and trace the vestiges of its ruined cities; and that, at his return, we shall know the arts and opinions of a race of men, from whom very little has been hitherto derived', (Samuel Johnson to Warren Hastings, letter of 30 March 1774), Bruce Redford, *The Letters of Samuel Johnson*. 2: pp. 135–7; p. 136.

52   In his celebrated letter to Nathaniel Smith, Director of the East India Company, prefixed to one of the founding works of Indology, Charles Wilkins' translation of the *Bhagavadgitâ* (1785), he declared: 'Every accumulation of knowledge, and especially such as is obtained by social communication with a people over whom we exercise a dominion founded on the right of conquest, is useful to the state: it is the gain of humanity: [...] it attracts and conciliates distant affections; it lessens the weight of the chain by which the natives are held in subjection; and it imprints on the hearts of our own countrymen the sense and obligation of benevolence. Even in England, this effect of it is greatly wanting. It is not very long since the inhabitants of India were considered by many, as creatures scarce elevated above the degree of savage life; nor, I fear, is that prejudice wholly eradicated, though surely abated. Every instance which brings their real character home to observation will impress us with a more generous sense of feeling for their natural rights, and teach us to estimate them by the measure of our own. But such instances can only be obtained in their writings: and these will survive when the British dominion in India shall have long ceased to exist, and when the sources which it once yielded both of wealth and power are

lost to remembrance', reprinted in *The European Discovery of India: Key Indological Sources of Romanticism*, Michael J. Franklin, ed., 6 vols (London: Ganesha Publishing/Edition Synapse, 2001), 1: p. 13.

53   Hastings wrote to his Persian Translator, Jonathan Scott, on 9 December 1784: 'My letter to Mr Smith introducing Mr Wilkins' Translation of the Gheeta is also Business, though began in Play. It is the effect of part of a System which I long since laid down, and supported for reconciling the People of England to the Natives of Hindostan', Hastings to Jonathan Scott, 9 December 1784, BL Add MS. 29129, f. 275.

54   See Michael J. Franklin, *Sir William Jones: Selected Poetical and Prose Works* (Cardiff: University of Wales Press, 1995), pp. 356–67.

55   Garland Cannon, ed., *The Letters of Sir William Jones*, 2 vols (Oxford: Clarendon Press, 1970), 2: p. 652.

56   'I blush to feel how superior to all that Christianity can boast, of peace and good-will towards men', *Hartly House*, pp. 75–6.

57   See Michael J. Franklin, 'Radically Feminizing India: Phebe Gibbes's *Hartly House, Calcutta* (1789) and Sydney Owenson's *The Missionary: An Indian Tale* (1811), in *Romantic Representations of British India*, Michael J. Franklin, ed., (London: Routledge, 2006), pp. 154–79.

58   Michel Foucault, *The History of Sexuality: An Introduction*, transl. Robert Hurley (New York: Vintage, 1990).

59   William Dalrymple, *White Mughals; Love and Betrayal in Eighteenth-Century India* (London: Harper Collins, 2002).

60   Sophia explicitly makes the point that her mother had earlier accompanied her father to India (leaving Sophia in the care of Arabella's aunt who superintended her education) for motives of love. She also stresses that her demise 'in the grave of thousands' was on account of a consumptive tendency rather than as a result of contracting an 'exotic disease'.

61   The alternative versions of 'Goldsborne' and 'Goldsborn' also occur in the novel; such variation might have resulted from the difficulty of interpreting Gibbes's handwriting.

62   *The Western County Magazine*, IV (1790), pp. 316–17. The letter is simply signed 'Middleton' in large capitals, suggesting to an inattentive reader that it might have been written by Nathaniel Middleton (1750–1807), Hastings' representative at the court of the nawab wazir of Oudh, Shuja ud-Daula, in Lucknow, 'Memory Middleton' had obviously forgotten that his own fortune had been made in a remarkably similar fashion as he penned this moralistic contribution from the comfort of his splendid Hampshire estate, named with perfect macaronic Anglo-Indian poise: 'Midanbury'. The sharp-eyed Phebe Gibbes would have noted that this 'letter' was a plagiarized

version of a section of Lord Clive's 30 March 1772 Commons speech in defence of himself, with inserted topical references to Hastings and Major Scott. Reading this speech in *The London Magazine*, 41 (May 1772), pp. 203–8 or elsewhere might have encouraged her to send Anthony to Bengal.

63   See P.J. Marshall, 'Masters and Banians in Eighteenth-Century Calcutta', in *The Age of Partnership: Europeans in Asia before Dominion* Blair B. King and M.N. Pearson, eds (Honolulu: University Press of Hawaii, 1979), pp. 191–213, and Lakshmi Subramanian, 'Banias and the British: The Role of Indigenous Credit in the Process of Imperial Expansion in Western India in the Second Half of the Eighteenth Century', in *Modern Asian Studies*, 21: 3 (1987), pp. 473–510.

64   Calcutta was evidently in the van of this 'rage' for women drivers of *ton*. In London, the fashion was satirized on stage; Lady Sarah Savage, 'one of those ladies call'd female phaetoneers', drives four in hand, but has to be rescued when 'the horses take fright'; Frederick Reynolds, *The Rage: a Comedy* (London: Longman, 1795), p. 9.

65   Felicity A. Nussbaum, *Torrid Zones: Maternity, Sexuality, and Empire in Eighteenth-Century English Narratives* (Baltimore and London: John Hopkins University Press, 1995), p. 176.

66   'The rustling of fine linen, and the general hum of unusual conversation, present to his mind for a moment the idea of an assembly of females. When he ascends upon the deck, he is struck with the long muslin dresses, and black faces adorned with very large gold ear-rings and white turbans [...] besides this, the European is struck at first with many other objects, such as women carried on men's shoulders on pallankeens, and men riding on horseback clothed in linen dresses like women: which, united with the very different face of the country from all he had ever seen or conceived of, excite the strongest emotions of surprise!' William Hodges, *Travels in India* (1793), reprinted in Michael J. Franklin, *The European Discovery of India*, 3: p. 2–4. Cf. Mrs [Jemima] Kindersley, *Letters from the Island of Teneriffe, Brazil, the Cape of Good Hope, and the East Indies* (London: Nourse, 1777), reprinted in Caroline Franklin, ed., *Women's Travel Writing: 1750–1850*, 8 Vols (London: Routledge), 5: p. 197. Harriet Guest notes how Hodges' feminization of Hindus is balanced by the representation of Muslim men as excessively masculine; see Harriet Guest, 'The Great Distinction: Figures of the Exotic in the Work of William Hodges', in *New Feminist Discourses: Critical Essays on Theories and Texts* Isobel Armstrong, ed., (London: Routledge, 1992), pp. 296–341.

67   A suitably outré role-model for Sophia was Miss Emma Wrangham, the 'Chinsurah Belle'; see note to p. 40.

68   In terms of humbler shopping for provisions, the documentary accuracy of
      Hartly House, Calcutta may be indicated by comparing the listing of prices
      with that furnished by the equally bourgeois Eliza Fay, whose letters were
      written from Calcutta at almost exactly the same time as Sophia's fictional
      ones. 'Claret expensive indeed five rupees (twelve and sixpence) a bottle'
      (p. 35). '[S]ix fine ducks are sold for a rupee, two and sixpence. Bread is also
      good and cheap; fish both excellent and cheap. Likewise fowls, eggs, and
      milk, very cheap; butter dear—geese cheap, turkies—dear; and Arabella,
      half a sheep is often bought for one rupee' (pp. 77–8). Mrs Fay's shopping
      list in a letter of 29 August 1780 is remarkably similar: '[E]xcellent Madeira
      (that is expensive but eatables are very cheap)—a whole sheep costs
      but two rupees: a lamb one rupee, six good fowls or ducks ditto—twelve
      pigeons ditto—twelve pounds of bread ditto—[...] good cheese two months
      ago sold at the enormous price of three or four rupees per pound, but now
      you may buy it for one and a half—English claret sells at this time for sixty
      rupees a dozen'; Eliza Fay, *Original Letters from India (1779–1815)*, with
      introductory and terminal notes by E. M. Forster (London: L. & V. Woolf,
      1925), pp. 181–2. Sophia's letters were cited as an authoritative source of
      information on Calcutta by H.E. Busteed, who takes them to be genuine
      epistolary correspondence; see H.E. Busteed, *Echoes from Old Calcutta:
      being chiefly Reminiscences of the Days of Warren Hastings, Francis, & Impey*
      (Calcutta: Thacker, Spink & Co., 1882).

69   Kumari Jayawardena, *The White Woman's Other Burden: Western Women
      and South Asia During British Rule* (London: Routledge, 1995), p. 4.

70   The arrival of Earl Cornwallis prompts this further paean to the 'self-enno-
      bled' Hastings from Sophia who will not 'forget the Governor I have known
      [...] Hereditary advantages, however brilliant their effects, are but secondary
      recommendations;—the self-ennobled individual, and him who disgraces
      not the memory of his illustrious forefathers, being the only highly-revered
      characters in this land of commerce and plain understanding' (pp. 149–50).

71   Edmund Burke, *The History of the Trial of Warren Hastings, Esq.* ... (London:
      J. Debrett and Vernor and Hood, 1796), part ii, p. 3.

72   P.J. Marshall, ed., *The Writings and Speeches of Edmund Burke, VII India: The
      Hastings Trial 1789–1794* (Oxford: Clarendon Press, 2000), pp. 36 and 54.

73   Edmund Burke, *The History of the Trial of Warren Hastings*, part ii, p. 77.
      Richard Brinsley Sheridan, in the June of 1789, also played his rhetorical and
      histrionic part in the blurring of fact and fiction as he attempted to convince
      a Westminster Hall audience of the 'high crimes and misdemeanours'
      authorized by Warren Hastings in the *zenana* (women's apartment) of the
      Begums.

74 Burke was referring to his speech of 18 February 1788 which, in its minute description of repulsive sexual tortures allegedly committed by Devi Singh, a revenue farmer appointed by Hastings, had plumbed graphic depths unknown even in the Gothic novel. A contemporary editor commented: 'Mr Burke's descriptions were more vivid—more harrowing—than human utterance on either fact or fancy, perhaps, ever formed before. [...] Mrs Sheridan was so overpowered, that she fainted. [...] Mr Burke was here taken ill [...] too exhausted to be able to proceed', *ibid.*, part ii, pp. 7–8. See Michael J. Franklin, 'Accessing India: Orientalism, "Anti-Indianism" and the Rhetoric of Jones and Burke', in *Romanticism and Colonialism*, Tim Fulford and Peter Kitson, eds (Cambridge: Cambridge University Press, 1998), pp. 48–66, pp. 53–5.

75 See Burke's comments on 'the beggary of the Nabob of Bengal', Speech on Mr. Fox's East India Bill, 1 December 1783, in P.J. Marshall, ed., *The Writings and Speeches of Edmund Burke*, vol. V *India: Madras and Bengal 1774–1785* (Oxford: Clarendon Press, 1981), p. 400.

76 Ghulam Husain Khan Tabatabai, *A Translation of the Sëir Mutaqharin; or, View of Modern Times, being an History of India, from the Year 1118 to the Year 1195 (this year answers to the Christian year 1781–82)*, 3 vols (Calcutta: James White, 1789 [1790]), 2: p. 533.

77 See Michael H. Fisher, ed., *The Travels of Dean Mahomet: An Eighteenth-Century Journey through India* (Berkeley: University of California Press, 1997), pp. 60–61; Michael H. Fisher, *The First Indian Author in English* (Delhi: Oxford University Press, 1996); Michael H. Fisher, 'Representations of India, the English East India Company, and Self by an Eighteenth-Century Indian Emigrant to Britain', *Modern Asian Studies*, 32: 4 (1998), pp. 891–911. See also Kate Teltscher, 'The Shampooing Surgeon and the Persian Prince: Two Indians in Early Nineteenth-century Britain', *Interventions*, 2: 3 (2000), pp. 409–23.

78 *Fifth report from the select committee, appointed to take into consideration the state of the administration of justice in the provinces of Bengal, Bahar, and Orissa* (London, 1782), p. 24.

79 William Hodges, *Travels in India, during the years 1780, 1781, 1782, & 1783*, reprinted in Michael J. Franklin, *The European Discovery of India*, 3: p. iii.

80 Constantin-François Volney, *The Ruins, or a Survey of the Revolutions of Empires* (London: J. Johnson, 1795), p. 28.

81 The first citation is from 1810; the second being Byron's celebrated advice to Thomas Moore: 1813 BYRON *Letter* 28 Aug. 1974 III. 101, 'If it had any success, that also will prove that the public are orientalizing, and pave the way for you', *OED*.

82   For a scholarly and accessible survey of such writings, see Ketaki Kushari Dyson, *A Various Universe: A Study of the Journals and Memoirs of British Men and Women in the Indian Subcontinent, 1765–1856* (Delhi: Oxford University Press, 1978).

83   In an undated letter Owenson expresses her thanks: 'I have at last, waded through your *Oriental Library*, and it is impossible *you* can ever feel the weight of the obligation I owe you, except you turn author, and some kind friend supplies you with rare books that give the sanction of authority to your own wild and improbable visions. Your Indian histories place me upon the fairy ground you know I love to tread, "where nothing is but what is not", and you have contributed so largely and efficiently to my Indian venture, that you have a right to share in the profits, and a claim to be considered a silent partner in the firm', W. Hepworth Dixon and Geraldine Jewsbury, eds, *Lady Morgan's Memoirs: Autobiography, Diaries, Correspondence*, 2 vols (London: W. H. Allen, 1862, revised, 1863), II: p. 388.

84   See Michael J. Franklin, 'Passion's Empire: Sydney Owenson's Indian Venture, Phoenicianism and Orientalism', *Studies in Romanticism*, 45 (Summer 2006), pp. 181–97.

85   A brief comparison of relevant passages will here suffice. 'The Bramins, however, affirm that he bequeathed them a book called the Vidam, containing all his doctrines and institutions; and that, though the original is lost, they are still possessed of a commentary upon it, which they name the Shahstah, written in the Shanscrita language; a dead language at this time, and known only to the priests who study it', *Hartly House, Calcutta*, p. 74. Cf. 'The bramins [...] pretend that he bequeathed to them a book called the Vidam, containing his doctrines and institutions; and that, though the original is lost, they are still possessed of a commentary upon it, called the Shahstah, written in the Sanscrit language; now a dead language, and known only to the bramins who study it', William Guthrie, *A New Geographical, Historical, and Commercial Grammar; and Present State of the Several Kingdoms of the World*, 9th edn. (London: Charles Dilly, G.G.J. and J. Robinson, 1785), p. 678. Cf. 'The Bramins, say, that Brumma, their law-giver, left them a book, called the Vidam, which contains all his doctrines and institutions. Some say the original language in which it was wrote is lost, and that at present they only possess a comment thereon, called the Shahstah, which is wrote in the Sanscrit language, now a dead language, and known only to the Bramins who study it', Luke Scrafton' *Reflections on the Government of Indostan* (London: Strahan, Kearsley, and Cadell, 1763), p. 4.

86   William Jones, *Sacontalá; or, the Fatal Ring: an Indian Drama. By Cálidás.*

Translated from the original Sanscrit and Prácrit (London: printed for Edwards, by J. Cooper, with his new-invented ink, 1790).

87 I have argued elsewhere that the cult of Sensibility rendered European Romanticism particularly susceptible to the Sanskrit literary concept of *rasa*, with its emphases upon the cultivation of the emotions, as displayed par excellence in *Sakuntala*, see Michael J. Franklin, *The European Discovery of India*, 3: pp. xiv-xvi.

88 'I felt myself in danger of becoming a *Braminate*, though all the wealth of Indostan could not bribe me to become a Mahometan', *Hartly House, Calcutta*, pp. 111–12. In this prejudice she follows Orientalists such as Nathaniel Brassey Halhed, a protégé of Hastings, friend of Jones, and author *A Code of Gentoo Laws* (1776) and *A Grammar of the Bengal Language* (1778), in whose writing a certain anti-Islamic bias may sometimes be detected. For a comparative study of the two friends' representations of Islam and Hinduism, see Michael J. Franklin, 'Cultural Possession, Imperial Control, and Comparative Religion: The Calcutta Perspectives of Sir William Jones and Nathaniel Brassey Halhed', *Yearbook of English Studies*, 32, (2002), pp. 1–18.

89 *The Works of Anna Lœtitia Barbauld*, 2 vols (1825); repr. with an introduction by Caroline Franklin (London: Routledge Thoemmes, 1996), 2: p. 83.

90 Raymond Schwab, *The Oriental Renaissance: Europe's Rediscovery of India and the East 1680–1880*, trans. Gene Patterson-Black and Victor Reinking (New York: Columbia University Press, 1984).

91 Nussbaum, *Torrid Zones*, p. 189.

92 Indira Ghose, *Women Travellers in Colonial India: The Power of the Female Gaze*, (Delhi: Oxford University Press, 1998), p. 5.

93 'When confronted with the dark sublime of India, having finally represented it as uncatalogable and unclassifiable, Sophia domesticates and simplifies race, class, and gender relations', Nussbaum, *Torrid Zones*, p. 190.

94 Betty Joseph, *Reading the East India Company, 1720–1840: Colonial Currencies of Gender* (Chicago and London: University of Chicago Press, 2004), p. 28.

95 *The Writings and Speeches of Edmund Burke*, vol. vi *India: The Launching of the Hastings Impeachment, 1786–88* P.J. Marshall, ed., (Oxford: Clarendon Press, 1981), p. 110.

96 He continues in propagandizing mode: 'How much to the honour and credit of our government!—how highly to the dignity and importance of the British Empire! In our own dominions we have the satisfaction of beholding people, protected in their persons and property, by a mild and just government, reaping the fruits of industry in peace and happiness!' see Charles William Madan, *Two Private Letters to a Gentleman in England, from his Son*

who Accompanied Earl Cornwallis, on his Expedition to Lucknow in the year 1787 (Peterborough: J. Jacob, 1788), pp. 52–3.

97   Isobel Grundy, '"The barbarous character we give them": White Women Travellers Report on Other Races', *Studies in Eighteenth-Century Culture*, 22 (1992), pp. 73–86; p. 80.

98   Gibbes's feminization of a Hindu India, of course, conforms to current cultural stereotypes, but this is balanced by a representation of Mughal potency in the portrayal of the Nawab Mubarak ud-Daula.

Hartly House

Volume I

Hartly House – I

Arabella

Bay of Bengal.

The grave of thousands!—Doubtless, my good girl, in the successive years of European visitation, the eastern world *is*, as you pronounce it, the grave of thousands; but is it not also a mine of exhaustless wealth! the centre of unimaginable magnificence! an ever blooming, an ever brilliant scene? And moreover, I have to inform you, that all the prejudices you have so long cherished against it must be done away; and for this plain reason, that they are totally groundless. Yes, Arabella, the mother I have lost, and your so much lamented friend, fell not, as we have conceived, a victim to this ardent climate; her pulse was not suspended by exotic disease; the arrow of death was lodged in her gentle bosom *before* she left her native country, and she alone debarked,[†] to expire on this coast.—But take the melancholy fact, as my father was drawn out to relate it, during our voyage.

That the marriage of those to whom I am indebted for my existence was a marriage of affection, sanctified nevertheless by the approving voice of their parental relatives, is a circumstance you are well acquainted with; but, perhaps, it may be as new intelligence to you as it was to me, that, from the tender distress mutually experienced on their first separation, in consequence of my father's profession, they resolved, on their reunion, never to separate more.

My birth gave them, however, a different turn of sentiment, though it in no degree lessened their conjugal attachment; my infant period being an insurmountable impediment to my mother's making an East India voyage, and my education a claim upon their feelings not to be dispensed with, until their confidence in the good understanding and excellent principles of your aunt at length persuaded them their personal superintendence might, for a time at least, be safely intermitted; then the firmness with which my mother bade me adieu, astonished all who knew her.

The India fleet was detained in the channel by adverse winds; and, in an excursion to Portsmouth, my mother caught a cold, which terminated in a cough.—Yet did the extreme delicacy of her complexion, and uncomplaining turn of temper, prevent the discovery of a consumptive tendency, until it was too late to try the efficacy of softer climates than are to be met with in an East India voyage. She laboured, suffering angel as she was, to give her husband hope, even when she herself despaired; talked, in the most touching terms, of the treasure they had left in England; and when the pious fraud could no longer be kept up, died, conjuring him to live for my sake.—But I will not dwell upon so heart-wounding a subject; I indeed cannot, Arabella, for it has unhinged me, and I must quit my pen for a few moments.

If the packet I sent you from St. Helena (which was the first opportunity that offered) was put safely into your hands, or rather, if I could be assured that was the case, I might spare myself the trouble of accounting to you for what you call my wonderful departure from my native country; an epithet that surprises me not, when I recollect the incoherence and agitation with which I told the story of my approaching embarkation; but as I must remain for months uncertain whether it reached you or not, I will, on this occasion, give you the particulars of my motives and consequential conduct; for I love you too well to suffer you to suppose caprice, or the wild curiosity of seeing foreign sights had any share in my instantaneous resolution to visit the eastern continent.

Having attended my father, as you well know, to Deal, in order that we might enjoy each other's company to the last possible moment, I found, Arabella, on every renewed good-night we exchanged, irrepressible sighs escaped him.

The wind began to waver, and was expected to come round to the favourable point before the next morning's dawn.—I was retiring, and the final farewell appeared to tremble on my father's lips; again I approached, and again, to embrace him.—My manner unspeakably affected him.—It was nature's work; and when did nature ever work in vain?

He held me for a short space, with silent anguish, in his arms, and I could alone articulate, 'My father!—my dearest father!' 'Alas! Sophia,' said he at length, 'are my feelings prophetic; shall I never more behold thee?' 'Oh, Sir!' cried I, 'revoke, I conjure you, your own decree; nor be so cruel to yourself, when it is my anxious wish to accompany you, as to leave me behind.'

He lifted up his eyes and hands; but made no reply.

I dropped instinctively on one knee before him. 'My dearest sir,' resumed I, 'if you persist in refusing my request, and I live not to welcome your return to England, can you charge the calamity on aught but your own fiat; for it is you, not Heaven, that forbids my sharing your destiny; or, should I survive you, do not flatter yourself the tidings of your dissolution could be supported by me; for who could convince me my presence might not have been soothing, or enable me to believe that somewhat of my suggesting might not have been salutary, and prolonged your most valued life?—Your heart relents (perceiving I had subdued his resolves); I read it in your countenance; and I take upon me, short soever as the time may prove, to be prepared to go with you.' He laid his pocket-book open on the table, bade me use the contents without reserve, and, to hide his emotion, hastily retired.

With what alacrity and expedition I provided the necessaries for my voyage I need not mention; for who has not heard of the all-creative power of gold, and the rapid movement of the wings of inclination?

We embarked together, and have without one alarming (that is unusual) incident, made the Bay of Bengal.—This letter shall

Hindustan ? India ?

therefore be constituted the repository of a private vow I have
entered into with myself, never to marry in Indostan, lest it
should become difficult, at some future period, to ascertain, my
genuine impulse for quitting the country of my birth; a vow, take
notice, Arabella, I will not violate to be a nabobess. *Nawab ?*

And thus concludes my last epistle, unanimated by oriental
suns, and unperfumed by oriental breezes. An indescribable
degree of vivacity already diffuses itself through my heart, insomuch that I hasten to tell you, in the cold language of European
friendship (before I blush to have known its frigid influence) that
I am your's affectionately,

SOPHIA GOLDBORNE

LETTER II

Hartly House, Calcutta.

The splendor of this house, as it is modestly styled, is of itself,
my Arabella, sufficient to turn the soundest European head; but
I am well aware, was I to plunge at once into a description of it,
I should have my veracity, if not my intellects, impeached : low-
ering myself, therefore, to your narrow conceptions, I will begin
with the circumstances of my first arrival, and so contrive to
temper, though I cannot, like Mr Apollo, lay aside my rays, that
your optics shall be enabled to contemplate, however brilliant,
the dazzling objects I gradually open on your view.

The island of Sawger,† at the mouth of the Ganges, is the
first land you encounter; but as it is alone inhabited by tygers,
alligators, &c. &c. you will believe me when I tell you I had not
the smallest *penchant* for visiting it. Pilots, however, come down
to this distance (some hundred miles) from Calcutta, for the safe
convoy of ships; the tide of this eastern river being subject to no
less sudden than impetuous changes, insomuch that the ablest
seamen are often drifted by it.

We proceeded on our voyage up the river to one of the stations for Indiamen,[†] called Culpee,[†] 150 miles from Calcutta, where my father received the most affectionate greetings from his old acquaintance; and we were told, that three *bugeros*[†] were on their way to welcome and accommodate us.

This sound having no semblance whatever of the eastern dignity, I begged my father to inform me what a *bugero* was:—He smiled, and bid me wait their arrival, nor seek to anticipate my own discoveries in a single instance.

We next passed the second station, called Cudgeree;[†] when lo, the *bugeros* appeared in view; and judge, if you can, of the pleasure it gave me, after having been so long confined to one set of company, to perceive I was on the point of tasting the boundless joys of eastern magnificence.

You have seen, as you suppose, some very handsome barges on the river Thames; but how poor a figure the handsomest would make, in comparison with the *bugeros*, or barges of Calcutta, I will endeavour to convince you.

As they approached, my ears drank in the most delightful sounds; a band of music, as is the custom, occupied each of them, playing the softest airs; and from the *tout ensemble*, brought Dryden's Cydnus[†] and Cleopatra to my recollection.

The company in the first that came along-side of us were seated upon deck, with kittesan[†] boys, in the act of suspending their kittesans,* which were finely ornamented, over their heads; which boys were dressed in white muslin jackets, tied round the waist with green sashes, and gartered at the knees in like manner with the puckered sleeves in England, with white turbans bound by the same coloured ribband; the rowers, resting on their oars in a similar uniform, made a most picturesque appearance.

My foolish heart was in the *bugero*, before my father, at the earnest solicitations of his friends, and a look of desire from me, assisted me to descend from the ship; but, when descended,

* Umbrellas. [Author's note.]

my astonishment and delight so abundantly increased at each advanced step, that the European world faded before my eyes, and I became *orientalised*[†] at all points.

Eight gentlemen, three of whom were my father's particular friends, and four ladies, were the party; and it appears to me, Arabella, that I shall find every poetical description realised in this enchanting quarter of the globe; for be it known to you, in the language of Southern's *Oroonoko*,[†] that when presented to the gentlemen as my father's daughter, I *bowed*, and *blushed*; and, if I have any skill in physiognomy, they *wondered* and *adored*; and such, I already understand, is the court paid to ladies at Calcutta, that it would be well worth any vain woman's while, who has a tolerable person, to make the voyage I have done, in order to enjoy unbounded homage.

The chief article of refreshment was claret, which was drank with great freedom, under the name of *Loll Shrub*.[†] Coffee, tea, sweetmeats, &c. &c. were offered, but in general refused, except by my father, who is fond of coffee to a degree that I think will not accord with his health in this relaxing climate.

A kittesan boy instantly took his stand behind my chair, and an attendant, called a Bearer, flew backwards and forwards in my service; and in this state we reached Diamond Point,[†] a place of debarkation,[†] where we found a suitable number of Palanquins in waiting to accommodate us all.

I was startled, Arabella, however prepared, on finding myself hoisted on the men's shoulders; for I need not observe to you, the only difference between a palanquin[†] and a London sedan-chair, (except the travelling ones) is their having short poles fastened to the central part of the sides, the front pair of which have a curve for the bearers better hold—Venetian blinds instead of glass windows—and in the mode of carrying.

It was evening; I therefore, as well as my father, and the rest of the company, had two harcarriers,[†] or flambeaux-bearers, running before me; and I felt all the dignity of my transition; though I will confess to you, the *Tok, Tok*,[†] their almost perpetual cry, to clear the way, did not fall so agreeable on my ear as I could have wished; nor was I able to suppress the invocation of *aura veni*[†] at every foot step.

From the point where we landed, to the Esplanade, (a place I shall describe to you on my own acquaintance with it) is almost four miles; and swiftly did we pass along; for it seems these palanquin-bearers (with proper relays, as is the case with those that perform journies) are so expert, that in defiance of the heat, &c. &c. they go at the rate of from nine to twelve miles an hour.

I could only observe by the light of the flambeaux (though a host of servants poured forth to receive us) that the entrance to Hartly House was by means of a double flight of stone steps, at the top of which we found a spacious balcony, called a veranda, covered in by Venetian blinds, and lighted up with wax candles, placed under glass shades, to prevent their extinction from the free admission of the evening breeze; together with a couple of card-tables, furnished at all points, for those disposed to occupy them, with very many other polite *et caetera's*.

Here I met with new homage, in the form of congratulations on my safe arrival; but recollecting, it would not be to forfeit it in future, if I declined it at the then moment, I complained of fatigue, and was conducted to an apartment that would have satisfied a princess, though neither more nor less than a common genteel sleeping-room.

The furniture was all Chinese,[†] of the elegant materials and manufacture of which, even you people in England have a very tolerable idea; but the vases and the perfumes were superior to every thing of the kind within my knowledge, and as such had a fine effect on my feelings.

My musketto[†] curtains are made of beautiful muslin, extremely full, and capable of considerable expansion; and it is the custom for the servants to beat them immediately before going to bed, to clear them of those insects; when they are just sufficiently opened to admit the party, and suddenly closed to exclude those troublesome nocturnal companions; then, being spread out wide, they admit the air in the most refreshing degree. Apropos of muskettos; I must tell you, though I shudder at the bare recollection of so vulgar a nuisance, that, in like manner with the bugs in London,[†] they mercilessly annoy all new-comers, blistering them, and teazing, if not torturing them continually; and in a great measure spare those who are seasoned to the climate.

And now let me ask you your opinion of my attachment to you, when I can thus forego the highest earthly pleasures, flattery and luxurious accommodation, for your amusement.—But perhaps, instead of thinking yourself obliged to me, you will, with the true European *sang-froid*, suspect me of self-gratification in my descriptions;—beware, however, of such erroneous conclusions, as you value the future favours of your own

Sophia Goldborne

P.S. We are, they tell me, (yet such is the present warmth, that, without the information, I should not have supposed it) arrived at the commencement of the temperate season,[†] and I am taught to expect a very fine climate for five successive months, the monsoons not coming on until February, when agues and fevers are epidemic; and my constitution, no doubt, Arabella, must undergo its naturalization; for few indeed are the exceptions to these severe attacks, which often lead down to final dissolution.—The idea shakes my constancy! Oh! pray devoutly with me, that my dearest father may be spared in his own health, and unwounded in mine; for well do I know he could depart in peace, if his child was not to be left behind.—And to survive her!—Can any thought be more killing? Good night!—I will try to lose it, and all my cares, in that sweet balm of our existence, sleep. Once more, therefore, good night!

❧

Letter III

——————————Prime cheerer! light,
Of all created beings first and best!
Efflux divine!†

It is morn, you must understand, Arabella, with us sons and
daughters of the East, six hours at least before you enjoy the glorious, however weakened sun-beams; and I awoke to encounter
new wonders.

Having breakfasted, (which I find is the only *degagé*† meal I
must hope to enjoy, every one ordering what is most agreeable to
their choice, and in elegant undress chatting *à la volonté*;† whilst,
on the contrary, dinner, tea, and supper are kind of state levees†)
knowing that in the next apartment to mine, a *country-born*† young
lady—as the phrase is, to distinguish them from Europeans—
was lodged, whom I had found extremely winning in her address
during our voyage in the *bugero*, and declaredly ambitious to be
admitted on the list of my friends; I took it in my head to visit
her *en passant*, and make her a morning compliment; and this
the more particularly, because she had not given us her company
at breakfast, and I imagined she might have taken cold on the
water.—But judge my surprise, Arabella, when, on entering her
chamber, I found her under the hands of her hair-dresser, actually smoking a pipe.

But let me caution you against every plebeian idea on the
occasion, for that pipe was a most superb hooka,† the bell filled
with rose-water; and instead of odious tobacco, a preparation
of the betel-root, rolled up, and wetted, was placed in the bole,
which bole was beautiful china-ware, covered with a filligree
silver cap, with a mouthpiece of the same materials.—Nor can I
give you a conception of the graceful manner in which the snake
(the long ornamented tube) was twined through the rails of her
chair, and turned under her arm, so as not to have incommoded

any person seated by her; or the genteel air with which she drew out the soft fume, and puffed it forth, alternately (for none of it is retained.)—In a word, I wished to have taken her portrait on the spot, for her form is elegant, her complexion near the European standard, and the novelty of her attitude such, as rendered them altogether an admirable subject for the pencil.

This kind of smoking is, I am told, the characteristic custom of the *country-born* ladies; and the servant, dressed as I have already described, whose sole business it is to arrange the snake, feed the fire on his knees, and take care of the whole apparatus, is called the hooka-bearer, and is an indispensable appendage of eastern state and etiquette. The gentlemen, without distinction, indulge themselves this way, and as naturally, I am informed, fill up the period of their hair-dressing with their hookas, as those in England with perusing the daily prints, and unquestionably to a more beneficial purpose; for the health is preserved or promoted by the practice: whereas news-paper reading, in your fashionable world, only furnishes the head with politics, and the heart with scandal, no very estimable acquisition, I hope you will grant me, for a rational member of the community.

I have this morning enabled myself to give you some idea of the houses at Calcutta—for all of them, of any consequence, are, I am assured, built upon a similar plan, though not all with similar advantages of situation. To begin with

Hartly Mansion[†]

The centre part of the building is much higher than the rest, and terminates in a point at the top, forming an obtuse angle (if I may properly so call it) when the projecting lines are downwards; and extend to the wings on each side; the roof whereof covers a most magnificent hall, or saloon, the whole length and breadth of this central space, ornamented at back fronts with balconies, or verandas, that open by folding glass-doors, of inconceivable grandeur, into the above-mentioned apartment; and the architecture, having the advantage of every possible decoration, (together with large-sized windows over the balconies) has a striking effect on an European beholder.

From this grand centre the wings project, each of which consists of a suite of elegant rooms, all on one floor—(for the utmost elevation from the ground is the flight of steps at the entrance) with a view of the esplanade[†] in front, a kind of immense park; and a large garden, with a fine tank or fishpond, behind—such as sleeping-rooms, dressing-rooms, withdrawing-rooms, &c. &c. in a style, no set of words I am mistress of can convey to your imagination;—and under this prodigious structure are the family offices in general; the exceptions are store-houses, with the offices, at a distance, instead of gardens. The hall is, it seems, on all occasions, the place where dinner and supper are served up; and, when illuminated, as the lustres[†] and girandoles[†] bespeak, must be fit for the reception of a royal guest.

The outside of the walls is washed with a white composition, called *chinam,*[†] that, in like manner with the scenes in your theatres, has no glare, and of course is not painful (how powerful soever the sun's rays may be) to the sight; which *chinam* is a pleasing contrast to the lively green of the verandas, or Venetian blinds, (universally used, whether the windows are glass or not), and are reliefs to each other; but glass, you must know, is a dear commodity at Calcutta, and imported solely from England; on which account the Governor's house[†] is almost the only one that can boast that distinction.

The Venetian blinds[†] (or *verandas,*[†] as I shall accustom you to call them) answer two most desirable purposes—shade, and the free current of air, without which there would be no existing.——— Eastern pomp, splendor, and magnificence, support me in this trying moment! when, almost expiring with heat, (and the seldom heard of, in Europe, misery of laboured respiration) I am on the point of confessing, no happiness can equal the happiness of a temperate climate, and the social intercourse of the sons and daughters of Liberty and intellectual cultivation; for, my dear Arabella, too true it is, that the best pleasure of the East is, being a kind of state-prisoner, enfeebled and fettered by vertical suns, and the fatigue of veiling our distresses from vulgar optics, by gaudy trappings and the pomp of retinue; nor can I suppose it possible, I should ever become habituated to what I now languish under, and cease to sigh for one delightful strole in St. James's Park, unincumbered by palanquins, kittesan-bearers, the clamour of har-carriers, &c. &c.

I reprobate all I have written.—My father has this instant filled my purse with gold mohrs,[†] value forty shillings, or sixteen rupees, each; has purchased me a palanquin (what prophanation have I not been guilty of against palanquins!) and my mind is restored to the pinnacle of grandeur, from which it had so meanly fallen.—I am nevertheless, in despite of myself,

Yours, as usual,

S.G.

LETTER IV

> 'Tis raging noon, and vertical the sun
> Darts on the head direct its forceful beams;
> O'er heaven and earth, far as the ranging eye
> Can sweep, a dazzling deluge reigns.[†]

Thomson certainly passed a part of his life under this meridian, so applicable are the above lines to my present situation.—You cannot therefore wonder, if you give them an attentive perusal, at the weakness into which I was surprised at the conclusion of my last letter, or that the poet's words,

> All-conquering heat! O intermit thy wrath,
> And on my throbbing temples potent thus
> Beam not so fierce.[†]

should at this moment spontaneously flow from my pen.—But we will talk no more of it.

The royal levee was never more crowded than mine—fine fellows, Arabella, without number!—the East India Company's servants! the English sovereign's servants!—I trust I shall not dwindle again into my former self, or yawn away my days under your gloomy atmosphere.—But I wander wide from my intended subject.

I have been at church, my dear girl, in my new palanquin, (the mode of genteel conveyance) where *all* ladies are approached, by sanction of ancient custom, by *all* gentlemen indiscriminately, known or unknown, with offers of their hand to conduct them to their seat; accordingly, those gentlemen who wish to change their condition, (which, between ourselves, are chiefly old fellows, for the young ones either chuse country-born ladies for wealth,[†] or, having left their hearts behind them, enrich themselves, in order to be united to their favourite dulcineas[†] in their native land) on hearing of a ship's arrival, make a point of repairing to this holy dome, and eagerly tender their services to the fair strangers; who, if this stolen view happens to captivate, often, without undergoing the ceremony of a formal introduction, receive matrimonial overtures,[†] and, becoming brides in the utmost possible splendor, have their rank instantaneously established, and are visited, and paid every honour to which the consequence of their husbands entitles them.—But not so your friend; for, having accompanied my father to India, no overtures of that nature will be attempted, previous to an acquaintance with him, or at least under his encouraging auspices; nor did any gentleman break in upon the circle of my surrounding intimates, on this first public exhibition of my person, though every male creature in Calcutta, entitled to that privilege, bid Mr and Mrs Hartly[†] expect an early visit from them.——On my mentioning the church,[†] you will perhaps fancy I ought to recount to you its magnificence and style of architecture; but the edifice dignified at present with that appellation does not deserve notice. It is situated at the Old Fort, and consists solely of a ground-floor, with an arrangement of plain pews; nor is the Governor himself much better accommodated than the rest; and of course the Padra, as the clergyman is called, has little to boast of; the windows are, however, verandas, which are pleasing to me in their appearance, independent of the blessing of air enjoyed through that medium.—But at the New Fort there is a new church erecting,[†] on quite an European model, with galleries, a set of bells, and every suitable *et caetera*; the plan and foundation of which I have seen, conversed with the architect, and, from the whole, form very high expectations of the superstructure. One remark, however, is a-propos on this subject; namely, that the house of prayer, at Calcutta, is not the house of sepulchre. Burying-grounds are provided some miles from the town, which, I am given to understand, are well worth the visit of a stranger. I will only add, that though this measure may have arisen from the fervid heat of this climate (where death is busy) which gives the idea of rapid putridity, yet surely it is disgracing the temple of the Divinity, (admitting even that in England no bad consequence results from such deposits) to make it a charnel-house.—Let this suffice for churches, except the mention, that at Calcutta Sunday is the only day of public devotion, and that only in the morning; though the Padra's salary[†] is liberal, and his perquisites immense.

Think you, Arabella, that on mentioning the awful repositories of the dead, I forget my dear mother's sacred remains[†]—Surely no.—But I wish not to hang unnecessary weights on your spirits, and therefore reserve all I have to say on that heart-searching subject, for the period that enables me to tell you, I have beheld her hallowed tomb, and paid the best tribute in my poor power to her beloved memory!—Adieu! adieu!—I will resume my pen the first opportunity; but can no more at present.

S.G.

❦

Letter V

You would, my Arabella, be enraptured at the extreme neatness of even the meanest attendant; but besides the beauty and the virtue of cleanliness,[†] it is the only fence in the East against putrid diseases. That unerring guide, Nature, who teaches the people of the North to fortify themselves with furs against their inclement seasons, bids the inhabitants of Indostan be correctly delicate in their persons, and personal attire: to which the circumstance of all the servants being Gentoos[†] not a little contributes; for diurnal immersion in the river Ganges is one of the strict articles of their religion, at the same time that it is a general benefit to the Europeans.

The Moors, or Mahometans, and the Gentoos, compose the chief body of the public; but perhaps, Arabella, you may wish and expect I should present you with some account of the ancient inhabitants of this astonishing empire,[†] before I introduce you to an acquaintance with the moderns, as the living generations may possibly be deemed by you.—You must, however, excuse me; historical anecdotes are not compatible with either the taste or leisure of a fine lady at Bengal. I will indeed advance so far on this heavy ground in your service, as to inform you where you may meet with such matter of fact, and spare myself the drudgery, as well as the disgrace, of exercising my pen thereon.—Yet, when I turn my thoughts that way, I must believe it will cost me less labour to write the little it is necessary for you to read, than to refer you to the chapter and verse of those authors who have treated of this world of wonders; for, in the first place, Arabella, take notice, the work of creation was performed in the East, and in the East Christianity received its birth; in consequence of which great circumstances, the sublime ideas[†] and discoveries perpetually opening themselves upon my mind, can alone be even faintly conceived by you, if you, (as I recommend it to you to do) travel over so highly-distinguished a region, traced out as it is on your globes, with the sacred and prophane writers of antiquity in your hand—when your entertainment will be ample. I speak from experience.—The other particulars run thus:—

India,[†] it is supposed, was first peopled from Persia, (which, in conjunction with the Indian ocean, is its western boundary) because, by its contiguity to that kingdom, it lies in the way of Mesopotamia, where, it is generally agreed, the descendants of Noah settled after the deluge.—Be this as it may, it is evidently the southern division, (for there is not a white man, or any complexion but black, amongst its numerous inhabitants) and was possessed by the Ethiopians: their colour, long hair, and regular features being markingly different from the blacks of Guinea; and, as a further proof of their Ethiopian origin, we read in our Bible, that the queen of Sheba (which Sheba is only another name for Ethiopia) sent presents to the wise king Solomon, of many fine spices—which alone grow in India, and were brought thither from Ethiopia for cultivation.

The next people who possessed the country were Arabians; for certain it is, that almost the whole coast was subject to Arabian or Mahometan princes, when the Portuguese arrived there in 1500; which Arabs, there is held little doubt, dispossessed the Ethiopians of their territories, and drove them up into the midland country, which they still inhabit.

The next invaders were the Mogul Tartars under Tamerlane, about the year 1400, who fixed his third son in the North of India and Persia; but the Southern provinces were not reduced under the dominion of the Mogul, until the reign of Aurengzebe, in 1667. This prince, it seems, had been shewn some of the large diamonds from the mines of Golconda (the grand magnet at this day), and was thence induced to attempt the conquest thereof; and a good substantial motive it was; whereas the mighty Alexander overspread the universe with his armies, for the sole purpose of restoring, in the form of a generous act, those kingdoms his superior force wrested from their lawful and peaceful possessors.—But to return to Aurengzebe. He made himself at length master of all the country as far as Cape Comorin, which, if

you look in your map, you will find to be the most Southern prom-
ontory of India; but the midland country being very mountainous
and woody, and subject moreover to several Ethiopian princes
called Rajahs, preserved, by their united efforts, their independence; insomuch, that they alone acknowledge the Mogul for their
sovereign, at the present period, in instances you will meet with
hereafter.

In the time of the famous Persian monarch, Khouli Khan,† the
Mogul throne was possessed by a great grandson of Aurengzebe,
who was made prisoner by that bold and enterprising Persian,
and obliged to cede to him all the North-west provinces of India,
to obtain his liberty. This invasion cost the poor Gentoos two
hundred thousand lives. As to the plunder made by Khouli
Khan, well-authenticated accounts speak it to be no less than
two hundred and thirty millions sterling; his own private share
of which was considerably above seventy millions, and may be
considered as terminating the greatness of the Mogul empire in
the house of Tamerlane: nevertheless, when he had raised all the
money he could in Delhi, he reinstated the Mogul Mahommed
Shah in the sovereignty, and returned to his own country.

A general defection of the provinces ensued, none being
willing to yield obedience to a prince deprived of the power
of enforcing it. The provinces ceded to Khouli Khan were only
a short time enjoyed by him; for in 1747 he was assassinated,
and Achmet Abdallah, his treasurer, equally unprincipled as
his royal master, being a man of great intrepidity, found means,
in the general confusion, to carry off three hundred camels
loaded with wealth, and, putting himself at the head of an army,
marched against Delhi with fifty thousand horse. Thus was the
wealth, drawn from this powerful city, made the instrument of
continuing the miseries of war, which it had at first brought upon
them. At present, the imperial dignity is vested, after manifold
revolutions, in a prince that is universally acknowledged to be
the true heir of the Tamerlane race; but his power is feeble,† the
city of Delhi, and a small territory round it, being all that is left
remaining to that ancient and magnificent house; and he depends

upon the protection of the English, whose interest it is to support him, as his authority is the best legal guarantee.

The point of prudence, however, in the East India Company, is, that their Governors should interfere as little as possible in the domestic or national quarrels of the country powers; peace and tranquillity best promoting their commercial interests. The wars with the Marattas, and Prince Hyder Ally,[†] indeed, prove, that these maxims have not always been properly adhered to.[†]—But I do not intend to pass myself off for a politician; and, therefore, leaving these modern particulars undiscussed, affirm, that this is historical knowledge sufficient for any reasonable woman, who is in the way of receiving more extensive intelligence from incidental observation and hourly occurrences. But I must beseech you to keep these matters in your head, that you may comprehend, on the instant, the references or elucidations I may present you with.

You will marvel at my reading and literary talents; but please to remember, that we alone know our depth of information or abilities, when occasion calls them forth,—I need not say how much I am,

Yours,

S.G.

LETTER VI

[†]This, Arabella, shall be a long letter; for it shall contain an account of one whole day, spent after the Calcutta manner; which, I conceive, will prove so close a copy of the general mode of living, that little more will be left for me to say on that subject; for the variations in amusement, exercise, &c. &c. cannot be considerable, in a place, where, to render existence supportable, is the sole end and purpose of elegance, as well as of industry.

At nine o'clock it is the custom of this family to breakfast; and I, who am no daughter of solitude, so soon as it is announced, become visible; for I have much pleasure in Mrs Hartly's conversation.

The fashionable undress, except in the article of being without stays (and stays are wholly unworn† in the East) is much in the English style, with large caps, or otherwise, as fancy dictates: it is, however, sufficient to say, no care or skill is left unexerted to render the appearance easy and graceful—a rather necessary circumstance, as you will grant me, when I add, that the gentlemen, in the course of their morning excursions (for they ride out on horseback at an early hour) continually drop in; and, from the numerous acquaintances this house can boast, I apprehend we shall seldom know a breakfast unaccompanied by these casual visitants—who say the prettiest things imaginable, with an air of truth that wins on the credulity, and harmonizes the heart.—Not, Arabella, but a fine woman, robed in white muslin, and with every other species of attractive drapery (let me tell you) is a very striking object, and, as such, honestly entitled to admiration.

You probably conceive, that, in this gay and enervating climate, industry is the last idea that would suggest itself to the mind of a fine lady: but you are mistaken; for the ladies at Calcutta are very fond of working upon muslin, of knotting, netting, and all the little methods of whiling away the time, without hanging weights on the attention.

At twelve a repast is introduced, consisting of cold ham, chickens, and loll shrub; after partaking of which, all parties separate to dress. The friseur† now forms the person anew; and those who do not chuse to wear caps, however elegant or ornamented, have flowers of British manufacture† (a favourite mode of decoration) intermixed with their tresses, and otherwise disposed so as to have an agreeable effect. Powder is, however, used in great quantities, on the idea of both coolness and neatness; though, in my opinion, the natural colour of the hair would be more becoming: but the intense heat, I suppose, renders it ineligible.

At three the day after my arrival, as is usually the case, the company assembled† in the hall or saloon, to the number of four-and-twenty; where, besides the lustres and girandoles already mentioned, are sofas of Chinese magnificence: but they are only substituted for chairs; what is called lolling, in the western world, being here unpractised.

The dinner table was covered with a snow-white damask table-cloth of the finest texture; and to every plate were arranged two glasses, one of a pyramidical and slender form (like the hob-nob glasses in England) for loll shrub, the other a common-sized wine glass, for whatever beverage is most agreeable; and between every two persons at table were also placed a decanter of water and a tumbler, for diluting at pleasure; with folded napkins, of equal elegance with the table-cloth, for all the company, marked by art with a variety of fanciful figures, which I reluctantly destroyed.

Such hosts of men on all occasions present themselves, that, at dinner, to the demolition of scandal and all other personal subjects, no two ladies are permitted, I find, in this country, to sit by each other. But the sexes are blended (I will not say in pairs, for the men are out of all proportion to the female world) so as to aid the purposes of gallantry and good-humour; and, during the whole period of dinner, boys with flappers and fans surround you, procuring you at least a tolerably comfortable artificial atmosphere.

The dishes were so abundant, and the removes so rapid, I can only tell you, ducks, chickens, fish (no soup[†], take notice, is ever served up at Calcutta) and all the *et caeteras* of an English bill of fare, according to their proper seasons, passed before my eyes.

But the mode of dressing these provisions is somewhat curious; for, I am told, fires of a particular kind of wood are prepared, which being burnt to a clinker,[†] the animal or joint intended to be roasted is placed *over*, not *before* them; where they are turned about until done in the greatest perfection; the fires being so judiciously fed, as to prevent both decay of heat, and smoke.

The attention and court paid to me was astonishing; my smile was meaning, and my articulation melody: in a word, mirrors are almost useless things at Calcutta, and self-adoration idle; for your looks are reflected in the pleasure of the beholder, and your claims to first-rate distinction confessed by all who approach you.

After the circulation of a few loyal healths, &c. &c. the ladies withdraw; and the gentlemen, I am told, drink their chearful glass for some time beyond that period, insomuch, that it is no unfrequent thing for each man to dispatch his three bottles of claret[†], or two of white wine, before they break up; having the bottles so emptied piled up before them as trophies of their prowess.

The ladies at Calcutta retire, not to enjoy their private chat, or regret their separation from their admirers; for to sleep is the object of their wishes, and the occupation of their time—a refreshment that alone enables them to appear with animation in the evening: accordingly, both ladies and gentlemen entirely undress, and repose on their beds, in the same manner as at the midnight hour; and, on awaking, are a second time attended by their hair-dresser; and thus, a second time in the twenty-four hours, come forth armed at all points for conquest.

But it shall not be concealed. Arabella, that so great an enemy to beauty is this ardent climate, that even I, your newly-arrived friend, am only the ghost of my former self; and however the lily has survived, the roses have expired: neither my lips (the glow, of which you yourself have noticed) or cheeks are much more than barely distinguishable from the rest of my face, and that only by the faintest bloom imaginable. Art, therefore, is here (as well as in Britain) a substitute for nature in ninety-nine instances out of a hundred. I hope I miscalculate my countrywomen in this comparison; but you know me too well to suspect me of a departure from my established custom. Notwithstanding all which, from being a new figure at Calcutta, my father's partiality for his only child (the only child of a woman he adored) is gratified beyond measure by the unending themes of my celebrity—my dress, my address, my judgment, my understanding, my language, my sentiments, my taste.—Fear with me then, my good Arabella, that I have cut out much distressing business for myself in the refusing line, by the rash vow I registered and transmitted you

from Bengal Bay, and by which I religiously conceive myself
bound to regulate my conduct.

I have slept little this morning—A whirl of ideas, I was unable
to regulate, was the cause.—I am, however, dressed; and my new
friend calls upon me to attend her to the tea-room.—I come, I
come.—She is gone without me, Arabella, from imagining me not
ready to present myself; and I will borrow so much time as just
to describe the household retinue of Mr and Mrs Hartly, and, of
course, of all the genteel families in Calcutta.

The ranks of natives from whence the domestic servants are
obtained, are Gentoos[†] (I think I told you as much in a former
letter; but no matter, the repetition will only confirm my report);
they do not board in the European families; but, receiving a
weekly stipend (and that a very slender one) feed at their own
hovels, on rice and fish, during the hours of their masters and
mistresses reposing themselves, and then, with renewed alacrity,
resume their several appointments and offices.

The suite of servants consists of a coachman and groom, which
are generally Europeans; a consumer,[†] who is a Gentoo (a kind
of house-steward and butler, for he provides every family article,
and attends the sideboard and tea-table in person, with bearers,
all Gentoos, of several denominations; the chief of which is called
the Seda-bearer,[†] who cleans the tables, places the glass shades
over the candles in the verandas, and has the care of his master's
shoes, which he puts on and takes off for him with the profound-
est respect); two pair of palanquin-bearers; a kittesan-bearer;
two harcarriers, or flambeaux-bearers; a hooka-bearer; and the
bearers who stand behind chairs, and act as waiters to and from
the tea-table: and so diligent and discerning are they, that they
read the commands of the company in their eyes, and seem
created for the sole purpose and sole ambition of serving the
Europeans.

The muslin dresses, &c. &c. which I mentioned to you on the
adventure of the bugeros, are, it proves, the family liveries of
the East; I mean the colour of the sashes and turban ribbands;

my colour is the Tyrian dye, which, I need not tell you, has a beautiful effect upon white.

I am sent for, and must for the present bid you adieu!

Three o'clock, morning.

You will, perhaps, Arabella, be so unbred as to conclude, some particular party or amusement has kept me up till this late hour; but know, two is absolutely a plebeian time of breaking up company at Calcutta.—Refreshed by your afternoon's sleep, and braced by the cool breezes of the evening, you consider time as made only for enjoyment, and repose as an outrage on conviviality.

My new friend, the country-born lady, met me the day after my arrival, and led the way to the tea party; but, instead of a parlour, &c. I found this party collected in the veranda, as on the preceding evening, and I drank my tea with a degree of satisfaction unknown in England in large companies; for, Arabella, instead of the exchanges (a most alarming and disgusting idea) to which you are there exposed, it is the delightful and sensible custom at Calcutta, for a bearer to convey your cup, when empty, to the consumer, without once letting it go out of his hands; and of course returns it you secure from every possibility of contamination.[†]—I think I never was so pleased with any one article of polite etiquette in my whole life.

At dinner we were cooled by artificial means; but the heavenly breezes of evening reached us through the verandas—cheered, enlivened, and rendered us quite another order of beings.

Tea and coffee over, three card-tables (for, sorry I am to tell you, card-playing is here, in like manner as in Europe, the fashionable propensity) were brought forward, and I, as a visiter, and a stranger, was not permitted to decline.—I was on the point of seating myself, when the stake was mentioned; but what was my astonishment, when I heard five gold mohrs (ten pounds)[†] spoke of as a very moderate sum a corner!

I drew back, Arabella, instinctively; for the little treasure my father had so kindly made me mistress of, my heart told me, at this rate, would literally make itself wings, and flee away.

Mrs Hartly, perceiving both my surprise and chagrin, asked me to honour her table with my company, where, the said, they were so humble as to stake only poor one gold mohr.—I gladly accepted her invitation; and endeavoured to remember with fortitude, that forty good shillings sterling would be either won or lost by me in the course of a few deals; whist being the polite game.

It is observed by some author,[†] (but I do not immediately recollect who) that intoxication is the vice of a barbarous, gambling of a refined, people; this is verified to a fatal proverb on this spot; for fortune, in the East (however refined the taste or manners of its possessor) appears alone to be acquired for the purpose of this wild dissipation of it; insomuch, that the *ultimatum* of European desires, the return to their native country, is sacrificed to the gratification of this pernicious propensity, as well as the peace and felicity of many most deserving families.—In a word, several hundred pounds were transferred from their possessors in the short period we were engaged.

At supper the saloon was superbly lighted, and the table sumptuously covered.—The same ceremony of parting the ladies was observed, as I have already described; so that the decanter and tumbler are evidently designed for her accommodation: and a band of music was introduced, which played all the evening.

I was requested to favour the company with a song, (vocal music[†] being highly esteemed by the *Calcuttonians*[†]); and so anxious were the gentlemen to discover, whether I had a voice tuned to melody or not, that doubt and expectation sat on each countenance.

I dispelled their doubts, and, if the goddess of Flattery (who certainly touched the lips of her votaries with peculiar eloquence on the occasion) may be relied on, exceeded all they could have hoped for from the first daughter of Harmony.—It must, however, be seriously acknowledged, that, from indolence, relaxed fibres, or whatever other cause or impediment, my little powers equalled the best efforts of my fair friends; and I have bound myself by a solemn promise, to be an *angel* on each succeeding evening.

A jingling of unaccustomed sounds to my ears now interrupted my eulogiums, and immediately six or seven black girls were brought in, dressed in white muslin, loaded with ribbands of various colours, with two or three gold rings in their noses, by way of ornament, and silver casnets[†] at their ancles and wrists, with which they beat time very agreeably to the tamborines that attended them. These are called *notch-girls*[†] (the word for dance), and their performance is called *notchee.*—They sang lively and tender compositions alternately, as was apparent by the movement of their eyes and hands, but to me otherwise unintelligible; danced with good effect; and, I could perceive, were well rewarded.—After which, the night being particularly fine, we were instantly conveyed in our palanquins to the Company's gardens;[†] late in the evening, or absolutely midnight, being the only walking time in this climate. The moon was near the full, and her silver beams, displayed unusual lustre.—Flowers of the most beautiful aspect and delightful scent, aromatic trees and shrubs, perfumed the breeze; and the vistos, or shady walks, had an air of enchantment! Thus was the evening terminated, or, more properly, Arabella, the new-born day welcomed with luxurious glee; the senses flattered; the heart softened; and love and friendship the prevailing sensations of the soul!—For, where the mind is pure, under such auspices as I have described, love is friendship, and friendship affection.

You are now, my dear girl, thinking of your temperate and solitary supper; and may a repose succeed, tranquil as your nature.

Adieu!

S.G.

❧

Letter VII

Bear me, Pomona! To thy Citron-groves;
To where the Lemon and the piercing Lime,
With the deep Orange, glowing thro' the green,
Their lighter glories blend: lay me reclin'd
Beneath the spreading Tamarind, that shakes,
Fann'd by the breeze, its fever-cooling fruit:
Deep in the night the massy Locust sheds,
Quench my hot limbs; or lead me thro' the maze,
Embowering endless, of the Indian Fig:
Or, thrown at gayer ease on some fair brow,
Let me behold, by breezy murmurs cool'd,
Broad o'er my head the verdant Cedar wave,
And high Palmetos lift their graceful shade:
Or, stretch'd amid these orchards of the sun,
Give me to drain the Cocoa's milky bowl,
And from the Palm to draw its fresh'ning wine,
More bounteous far than all the frantic juice
Which Bacchus pours! Nor on its slender twigs,
Low-bending, be the full Pomegranate scorn'd;
Nor, creeping thro' the woods, the gelid race
Of Berries—oft in humble station dwells
Unboastful worth, above fastidious pomp;
Witness, thou best Anana, thou, the pride
Of vegetable life, beyond whate'er
The poets imag'd in the golden age:
Quick let me strip thee of thy tufty coat,
Spread thy ambrosial stores, and feast with Jove.[†]

To taste the beauties of this poet's pencil, Arabella, you must
visit Bengal, where, I am more than ever convinced, he penned
his glowing descriptions of a climate and its characteristics,
Fancy, with all her fire, could not, unassisted by facts, have suggested.—The produce of this Eastern soil[†] is the palm, the cocoa-
nut, the tamarind, the guava, the orange, lemon, pomegranate,
pine, &c. &c. in the highest perfection; nor can they be spoken

of, by an animated beholder, in terms of common approbation.
For my part, my mental exclamation is, 'O for a muse, adequate
to the sublimity of the subject! that the wonder-working hand of
Nature[†] might be fitly celebrated by me!'—for, as Thomson again
expresses himself,

> Great are the scenes————
> ————that see, each circling year,
> Returning suns and double seasons pass:[†]

and poetry, Arabella, is the natural language, where all is loveli-
ness, and magnificence, and power exhaustless as infinite.—But
I am lost, you will perceive, in the immensity of my subject:
'Come, then,' as my favourite bard has it, of the Deity, on a
similar occasion—

> Come then, expressive Silence! muse his praise.[†]

On so vast a scale, indeed, are all things in this country,
both human and divine, that if any earth-born creature could be
pardoned the sin of ambition, it would be the Asiatics; nor can
I doubt, from all I have already seen and heard, that numbers of
them are proud enough to believe, and apply to themselves, the
poet's language:

> For me the mine a thousand treasures brings;
> For me health gushes from a thousand springs;
> Seas roll to waft me, suns to light me rise;
> My footstool earth, my canopy the skies.[†]

At least, we may fairly conclude the Moguls, in their day of
splendor, were of this haughty faith, if we read the following
description of their encampments:

His residences (the Mogul emperor)[†] during the temperate
season, which lasts four or five months, are in the field; and
few curiosities in the Eastern world were more striking than his
camp; for, besides the military men, (which amounted to above
100,000, who carried their wives and families with them) he was
attended by most of the great men in the empire, and followed, by
all kinds of merchants and tradesmen from the capital cities—in

the whole, above a million of people; and, with this retinue, he made a tour of a thousand miles every year, through some part of his dominions; and heard the complaints of his meanest subjects (an astonishing trait in so lofty a character!) if they happened to be oppressed by his nabobs or viceroys.

A caravan, of ten thousand camels and oxen, constantly attended the camp, and brought provisions from every part of the country; the commander of which was styled a prince, and vested with great power; his office being to furnish the camp with provisions.

The camp was at least twenty miles in circumference, and formed in a circular manner; the Mogul's tent and his women's being on an eminence in the centre, and separated from the rest by a high screen or inclosure; next to which were the nobility, generals, and people of distinction, in another circle; the rest succeeding in circles, according to their quality; the inferior people being nearest the outside of the camp[†]: nor do I marvel, that such an emperor, at such a period, should be induced, in the vanity of his heart, to style himself the Governor of the Universe, the Ornament of the Earth,[†] &c. &c. as is the custom, on the assumption of the imperial diadem; though, in the present circumscribed condition of the empire, those high-sounding titles are totally inapplicable.—But to descend to humbler subjects.

The East India Company, I find, pay the rent of such houses as the captains of their ships occupy during their residence at Calcutta; and it is well they do, or it would be a heavy tax upon their purse; for, could you suppose it possible such a sum as 500 sacre rupees[†] (sixty pounds) per month, could be decently demanded, or chearfully paid, by these birds of passage?[†] it is, nevertheless, the fact: accordingly, those gentlemen, who have it in their power, build elegant dwelling-houses, at the expence of 30, 40, 50, and 60,000 rupees, for the purpose of letting them ready furnished; and, I am assured I shall see many, which bear the astonishing rent[†] of 900 and 1000 pounds sterling per year, without a table, chair, or one necessary unhired at an equally extravagant rate.

The streets of Calcutta, at the part of the town inhabited by trades-people (who, by the way, are all Blacks, except what are called the Europe shops, of which I shall speak hereafter) are distinguished by the name of the *beisars*,[†] or traders, by which they are occupied; as, the bada beisar[†] (fruit and pastry); the muchee beisar[†], (the fish-market); the dewdwallar[†] beisar (milk-sellers); suedwallar[†] beisar (hog-merchants); chine beisar[†] (sugar-venders); &c. &c. Moreover, cards form a separate article of merchandise, and the shops for selling them furnish one whole street—a proof of their great consumption and value in the East.

The Europe shops,[†] as you will naturally conclude, are those ware-houses where all the British finery imported is displayed and purchased; and such is the spirit of many ladies on visiting them, that there have been instances of their spending 30 or 40,000 rupees in one morning, for the decoration of their persons; on which account many husbands are observed to turn pale as ashes, on the bare mention of their wives being seen to enter them: but controul is not an article of matrimonial rule at Calcutta;[†] and the men are obliged to make the best of their conjugal mortifications.

Five streets, well built, and inhabited alone by persons of genteel rank, open on the Esplanade, which is ornamented to a great extent, in view of the first houses of each (one of which is the Governor's[†]) with iron palisades, and makes a magnificent appearance. I shall enlarge upon this subject as soon as I have made my intended tour through the town; the whole of which, however, is a flat situation, and the habitations are scattered over a great space of ground; for the gardens, particularly the Company's and Governor's, are extensive; nor are the private ones small; for, as it is one of the chief pleasures of the country, to admire the beauties of vegetation, enjoy the shade, and feed on the delicacies so bountifully bestowed by Nature, it is their pride to possess them all together in their prime excellence, to speak at once their fine taste, and abundant fortune, to every beholder.

What a motley epistle is this! the great sublime, succeeded by the most inferior topics; but, Arabella, these transitions are not to be avoided, on a spot, where vivacity and dignity of mind is transient, and a low ebb of both the one and the other, the consequence of languor not to be resisted, and of gusts of heat not to be described.

I am,

Yours, as usual,

S.G.

LETTER VIII

How prophetic were my words, Arabella, where I mention my apprehensions of the refusals I should be called upon to make!—A painful task to a feeling, and not illiberal mind; but we must all submit to our destiny.

An *old* fellow,[†] with an incredible fortune, ogles me, and professes his life depends on his obtaining the honour of my hand— my father smiles—and I, with an air of indolent complacence (the air of the country) receive his devoirs as the just tribute of my transcendent charms; which charms (it is already got into circulation) are held by me above all price (for the fetter of my vow has not yet transpired); which may possibly tend to a diminution in the train of my adorers, at least on the arrival of the next ships; for, as the life of a butterfly is but an hour, so the ladies, who wish to see themselves advantageously disposed of, must reprobate the antediluvian practice, and be careful not to let the iron grow cold on the anvil; which, with few exceptions, is the universal conduct: so that, I doubt not, I shall soon behold this love-stricken grey-beard at the feet of some more yielding damsel:—and may she make him as happy as she will flatter herself his wealth can render her; nor once experience the common fate of such expectations—finding she has been self-deceived!

Here is also a little dapper fellow, in a yellow silk coat, that buzzes soft things in my ear, and affects to keep all the rest of his sex at a distance: but I have given it in commission to Mrs Hartly, to hint to him, that such behaviour is not lawful; the accepted lover alone being entitled to monopolize his fair one. I suppose we shall have him in the pouts on the occasion; this is, however, no formidable circumstance at Calcutta, where you may chuse and refuse at will. What gives the men such constant access to the ladies their rank entitles them to visit, is, that on being once introduced, you make their abode an home—walk in and out at pleasure—have your chair and attendant ready for you, as a matter of course—and the only wonder is, what can have become of your new friends, if they happen to absent themselves without a declared engagement. At breakfast, they tell me the news of the day; at dinner, solicit me to drink so many glasses of wine with them, that I ring unending changes on negative phrases[†] (and those the best chosen) to prove my fund of polite language, and soften my cruel denials; at the card-table they lose their money with a good grace; and, at supper, are brilliant companions: nor be it unobserved by you (tho' your matrimonial chance is beyond measure critical) you do not forfeit your claims to homage or adoration, on becoming a wife; whence Slander is often busy. The opportunities are, indeed, inconceivable for amour, if the inclination be prompt; but I verily believe, that gallantry at Calcutta is, like gallantry in France,[†] carried on by friendly compact amongst all parties: I trust you with my wife—you trust me with yours;—and that the abuse of such well-bred confidence is a rare instance of the ill effects thereof.

One or two offers, for their generosity and respectability, have been noticed by my father; and, with every profession of gratitude, declined by me. Mrs Hartly remonstrates, from looking forward (she kindly says) to alarms such conduct gives rise to— from implying some European engagement, that must eventually deprive her of my company. I assure her, she is mistaken, I perceive, in vain; for it appears to her an absurdity, to believe, a heart, that possesses its freedom, should shut the door against unexceptionable overtures. I own, Arabella, I cannot account for it myself, unless it can be possible, that the multitude renders me indifferent to individuals; and, true it is, that you have not leisure for the observations, so necessary to be made previous to an union for life, in these crouded scenes; or (if you can pardon the seeming levity) sufficient time to know your own mind; one agreeable impression being immediately, if not chased away, blended with another: in short, my hour of attachment is not come; and I never will be prevailed upon to separate, or (what is the same thing) endanger the separation, of my hand and heart.

Was there any prospect of your coming to Bengal, I might, perhaps, think otherwise than, I am convinced, I ever shall do, with the reflection on events that would prevent our ever meeting more.

I am, &c.

S. G.

Letter IX

I adore the customs of the East.[†]—Instead of having their servants, or beisars (trades-people) speaking in broken words, and mistaking, consequently misrepresenting, what their superiors say, the dresses and accommodations of the Europeans do not more perfectly discriminate them than their language; every person taking the trouble, or rather considering it their amusement, to learn to ask for what they want in Gentoo phrases; and making English the vehicle only of polite conversation.

Early this morning, the weather beginning to be settled, I took advantage of a cool breeze, and was conveyed in a phaeton[†] through the town and its environs.

The Writers Buildings,[†]

Arabella, in like manner with our inns of court, are divided into chambers, more or less elegant, according to the rank and consequence of their owners. This, I need not tell you, is the nursery of all the great men; for, from being writers, they are advanced, as their abilities enable them, to the highest civil offices, or even military, if their genius inclines them that way. I was struck by them altogether, as the monument of commercial prosperity; and made some comments on the subject, that did credit, I was told, to my sensibility and understanding;—but I seek not to shine in your sight, Arabella; you know the height and depth of my intellectual endowments, and honour me accordingly. A little ostentation is necessary in the East; but English estimates run upon the softer merits; for we are there taught to believe, that a woman's noblest station is retreat:—for that, as the poet says,

> Her fairest virtues fly from public sight,
> Domestic worth, that shuns too strong a light.[†]

But, be it always remembered by you, that Indostan is the land of vivacity, rather than of sentiment.[†]

At the back of the Writers Buildings is the

CALCUTTA THEATRE;[†]

the inside of which I have not yet seen; but am informed, from good authority, that it equals the most splendid European exhibition. The performers, Arabella, are all gentlemen, who receive no kind of compensation, but form a fund of the admission-money, to defray the expences of the house. It consists only of pit and boxes: to be admitted to the first of which, you pay eight rupees (twenty shillings);[†] to the last, a gold mohr (forty shillings): it is not, therefore, wonderful it should be rendered a brilliant spectacle.

I was also shewn, *en passant*, a tavern, called the London Hotel;[†] where entertainments are furnished at the *moderate* price of a gold mohr a head, exclusive of the dessert and wines—two very expensive articles indeed! for claret, notwithstanding its free consumption, is in private families five rupees (twelve and sixpence) a bottle.—Of their desserts I shall speak hereafter.

At the coffee-houses[†] your single dish of coffee costs you a rupee (half-a-crown); which half crown, however, franks you to the perusal of the English news-papers, which regularly arranged on a file, as in London; together with the *Calcutta Advertiser*, the *Calcutta Chronicle*, &c. &c.—and, for the honour of Calcutta, be it recorded, that the two last-named publications *are*, what the English prints formerly *were*, moral, amusing, and intelligent. I wish, Arabella, you could turn this hint to profit; but much fear, the frenzy of politics, and the fever of scandal, are confirmed diseases, and, as such, incurable.

Nor is Calcutta unfurnished with Livery Stables, riding being much the fashion at certain seasons of the year. And I had a distant view of the Hospital,[†] a building that deviates from the general plan of architecture, being three stories high; and, I am told, it deserves my particular notice and inspection.

At the Old Fort, which is situated at the extremity of those streets terminated by the Esplanade (I shudder to name it) are the ruins of the Black Hole,[†] where the no less memorable than tragical event took place in 1756; for, out of one hundred and forty-five British subjects, only twenty-three survived the horrors of one night's imprisonment: amongst those saved, was Mr Holwell, the Governor's chief servant, who has written a most affecting account thereof. The cause of this melancholy catastrophe was a quarrel of the Nabob, or Mogul viceroy, Surajah Dowla, with the Company—who suddenly invested Calcutta with a large body of black troops; the then Governor, and some of the other principal persons, threw themselves and their chief effects on board the ships in the river; whilst they who remained, for some hours bravely defended the place; but, their ammunition being expended, were compelled to surrender on tolerably flattering terms.

The Soubah,[†] a capricious and unfeeling tyrant, instead, however, of observing the capitulation, forced his prisoners into a secure hold, only about eighteen feet square, and shut them in from almost all communication of free air.—But I draw a shade over miseries I am unequal to paint; and will only add, that the seasonable arrival of our countrymen, Lord Clive and Admiral Watson, put the English once more (with some difficulty), in possession of Calcutta; the insensible Nabob, after plundering the place, having returned to his capital, under the persuasion that he had totally routed and subdued them; and the war was concluded by the battle of Plassey, as you may read in the British annals, won by Colonel Clive, and the death of Surajah Dowla; in whose stead Mhir Jaffier,[†] one of his Generals, a friend to the English, was advanced to the Nabobship; and Calcutta flourished more than ever, and became what we find it at this day.

The Old Fort is now totally deserted, and, except the church, has few buildings to boast; nor is its custom otherwise occupied than by the landing of copper, &c. &c. for the Company's service. The recollection of what I have related, so affected my spirits, that I begged to return home; and, having committed my morning's excursion to paper, shall endeavour to remember the concluding part of it no more.

One very singular circumstance at Calcutta is, Arabella, that there are no nurseries in any of the houses; nor does a child (with few exceptions) make its appearance.

Having made the observation upon repeated occasions (for you know I delight much in the company of children) I could not for-bear asking Mrs Hartly, how it came to pass that no little folks had met my eyes[†]—she, smiling, replied (for she is a sweet, amiable woman) 'Suspend your curiosity until to-morrow, and this mystery shall be unravelled.' Accordingly, at the usual early time the ensuing morn, we set off in our palanquins on a journey, the motive of which I was not aware of; and soon arrived at a most romantic and beautiful spot[†], at about five miles distance from our place of residence; where, it was revealed to me, the infant part of the family (as is the custom of the country) was situated; and I had the pleasure of making an instantaneous acquaintance with a boy and girl lovely as cherubs, and innocent as lovely.

These retreats (which in England we should know by the name of villas) are at Calcutta called *Bungilos*, and possess all the

charms and beauties of rural existence. The description of one
of them, however, will serve for all, with only the necessary
and natural abatements, fortune, taste, and liberality, produce in
every instance. Hartly Bungilo consists of a suite of apartments
on a ground floor, with a thatched roof and verandas, and stands
in the centre of a garden, I am wholly at a loss to describe to you.
Imagine, therefore, to yourself a spot, adorned with all the choic-
est flowers with which you are acquainted, formed into espaliers[†],
and encircling the fairest parterre[†] your eyes ever beheld; with
recesses, such as queen Dido[†] would have admired, and temples
the Graces might not disdain to visit; with, moreover, a spacious
tank or fish-pond at certain distances—every footstep appearing
fairy ground, and every breeze perfume.

My surprise and pleasure diverted Mrs Hartly exceeding-
ly.—'Take my advice another time,' said she; 'and, instead of
enquiring into things you are unacquainted with, endeavour to
behold them, and judge for yourself.' Had I told you, in so many
words, that my little boy and girl were, with whatever suitable
attendance, living in a thatched house, whilst I occupied what
you call a palace—would you not have shook your head, and
changed your opinion of a woman you now profess to esteem?—
whereas, beholding them lodged in the bosom of free air[†] and
tranquillity, jessamine and roses[†] forming their bed, and peace
and joy their pillow—will you not own, that mothers at Calcutta
have their children's happy condition as much at heart, as in a
country, where, at the top of the house, they are trusted to the care
of mere hirelings, and much farther removed from the maternal
superintendence than in our bungilos; though those bungilos
are under the regulation of well-educated and well-principled
gentlewomen, whose time and talents are devoted, in return for a
handsome stipend, to their service and benefit.

I had no reply ready; therefore only pressed her hand, in silent
approbation: but she is discernment at all points, and every
movement is to her intelligence.

Tell me, my dear girl, if you can, why the genuine delight of
conversing with children is so seldom sought for?—To me, next to

angels, I love and revere them. The dawnings of their reason are considered by me as so many emanations of the Divinity, and their artless turns of fancy the most rational of human entertainments.

My little new friends had not been five minutes presented to me before they found out the weak side of my character; and, having won me, to all intents and purposes, to their wishes, engaged me by a solemn promise (which I will actually perform) to visit them every morning I can contrive to steal from the company at Hartly House.—But most transient are our pleasurable moments in this world: I was summoned to re-ascend my palanquin, at the end of two hours, (the fleetest of all the hours I had spent at Calcutta) and was brought home with the actual loss of my heart—an acknowledgment that gave rise to innumerable effusions of Eastern gallantry, wholly unacceptable to me, and, as such, wholly disregarded.

It is usual, it seems, at a certain, to send the sons and daughters of this golden world[†] to England for education;[†] but great improvements having been made, during this last quarter of a century, in every branch of polite and valuable knowledge, among the Calcuttonians, this, together with the terrors of the ocean, which await such infant fugitives, has induced many fond fathers and mothers, as well as Mr and Mrs Hartly, to make it worth an accomplished Englishwoman's while to form their manners, &c. &c. under the parental auspices. The *gouvernante* at Hartly Bungilo, who comes precisely under this description, is the widow of a clergyman—has a pleasing person, and a well-stored mind—and was prevailed upon to make the voyage on the consideration of 250 gold mohrs (500 pounds) to be paid to her on her arrival; where she lives with as much discretion as elegance, and is esteemed and honoured by all who know her.

A large *bouquet* (every flower of which, by appearing more beautiful than the last noticed, I had selected from the multitude) was ordered to be carried for me to Calcutta. Nature is here lavish of her most beautiful productions;[†] and so peculiarly attentive to gratify the eye and the scent, that it is impossible to bring the island of your existence into the smallest competition

with the air I now breathe, or the objects I behold—a great
denial, you will perceive, to the unceasing remembrance of you,
I have so repeatedly assured you of; as a healer for which breach
of faith and truth, I have hit upon a proposal, that, if you are
human, must have attraction for you.—The Nabob,[†] Arabella, a
young smart fellow, lives but at the distance of four miles from
Hartly House. He has, it is true, several wives already; but you
shall be his wife of wives; and as for his copper complexion,[†]
you are too wise to make that an objection.—Come then, and
dwell only a short time with us—let him behold your face, and
have a few opportunities of discovering the perfections of your
temper, and he will think no price too high to purchase your
friendship and affection. I should rejoice to see you a Nabobess,
that you may surpass me as much in rank, as you surpass me
in every personal and mental accomplishment. But you are so
sentimental, there is no dealing with you; and I expect, in the
lines of your beloved Young, I shall be asked, by way of answer
to my wild question,

> Can wealth give happiness?—look round, and see
> What gay distress, what splendid misery![†]

which is so truly English, there is no standing : I therefore hasten
to conclude myself,

Your's, &c. &c.

S.G.

LETTER X

The manners of the ladies at Calcutta[†] are somewhat contradictory—now all softness and femininity, and now all courage and
resolution; as you shall hear:

They take a particular pleasure, on the one hand, in obliging and informing strangers—melt into tears at every tale of

sorrow—and sweetly sympathize with those whose spirits are depressed; on the other hand, you behold them so little attentive to female decorum, and so fearless of danger, that a scarlet riding dress, which gives them most the appearance of the other sex, enraptures them—and, to drive a phaeton and pair with a vivacity, a *dégagement*, or whatever may be the proper epithet, to mark their skill and unconcern, in the midst of numberless spectators, is their delight; whilst I, on beholding every such exhibition, say, with Dr. Young,

> ____ Such charioteers as these
> May drive six harness'd monarchs, if they please.[†]

for, to characterize them completely in your sight, I must add, that the ladies of gaiety and *ton* always make a point, on these occasions, of having a gentleman companion, who lolls at his ease; the office of managing the reins, &c. &c. being wholly assumed by the lady. I wish, nevertheless, you could see these phaeton enterprisers; for their attendance and accompaniments are in the high style of Eastern etiquette. A servant, in the dress I have heretofore repeatedly described, runs on each side the horses, with long-handled flappers in their hands, sometimes holding by their manes, and sometimes at a little distance; and the effect is both striking and pleasing. The phaetons are English built,[†] and ornamented with all the taste that country can boast, and all the expence the Asiatics are forward to incur, for their exterior importance;—the horses finely and splendidly set out, with silver nets to guard their necks from insects, and reins elegantly decorated;—and, to finish the whole, a kittesaw is suspended, not unfrequently, over the lady's head—which gives her the true Eastern grandeur of appearance.

Lady C—m—rs,[†] who, by the way, is one of the examples of the unions which here take place (I mean as to the disparity of age) is one of the most celebrated on this fashionable list; and, for attendant beaux, both as to smartness and variety, yields to no one.

Mrs Hartly is, however, quite another order of beings, and, like myself, is the daughter of an East India captain,[†] but conveyed by her father to Calcutta much earlier in life;—she has, therefore, or at least I imagine so, imbibed all their amiable prejudices, and thinks matrimony the duty of every young woman, who meets with an offer she cannot disapprove;[†]—for she persuades herself, and, perhaps, on experience, that esteem is the best basis of affection, and best security for our rejoicing in the choice we make; for what is called love (a propensity to approve, without the sanction of reason or the pause of sentiment) she affirms, blinds the understanding, and causes us to rest satisfied with pleasing manners, with too little attention to moral rectitude; an error in judgment, and a self-desertion, she asserts, we smart under to the latest moment of our existence.—I am, nevertheless, unconvinced, and unconverted.

She is, however, perfectly free from those traits, of affectation which are so generally conspicuous in a flattered woman, (and flattery at Calcutta is, literally speaking, our daily bread) has a cultivated understanding, and a feeling heart, and is at once the honour and happiness of her husband; my beloved mother, moreover, expired in her friendly arms: judge, then, if she is not dear to me!—But these are the very things that constitute my danger; for I know, though she knows it not, that without a congeniality of taste, of sentiment, of vivacity, and of serious-ness, there is no chance of felicity for me as a wife.—In a word, Arabella, my father is the model of him I can ever love, or ever wish to unite my destiny with; and, until I meet with this *rara avis*[†] (for well you know the treasures of his head, the treasures of his heart, and most agreeable person) I am determined to remain,

S. G.

❦

LETTER XI

I am half frantic with delight!—A review, Arabella!—What English *female* heart vibrates not at the bare mention of a review?—We are to dine in the New Fort,[†] at the commanding-officer's, (the Fort Major) whose house is situated within its circumference; and it is deemed one of the finest forts in the world, has a chain across the river, to secure the harbour from invasion, covers near five miles of ground, and has all the bustling charms of a garrison.

This fort, which was erected by the East India Company, at an immense expence, is, I find, the nursery for forming and disciplining the troops from England; and it is with pleasure I am enabled to assure you, that they are provided for in an ample manner, when in garrison, and kindly treated; which, in fact, is very different to the notions entertained, and the opinions circulated, in England.—It is true, that, when called forth into the field, their duty is not easily performed, the intense heat of the climate being hard to support; but, in order to throw in every possible softening, their pay is augmented to twelve rupees (forty shillings) a month, which augmentation is called *Batta-money*.[†]—And, as a proof of the advantages held out to them, one of these common soldiers, who was shewn to me a few days before he embarked, left India with seven hundred pounds[†] of his own acquiring, for England!—Yet it is doubtful whether he will remain there or not; for few revisit their native country, who do not, after a short period, re-enter the East India service.

The barracks, I am informed, are very fine, of course the men are comfortably lodged; and, as it is the interest, so it is obviously the desire of the Company, to keep them neat in their lodging, their persons, and their feeding, (death and dirt being synonymous in this climate[†]) the last is therefore diligently guarded against, to prevent the dire ravages of the first.

The garrison consists, you must understand, almost solely of the Company's troops,[†] the Government forces being seldom quartered there.—These soldiery are, however, held in high respect, and form a regular guard of centinels at the Governor's and the other great officers houses, and also patrole the streets, as members of the police, to clear them of such nuisances as they would otherwise be liable to, and particularly from sailors, when in a state of inebriety; and over this part of the military a Town Major presides, who belongs to the Company, and is the regulating officer, or general intendant, on all occasions.

Near the fort is the hospital I have already mentioned, erected for the reception of *all* indisposed persons, from whatever cause; throughout which, the wards or chambers are so neat and accommodating, that wretchedness reposes, and malady is put to flight.—It is lighted and cooled by verandas, and every possible means are adopted to procure the free circulation of air, &c. &c.; and it is allowed, by all who have seen it, to be superior to every thing under that appellation in the universe: nor could I forbear, on viewing it, exclaiming,

These are imperial works, and worthy kings.[†]

I was, however, informed immediately, by one present, of the source and nature of its establishment; and find it was built by the united contributions of the Europeans[†] of Calcutta, and the Company.—Yes, Arabella, this blessed asylum originates from commerce, and owes its support solely to commerce;—and observe, so charmed am I with the benevolence and the liberality of its institution, that, should I ever have an unwieldy fortune to leave behind me, the only hospital I will endow with it; shall be the Hospital of Calcutta.—But I am unable to impress you with the pleasurable sensations I enjoyed, on being an eye-witness of this invaluable place of refuge and accommodation for my diseased fellow-creatures and fellow-countrymen.

To gain admission into the hospital of Calcutta, there is no other interest or recommendation necessary, than being an European, and deprived of health. Moreover, men of honour and humanity,

tender of the lives of those received under their care, and tena-
cious of the just application of their subscription-money, are
its visitants and superintendants; no experiments can therefore
be tried, at the hazard of a worthy, though humble individual's
safety; no harpy keepers[†] can grind the face of the patients, or
riot in plenty, whilst they are expiring from wretchedness and
neglect; nor is a single nurse continued, that fails to perform the
duties of her engagement: and the manifold restored patients
prove the utility and the benevolence of the institution.

I blush, Arabella, to feel, that all I have written, as I have it
from my father's assertion, is an impeachment of the customs (in
this instance) in my native country; and it would be god-like in
you to promote new and salutary regulations, by publishing so
noble an example as I have thus set before you.

I am so struck with these matters, that I cannot forbear making
them the frequent subjects of my conversation; extolling the
country I now reside in, and sighing for the disgraces of the
country I have quitted; and, could you but behold the fixed
attention of my auditors, you would smile:—but, in the pastoral
language of Shenstone,

> They love me the more when they hear
> Such tenderness fall from my tongue.[†]

I was prevailed upon to be mistress of a phaeton in this
excursion; but so *outré* should I have exhibited myself,[†] that
I intreated my father would let me drive him. This was not
granted. An exchange was, however, settled, that was equally
to my satisfaction; for Mrs Hartly took my father with her, and I
had her husband for my cicisbeo.—O Arabella! if you knew half
Mr Hartly's virtues—filial, conjugal, paternal, universal—you
would rise up and say, this is a man worthy—worthy female
respect, worthy masculine celebrity; yet does he appear perfectly unconscious of his own merit, and is the first to praise,
and the last to condemn, every person living that is mentioned
before him. I think I must devote one entire letter to his history,
notwithstanding subject-matter flows in upon me so rapidly, that

I am at a loss what to give the preference to. I am, indeed, aware, that the colour of my own mind is apt to bias my choice; and that I rather entertain you with what interests my feelings, or flatters my fancy, than such particulars as may be best entitled to your perusal;—it is an error I will endeavour to correct, when I next give myself an opportunity of assuring you, that I am,

Your's, &c.

S.G.

✤

LETTER XII

The party to-day was brilliant—all that pomp and splendor could do, was done, to conceal the ravages of burning suns; and never were military gentlemen more animated, more obsequious, or camp more delightful; but Mars in the East, like Hercules at the court of Omphale,[†] has more gallantry than hostility about him.

Between Chitpore, the Nabob's house, and the Fort, at a place called Bugee Bugee,[†] a perpetual encampment, *in terrorem*,[†] I imagine, is kept up, to prevent any fatal surprize for the future; and a very pretty appearance it makes; but you will, no doubt, as it is situated in the very neighbourhood, hear more of it in future; for the review, of which I have been so happy a spectator, is quite a distinct and separate entertainment.

The troops performed all their evolutions[†] with equal credit to themselves and their commanders: nevertheless, from my acquaintance with the gentlemen, &c. &c. the whole display had, to me, more of a public shew, calculated to please the ladies, than to alarm the enemies of the Company by their skilful manoeuvrings; for which gay and giddy idea I beg the gentlemen's pardon—and very candidly acknowledge, that though their great complaisance has removed every idea of terror from my mind, yet the utility of these reviews may be very great; for (besides keeping the soldiers in practice) the minds they are intended to influence behold them in a quite different light, and tremble at the idea of their prowess.

We had a superb gala at the Fort Major's; who is so agreeable a man,[†] Arabella, that I detected myself in the act of enquiring, whether he was married or single. His lady, however, very opportunely appeared, to save my credit and reconcile me to myself; for she evidently merited and engaged my entire approbation, without any alloy.

She made me many pretty compliments; and, whilst I beheld her, and listened to her, I became impatient to know whether she had a little family or not (for it is my wish to be acquainted with all the children at Calcutta), and I have obtained her promise to introduce me at her Bungilo in a short time.

I am told, this passion for the society of children is the characteristic of an unvitiated taste: it may be so; but of this I am certain, that the politeness of the people of Calcutta is such, that what is not vice, they will exalt into virtue; and what is, they will melt down, by their charitable report, into error and misfortune.

You can have no notion of the *nonchalance* and *dégagement*[†] with which I conducted myself through the day; but you will recollect, that women, who are accustomed to live with a multitude of men, acquire a *modest* assurance (let me call it) private education cannot bestow.—Friendship and respect are the sentiments reciprocally professed, and chearfulness and joy the universal objects: therefore, those who can do the kindest, or say the pleasantest things, are unquestionably the most esteemed companions; for Othello's liberal-mindedness seems to prevail throughout (at least) all my agreeable connections.

> "'Tis not to make me jealous, to say my wife
> is fair, loves company, sings, dances well,
> &c. &c.; for, where virtue is, these are
> most virtuous."[†]

I am sensible I am not correct in my quotation;[†] but a visit to your library will enable you to read it at large, for both your instruction and amusement.

But, instead of ending this letter *en militaire*,† as was my intention, I must touch upon a circumstance that I advert to with a sigh.—In my (*dear*, I had almost called it) native country, existence is pleasing far beyond the period at which it becomes painful here; the early maturity of the natives leading down to early decay; insomuch, that you would be shocked to behold a woman of thirty; for her appearance, Arabella, is equal, in infirmity and wrinkles, at least, to the oldest-looking woman in England at three-score. Both sexes marry young, have families, decline, depart, and are remembered only in their offspring.— Not so the Europeans, even at Calcutta—having received their birth in the happy zone of your residence, Arabella, their nerves are much stronger strung; their youth, moreover, is passed under the same healthful meridian, which enables them to endure the Eastern sun, for ten or twelve years of their mid-life, with toler- able satisfaction; and their days are lengthened into old-age by their return to Britain.—But we will, quit this melancholy side of the prospect, if possible, for ever.

The Nabob, I need not tell you, is merely a viceroy to the Mogul, in like manner with your Lord Lieutenant of Ireland, and the representative of his most sublime master. Formerly his residence was at a distance from Calcutta,† and his intercourse with the Europeans restricted to embassies; but now his palace of Chitpore (for well does it deserve the name of a palace) is only four miles, as I have already told you, from Hartly House; and on such friendly terms does he live with the military gentlemen, that he gives them entertainments of dinners, fireworks, &c. &c. at an immense expence; but always eats alone;† according to the customs of the Asiatic Mahometans, seated on the ground, which is overspread by superb carpets (by the way, the only carpets I have heard of in India—the fine matting being, for coolness, substituted in their place); and, what will surprise you, is, that the captain or commanding officer of the Nabob's guards,† which consist of a whole battalion of black troops, is an Englishman, a younger brother of an ennobled family, and who paid 80,000 l. (acquired in this world of wealth) for the appointment.

The uniform of this battalion is the same worn by the Company's troops—red turned up with white,—with turbans to distinguish the divisions thereof.

The exterior of Chitpore in some degree bespeaks the grandeur of its owner; but I am informed few things exceed the magnificence of its interior architecture and ornaments. The apartments are immense—the baths elegant—and the seraglio, though a private one, suitable, in every particular, to the rest of the building: nor must the gardens be unmentioned; for they not only cover a wide extent of ground, but are furnished with all the beauties and perfumes of the vegetable kingdom. When he rides out, a detachment of his black troops attend him;—and observe, Arabella, the Nabob *Salam* (the word for compliment from his soldiers) is a most graceful application of the back part of the hand to the front of the turban, with a slight bend of the head.

But I should tell you, all persons of any rank have, in addition, to the servants I have described, a *Salam-bearer*; and the note or card, containing compliments of whatever kind, is called a *Chit*:†—nor is there a morning that my toilet is not covered with *Salams* and *Chits*, to the no small gratification of my pride, and support of my consequence.

Billiards are much played at Calcutta—a game well adapted, in my opinion, to the convenience of the country—it requiring no great exertions of either body or mind: but I retract that opinion on the instant; for the sums won and lost must keep the blood in a perpetual fever, even to endangering the life of the parties.—In private families, the billiard is a kind of state-room.—At the coffee-houses, you are accommodated with tables and attendants for eight *anas*, or half rupees,† by candle-light, or six by daylight, a certain number of hours—every coffee-house having at least two tables: so that men of spirit have as many fashionable opportunities of ruining themselves here, as you Europeans can boast. I lament this abuse of understanding; but fashionable vices are the hardest of all others to eradicate; and, that it will ever become fashionable to be moral or well-judging, I have my doubts and apprehensions. You, my dear girl, are a blessed exception. I have friends around me, at this moment, that are your counterpart, and models of all that is good or great in the human character.——I have written myself into the spleen,[†] and will therefore bid you goodnight.

I have told you, here are livery-stables. I now add, that horses are cheap at Calcutta;[†] and, what you would little expect to hear of, racers are bred for the turf.

The race-ground is a distinct part of the Esplanade; and the horses that run for a subscription-plate, as in England, are fed, they inform me, with meal, as you English feed pigeons;[†] and I shall soon have it in my power to give you a complete description of this amusement in the East, as the annual period is now not far distant. I have resumed my pen; for Mr Hartly and my father are not, I find, yet returned from spending the evening at the Governor's;[†]—and, though palanquins are safe conveyances, and their company numerous, I must hear they are come home before I attempt to repose for the night, or, more properly, morning; for it is now more than half after three.

Palanquins are, indeed, such state appendages,[†] that, if a gentleman at Calcutta (which is frequently the case) chuses to walk when on a visiting party, his palanquin must follow him in the same form, in every particular, as if he himself was within; a departure therefrom being deemed a solecism in polite etiquette.

Bless me! what do I hear?—Drums and musical instruments—and the streets are suddenly illuminated. What can it mean?—Mrs Hartly is, however, at my door; and I may, perhaps, have it in my power, before I conclude, to make amends for this very dull epistle.

A Gentoo marriage procession, Arabella, and an extreme pretty one too, was the novelty my ever-attentive friend to my amusement, Mrs Hartly, called upon me to be a spectator of.

The bride was carried in an elegant palanquin (Did I ever tell you the difference between a lady's and a gentleman's palanquin? I believe not) with tassels of immense finery (the distinguishing decoration for ladies) and near forty couple of men preceding, and an equal number following it; with wreaths of flowers beautifully fancied, and lights without number. After which came the bridegroom in his palanquin also, with great ceremony, and as many attendants as his bride; but not one woman, except herself, in the whole procession.

The musicians played the most lively tunes imaginable,[†] and the company danced in pairs as they passed along, making use of the wreaths with nearly as much taste and good effect as the figure-dancers in your London theatres; and in this manner they proceed, it seems, through the whole town—the Gentoos, and their Padras (the Bramins) living all around it.

They live, Arabella, (except from the austerities, in some instances, in their religion) the most inoffensively and happily of all created beings—their Pythagorean tenets[†] teaching them, from their earliest infancy, the lesson of kindness and benevolence; nor do they intentionally hurt any living thing:—from their temperance they derive health, and from the regulation of their passions, contentment; and come immediately under that description of Pope,

> They ask no angel's wings, no seraph's fire;
> But think, admitted to their native sky,
> Their faithful dog shall bear them company,[†]

I shall, however, make it my business, now my curiosity is awakened and interested, to learn all possible intelligence of a people so peculiar, and so distinct from the rest of the world— and one door of knowledge can be easily opened upon me; for the Sekars are all Gentoos (kind of brokers)[†] under whose care the East India captains put their merchandize, and who fix the rates of purchase according to the ebbs and flows of the supplies intrusted to their superintendence; and many of them amass large fortunes. Their profits are established, and their faith unimpeached; and they are found so necessary, that it is impossible to dispose of European goods without their assistance[†] or notice: moreover, any of the Company's servants who arrive in the India ships, and bring property with them, on application to a Sekar, are furnished with whatever money they stand in need of, without bond or other legal security; for a breach of moral rectitude on the part of the borrower would be productive of indelible disgrace and personal danger—the Company protecting these Gentoo brokers, notaries, or factors, in all their lawful rights.

My father, you know, is that sort of man, who steals the love of all who know him; accordingly, his Sekar, though a Gentoo, and tho' such intercourse is unusual, has attached himself to his employer by the heart-felt ties of friendship and affection—walks in and out of Hartly House at pleasure†—and converses by signs with me, with many marks of high approbation. He has moreover, I find, a relation that is a young Bramin; and (shall I own to you a most extravagant piece of vanity, which has recently sprung up in my mind?) an admirer, Arabella, of his character would be to me a proof of my attractions I should be proud of.

I will tell Mrs Hartly my whim, and engage his relation to introduce him. The compliments I at present receive, are all of the common-place kind, and may with equal propriety be addressed to any sister female; but to please a Bramin I must have perfections of the mental sort, little inferior to the purity and the benignity of angels:—in a word, my good dispositions would be cultivated and brought forward by such an acquaintance, and my bad ones corrected; and, as celibacy is their engagement, the soul would be the only object of attachment and admiration.

You will, I suppose, conclude, flattery has turned my head; but, to be serious, it would delight my peculiar taste to converse with beings of so superior an order, and to become an humble copy of their exemplary and beautiful simplicity.

What a transition!†—but it is not my fault; for my father, on coming home, told me, as an agreeable piece of news, that the theatre will open next week—and I rejoiced beyond measure to hear it.

Though, you must understand, the stage at Calcutta is under regulations which Britain has renounced; for there are no female performers;†—and I could most heartily wish that this reproach of morality could be done away in England. The custom, you know, is foreign, and alone imported by the polished Charles, on his return from exile in foreign lands; and you will not attempt, I am persuaded, to deny that this fatal change in theatrical politics has rendered the playhouses so many nurseries of vice, or public seraglios, far more censurable and licentious than any the Eastern world contains;—for the difficulty here is for any male individual (except their owner) to get into them; whereas, in your metropolis, every nocturnal exhibition, of even the most sentimental drama, is an advertisement where gentlemen, on certain conditions, may be accommodated with a temporary companion—and I blush to recollect the incompatibility thereof with delicacy and propriety.—But I will tell you more of my mind on this subject, when I have seen with what effect dress can bring forth (as ladies) the smart young fellows of Calcutta, on theatrical ground.

What a mistake did I fall into, when I imagined, that one day spent in domestic luxury would be a picture of all the succeeding ones I should pass!

Amusement is varied with every varying season of the year, except the months when the *hot winds* (what a paradox! yet is it a reality) annoy this coast, and the rude hand of sickness interrupts every scheme of pleasure; insomuch that, to guard your own life at every avenue, and fortify your mind against the wounds it must sustain in the persons of your dying friends, is the whole employment.

Heaven! how equal is thy bounty, and thy goodness to the children of men!—The scenes I now participate would be too highly fraught with felicity, untempered by the ravages of disease, and the distresses of heat; for, at the seasons I have mentioned,

> —— in blazing height of noon,
> The sun, oppress'd, is plung'd in thickest gloom:
> Still horror reigns, a dreary twilight round
> Of struggling night and day, malignant mix'd;
> For, to the hot equator crowding fast,
> Where, highly rarefied, the yielding air
> Admits their steam, incessant vapours roll.[†]

Whereas, in your soft climate, Arabella, such are your humble tables and humble pleasures, that all the transports of animation and of magnificence are unknown to you, and you creep through one dull track from infancy to age.

Adieu! adieu!—There is an oriental effusion for you! begun, I perceive, with too much solemnity for the turn I have given it;—but I must either be painfully serious, or idly gay, when I remember the days that are gone—days spent in the most rational delights—and in company with my (to me) lost Arabella.

Your's, &c.

S.G.

Letter XIII

On the race-ground, Arabella, (at a distance from the immediate track of the coursers, you will conceive) are two trees situated, whose spreading branches afford the most delightful shade, and under which I had it in contemplation to have voted for the erection of a temple.

But, behold! on mentioning them in terms of admiration, I was, to my surprize, told, they were called the Trees of Destruction[†]— and with great propriety, you will allow, when I add, that all the duels (which are not few in this country) are fought under them.

Duels at Calcutta!—my nature revolts at the idea!—Is not the angel of Death, then, sufficiently industrious in reducing the human race, that the arm of friend should be uplifted against friend (which I understand is the case) on as trivial provocation as in England, where the bills of mortality are so thinly filled?

But, Arabella, (for I will be gay, in my own defence, on even the gravest subjects) is it not a most mortifying abatement of my consequence, that these charms of mine have not yet sent two despairing, two passionate, or two any species of contending lovers and rivals, to die by the hands of each other, under these same trees, in my name?

Nay, so far am I from having occasioned a single duel, that I never suspected this convivial people of the bare idea of such a thing.—I must set to work, and, if possible, get at the knowledge of so extraordinary a circumstance; for I should suppose with Addison, (from all I have seen of their gallantry and their admiration) that, if they must quarrel, they would think nothing worth quarrelling about, except a fine woman;—and should it prove, (as that nevertheless favourite writer of mine affirms) 'that there is no quarrel without a woman in it,'† I shall be ashamed of my own insignificance, and break with all my male acquaintance for their light estimation of me.

If duelling is, as I am assured, the fashionable propensity, I shudder to think what dire ills a young and beautiful coquet might cause in this land!—But, for the peace of society, coquetry is practised at Calcutta in a new style;† for the handsome young women (except myself, Arabella) are all wives; and their adorers, you will perceive, could not, with any decent pretext, cut each other's throats; and few husbands are disturbed at the innocent freedoms of either manner or conversation in their *cara sposas.*†

You shall not, however, with that face of your's, come among us, until I am disposed of; for, though I am harmless where I have no competitor, having cast the eye of desire upon Chitpore, you would find me a formidable rival;—nor do I doubt (though tilting with the Nabob would be out of the question) but I could raise a little Army to oppose and combat such Europeans, at all points, as were capable of advancing your honour and glory at my expence.—And thus have I outlived the liberality of which my former letters brought you so striking a proof: but Chitpore was then unknown to me, and the Nabob, in appearance, out of my reach; whereas now I can throw out a lure whenever I please— and who can tell what dignities destined for

Your, &c.

S.G.†

END OF THE FIRST VOLUME

Volume II

Hartly House – II

I am this evening, Arabella, invited to a concert at the Governor's,[†] of gentlemen performers, who, I am told, are masters of the several instruments they undertake to exercise; for it is the common received opinion at Calcutta, in direct opposition to the Chesterfield tenet, that Nero himself, if he had not sunk the emperor in the fidler;[†] would have done honour to the imperial diadem by his musical taste and skill. But it was the pride of his nature alone that was gratified by his performances—his senses were untouched—his soul unharmonized—and enmity and death occupied his thoughts, even in the moment his fingers called forth sounds of delight: whereas, on the contrary, king David, who, as we have it on sacred record, not only played upon, but tuned his voice to his harp, was as great a king, and, with one only exception, as good a king, as any succeeding period can boast; neither his personal dignity, or his regal reputation, being lessened thereby.

I am going to make a distinction, which I expect you to subscribe to; and that is, the distinction between dressing to the best advantage, in order to do credit to our friends, and doing so for the purpose of gratifying our own vanity. Mrs Hartly is so proud of her guests, that she proclaims their imaginary, as well as real merits, far and wide: and I am sensible, in consequence of such partial reports, I am expected to be found the standard of fashion and good taste in the article of appearance.

Would it not therefore be to mortify her, and disgrace my father, if I was to fail in all possible and proper attention to my toilet?

I have not this day failed, I assure you; nor is the occasion a common one. The Governor is entitled to our respect, in honour of the British sovereign, in like manner as (on a court day) the British sovereign and his amiable consort are entitled to the *salams* and superb decorations of those who present themselves at St. James's.—And so much by way of apology for my splendid trappings; for, my dear girl, I have it yet to tell you, that a set of diamond pins from the very mines of Golconda[†] have been given me by my father, and a pair of bracelets of pearl, with gold clasps, studded with small brilliants, by Mrs Hartly, who declares to me, that whatever I behold of her prosperity originates from the friendly support of my father. I have also a necklace of pearl, of more value than I chuse to mention; and my hair will be decorated, my arms, and every part of my visible person, beyond all I can give you an idea of.

But, surprising to relate, Arabella—such is the corrected and confirmed principles of the Gentoos, that, though the diamond merchants travel with all their tempting treasures under their sole convoy, without fire-arms, &c. &c. not one of them has ever been deprived of an atom[†] of his property by this whole people.—What then are we Europeans made of? or how must we appear in their gentle and upright eyes, who have waded through the blood of millions,[†] to bring home gems of inconsiderable value, in comparison to what these travelling merchants are possessed of?—On such recollection, I am ashamed to know myself a European: nor can it be doubted.

If there are, as some tenets imply, a distinction of heavenly situations, will not this good-minded people occupy the first in rank; for nearest to the divine attributes of any thing you can have a conception of, is their kind-heartedness and probity.

I have had a harp presented me,[†] and am already complimented up on the delicacy of my finger. It is, you know, an instrument well adapted to this Arcadian climate; and I have played upon it at Hartly Bungilo by moon-light.—Can I go higher in my description thereof?

The ambition, Arabella, is, who shall have the honour of

adorning the top with a wreath, the daily offering of my host
of adorers;—and I wish you could behold the well-dissembled
dejection, and the well-dissembled delight, which mark the features of the rejected and approved votary: in a word, it requires
very peculiar gifts to believe one's self a mortal.

Apropos of mortality—I have visited the burying grounds[†],
which are to me scenes of melancholy entertainment, from the
affectionate fancy displayed in commemorating a departed friend;

For many a holy text around is strewed[†];

and the air of neatness, that proof of unabating attention, which
everywhere meets the eye, so unlike the crusts of dust which disgrace the labours of the sculptor in that first of royal sepulchres,
Westminster abbey, and the astonishing insensibility of the
French in this article (for in France, if we except the monuments
of their kings, not a stone tells where they lie)—the fairest, the
bravest, and the best, are alike unnoticed and unremembered.—
Strange and unaccountable circumstance!

You have visited St. Pancras, in the neighbourhood of London;
nay, I recollect we have visited it together, and together inter-
changed our sensations on the occasion; for there, as we read
it from the hand of the graver, are deposited the sacred and
beloved remains of infancy, of youth, of maturity, and of age.
Alas! Arabella, the Bengal burying grounds (for there are two of
them) though they greatly resemble that church-yard in monu-
mental erections, bear a melancholy testimony to the truth of my
observations on the short date of existence in this climate.

Born just to bloom and fade[†],

is the chief intelligence you receive from the abundant memori-
als of dissolved attachments and lamented relatives.

Obelisks, pagodas, &c. are erected at great expence; and the
whole spot is surrounded by as well-turned a walk as those you
traverse in Kensington Gardens, ornamented with a double row
of aromatic trees, which afford a solemn and beautiful shade: in a
word, not old Windsor churchyard, with all its cypress and yews,

is in the smallest degree comparable to them: and I quitted them with unspeakable reluctance.

There is no difference between these two grounds, but in the expence of the monuments, which denote that persons of large fortune arc there interred, and *vice versa*; whence, in order to preserve this difference in the appearance, the first ranks pay five hundred rupees, the second three hundred, for opening the ground; and they are disjoined merely by a broad road.

I intreated Mrs Hartly would lead me to my dear mother's last mansion—she started, and accused herself of the highest indiscretion, in consenting to my viewing a spot that could suggest such an idea to my mind; and so earnestly besought me, as a proof of my affection for her, to return home, and never again attempt to investigate a circumstance, so evidently desired by my father to be kept from my knowledge, that friendship and filial reverence prevailed over every other impulse, and I suffered her to put me into my palanquin without reply.

But palanquins are conveyances ill calculated to remove distressing thoughts; and, during my state of miserable sequestration from all social connection, I would gladly have exchanged places with any friend of yours, that enjoyed only a corner of a hackney-coach and your company. Nor shall I, from what I have this day experienced, ever be reconciled to this *sola*[†] condition, however conformable to the fashion of the country. This letter, my dear girl, will waft a sigh from your

SOPHIA GOLDBORNE

LETTER XV

Have I interested your curiosity by my mention of a concert? I can assure you, it well merits your notice and information.

It was performed in a grand hall or saloon, lofty and spacious beyond all I could have conceived. Dryden's *Timotheus*[†] was one of the pieces with which we were presented; the Coronation Anthem, a second; the overture to Artaxerxes, that *chef d'œuvre* of Arne[†], a third—of all which I was an inchanted auditor: yet were there moments, Arabella, when a painful pleasure, from the article of your absence, stole upon my heart, and traced out such correspondent lines in my countenance, that Mrs Hartly (whom nothing escapes) charged me with some soft recollections of England.—'Why will you not be sincere,' said she, 'with a woman whose heart is in your hand; and confess, what is so apparent, that your affections are not your own? Think you, I am not sufficiently liberal-minded to love those you love, and resign you, though one of the first pleasures of my existence, to the man of your choice?—O wherefore is he an inhabitant of a world I must never hope to behold again?'

Now, who shall say, that love and friendship are not the same?—for similar are the sensations of the tender regret separation excites, and similar the animated delight of a re-union: and we shall meet, my Arabella—we shall re-enjoy the satisfactions distance deprives us of; we shall—but all this plaintive language is very unoriental,[†] and shall be renounced; and more especially, as there is no due proportion between the strength of your attachment and mine—for I follow the fortunes of my father—the hand of destiny has torn me from you: whereas you are now, on the death of your aunt, perfectly mistress of yourself, and can, if your inclination prompts you, come to me with propriety; whereas I could not come to you, unaccompanied by my only parent, without dishonour—the dishonour of, violating my filial duty. Let me hear from you upon this point; and take care you well acquit yourself, or, on being weighed in the usual balance of even my warmest partiality, you will be found wanting.

The Governor's dress[†] gives you his character at once— unostentatious and sensible. His lady, however, is the great ornament of places of polite resort; for her figure is elegant—her manners lively and engaging—and her whole appearance a model of taste and magnificence.

Envy, malice, and uncharitableness[†]—how do those malign vices blemish and deform that last best work of Heaven, the human mind!—Perfection itself is not secure from their baneful breath. But I forget, upon this occasion, that there is a spur to their intent at Calcutta, beyond what they can generally plead. A change of Governor would introduce a change in Eastern politics; and numbers blaze forth, that are now unremembered. But, as I have told you before, I am no judge of these matters; and will not, therefore, trust myself on a subject that might mislead me. The heart will, I grant you, have its private decision, and its private election; and what power or fiat, less than divine, shall deprive it of its natural rights?

I foresaw that this concert would produce some great event. My father looked almost as young as his daughter;—a circumstance I premise as an apology for what is to follow. A widow lady[†] with thousands at her feet—a superior offer to every thing my youth and person has procured me—has insinuated, in so many very explicit terms, to Mrs Hartly, that she is ambitious to make him master of them.

Mrs Hartly executed her commission with a very grave face, and I laughed; but, I believe, looked chagrined, on my father professing himself much honoured, and that he would wait upon the lady.—Arabella, what do those words imply? that I have lost my father?—Was he not wedded to my mother's memory when in England, when whole oceans rolled between him and her hallowed remains? and can he, will he insult—But I have done: we are none of us angels, my dear girl—we are frail, frail mortality.

But should it be possible for so astonishing an event to take place, farewell India, farewell for ever! My father's blessing, his permission to end my days with you, and once, but once, to behold my mother's tomb, is all I will ask: for my grandfather, you know, has left me a sufficient provision; and I will constitute it my sole support. My mind, so little power have I over it, although I write so calmly, is all a chaos.—My father calls for me: I will instantly attend him—receive his commands with firmness, with resignation; nor dare so far to invert the order of things, as to hope or wish he should regulate his conduct by my will and pleasure. He is my father, Arabella; and I have only to forget he was the husband of my mother, to approve all his conduct.

The trial is over, and you shall judge how I supported it, without one anticipating reflection escaping me.—I found him alone in the garden veranda, and unusually serious. He rose when I entered—smiled—and looked my father.

'My dear Sophy,' said he, seating both me and himself—'I am this instant returned from a very affecting scene.' I sighed and was silent.

'You heard what Mrs Hartly said last night, and must recollect my reply.'—It was the nearest of all remembrances to my heart; but I only bowed in answer.—'The lady,' continued he, 'has a noble mind'—(I trembled as he spoke, but he was too much taken up with his subject to notice it)—'she deserved every polite attention in return for the high compliment she made me—and all things are settled between us.'—'My mother!' exclaimed I, in a scarce articulate voice, and fainted in his arms—A fine piece of heroism, after all my preparation and resolves!—I instantly revived, complained of heat, and begged he would proceed.

'You are sensible, my beloved girl,' said he, 'how awkward the situation of a young unmarried woman is at Calcutta;—you have declined every overture made you, though some of them deserved a better fate: but your inclinations are your own—I am the friend, not the tyrant of your heart, Sophia; and such I will prove myself.

Ah! sighed that rebellious heart—am I to be the saving consideration for your conduct?

'A woman of honour, fortune, and merit,' continued he, 'is not an offer a man of my time of life could have thought of; and the opportunity of giving my child a protector of her own sex, is an opportunity not to be left unimproved. She will not return to England without you; and, with a greatness of soul you will respect, has transferred her affections from the father to the

child.——Yes, my Sophia, she reveres my sorrows—acknowledges my heart cannot be recalled from the mansions of the
dead—asks only my friendship, your friendship, and will prove
herself an ornament to her sex.—Our inclinations, I repeat it,
will not always obey our voice; whence I shall ever leave my
child's unfettered:—but, though we cannot bestow them, we can
regulate them at will, and make an act of stern necessity an act
of choice, in every thing but delivering up our persons to an
unbeloved object.'

I wept aloud, Arabella—embraced my father—besought his
pity, and his pardon; and all this without his discovering my
motive—for, unconscious of deviating in a single thought from
what was excellent and amiable in his own character, it never
once occurred to him, that little mean suspicions occupied my
breast.

We are to dine with her tomorrow; and, next to Mrs Hartly,
I have assured my father I will love and revere her : but, from
knowing Mrs Hartly first, she has got possession, said I, of the
very next place to my Arabella in my affections, and I do think
can never be superseded. My father smiled at my mental etiquette, and left me with a full purse to collect myself at leisure.

Well do I now know my father is incapable of changing:—but
beware, Mrs D————, how you flatter, lest you should deceive
yourself; for such a friend, Arabella, as my father, must be dangerous to such a heart as Mrs D————'s; which, having once
loved to the height of revealing its sentiments—of rising superior
to the bars of decorum, and the chains of custom—cannot answer
for its feelings, or in future hope to restrain them by any human
fiat. Yet hopeless love, my father says, where the principles are
pure and upright, always subsides into friendship: it may be so;
but I would not chuse to adopt Mrs D————'s example in this
instance, however unexceptionable I may find her in every other.
Is this a mark of a narrow or a liberal way of thinking? I will take
your word for it, though I cannot my father's: he is no judge in his
own cause, and entertains too great an opinion of the force of just
sentiments and the authority of reason.

This is an eastern adventure we had not taken into our account;—but all females do not come under our British bard's description,

> ——She never told her love,
> But let concealment, &c. &c.[†]

for who does not know the lines as well as I, the writer of this epistle? and it is impertinent to assume the credit of information we cannot give.

I shall to-morrow morning exchange the soft passion for the subjects I have till now uninterruptedly pursued—my accounts of Calcutta, &c. &c.

Your own,

S.G.

❀

LETTER XVI

Weddings here, Arabella, are very joyous things to all parties; especially, I should suppose, to the padre or clergyman, who frequently receives twenty gold mohrs[†] for his trouble of performing the ceremony. The bride and bridegroom's friends assemble, all elegantly dressed, at one or other of the young couple's nearest relatives, and are most sumptuously entertained; and the congratulatory visits on the occasion put the whole town in motion. It is a festival I have not, however, the smallest desire to treat my friends with; for, even was my choice fixed, and every obstacle obviated, I should have unconquerable objections to making so public an exhibition of myself on so solemn a change of condition—an idea I cannot say I have in common with my acquaintance; for I have reason to believe, I am the only person in Calcutta, not even my well-beloved Mrs Hartly excepted, that has the same idea in this instance—which is entirely the effect of custom.

A very pleasing, because a very singular circumstance, is, that in this country the head gardener is a professed botanist,† and of course conversible on every part of creation around him : hence the classes and characters, as well as the beauties, of those shrubs and flowers that attract my notice most, are my frequent topics of observation and enquiry. And besides the entertainment, the benefit is abundant of having a well-educated person in this capacity; for his judgment is the household land, where the garden is concerned; and you are sure to have your table supplied, and your flower vases furnished with good sense and propriety. Moreover, I can mention ladies, (and myself, Arabella, for one) who, when at a loss for a subject, are enabled, by this gentleman's assistance, to read a lecture on the several articles of which their bouquet is composed. But to be serious, to me it is highly agreeable, let the art or science be what it may, to meet with people of information and good address: it is giving you a companion wherever you go, and promoting that disposition for local enjoyment so much recommended by moral writers, and which undeniably forms a large portion of our happiness. Accordingly, I have already learned to distinguish the native and exotic beauties of the parterre, and with no small pleasure (I might say pride, for I certainly have much nationality about me) discover that many English plants and trees, particularly apple-trees, which are hard to rear, and consequently their fruit of great value, are treated with all the attention and tenderness foreign products are honoured with in England.

Besides, do but conceive the advantage to a man or woman of fashion, who has taste without leisure, and a desire of knowledge without the smallest inclination for study, to have a liberal-bred officer (I may properly call it) of their household, capable of qualifying them to figure away upon subjects that are an honour to human nature, with whom they can converse at will on the most rational and delightful topics. If you love me, fail not to enforce these considerations on your wealthy and right honourable friends, and at least put them in possession of one means of shining. Nevertheless, my sweet friend, amidst all the joys our double seasons yield, the following lines frequently occur to me; and, if you can feel their truth in Britain, conceive how strongly they must affect my mind in this all-subduing climate—

> Who can unpitying see the flow'ry race,
> Shed by the morn, their new-flush'd bloom resign
> Before the parching beam?[†]

Three of the gentlemen, who so largely contributed to our entertainment at the concert, are, I find, theatrical performers; the Patty and Miss Sycamore of *The Maid of the Mill*,[†] the Rosetta and Lucinda of *Love in a Village*; and such are their agreeable persons, that I doubt not but, by the aids of the toilet, they fill up those several parts without dissatisfaction to either the ear or eye.

I have not yet described to you the wonders of a dessert. Ices,[†] Arabella, (could you have supposed such a thing?) ices, in the highest perfection, are, in the months of November and December, presented you at Calcutta.—This circumstance of the ice was to me so wonderful, that I was earnest to have it accounted for; and I find, that this temporary luxury is procured from some of the slender inland (if I may so express myself) branches of the Ganges, which are cut out into canals, or flow in rivulets, under various names. A thin plate of ice forming itself thereon, in some of the coldest nights the coldest season affords, is taken from thence with great care, and manufactured for the first tables: nor do some of the tanks or fish-ponds less advance the purposes of elegant accommodation in this respect, when the evenings are such as you have in April, or the mornings somewhat like your month of October.

At supper last night I drank a glass of excellent London porter,[†] with sensations of recognition you may much better imagine than I can describe. Mrs Hartly tells me, it is always on the sideboard, for those who like it; but I never before heard it mentioned. We have also small-beer, perry, and cyder, from my native country, and fine spruce-beer, the produce of Bengal; and, having more company than usual, we did not retire until after four o'clock:

and I begin almost to think it just, that those who thus continue to have two days in one, should live but half as long as those people who divide their existence, upon even a fashionable average, between sleep and amusement.

Had Thomson never been in India, how, let me ask you, could he have so admirably described an animal, that, to be known in all its terrors, must be seen?

> Lo! the green serpent, from its dark abode,
> Which e'en Imagination fears to tread,
> At noon forth issuing, gathers up its train
> In orbs immense, then, darting out anew,
> Seeks the refreshing fount; by which diffus'd,
> He throws his folds: and, while with threat'ning tongue,
> And deathful jaws erect, the monster curls
> His flaming crest, all other thirst, appall'd,
> Or shiv'ring flies, or check'd at distance stands,
> Nor dares approach.[†]

To-morrow I am to be presented to Mrs D————. I feel an awkwardness, I know not why; for, from the accounts I have received of her, any other worthy man but my own dear father should have my warmest vote to obtain her. Her fortune, Arabella, is her smallest merit; for she possesses, it seems, much intellectual cultivation, and has an excellent heart;—a *soft* one she has proved it to be. Good night: read not the last two or three lines with attention, that you may not condemn

Your most affectionate,

S.G.

Letter XVII

The visit is over—and, if my father can resist the merits and winning graces of this woman, I will only say, he is more than human.

Ah! Arabella, with what nice attention had she prepared for our reception!—her house is a palace in miniature, and her servants the best-formed and disciplined, if I may so express myself, I have ever yet seen.

I approached her with a somewhat of awe and reserve I could not get the better of; but her countenance is open as day, and her smile engaging.—'By permission, Madam,' said my father, with an air of humility I am confident touched her to the soul, 'by your permission I bring my daughter to solicit your friendship; she is prepared to honour you, and your indulgence will soon teach her to love you; and may this first interview be ever remembered by you both with the pleasure it gives to me.'

'You have deceived me, Sir,' said she.—'Is this your child, that stands in need of countenance and support?—What may she not command at Calcutta!—She exceeds my utmost expectation.'

'Sophia,' replied he, 'is a good girl, Madam, and has continued to lay her father under the greatest obligations; her voyage to India was solely for my sake; she has left friendships behind her that are not easily supplied: it is incumbent upon me, therefore, to procure her every possible compensation.'

A polite and animated return was made by the lady to this speech, and perfectly became her; for, as she does not call herself young, she has a licence to speak in terms that would be too assuming for you or me. But I have a discovery to communicate, that alarms me, perhaps, without a cause;—she has a son, Arabella; and, as their heads at Calcutta are full of lovers and husbands, I am more than half afraid there is some plot in this sudden acquaintance and friendship.

I watched her eyes with diligence; but her whole demeanor was unexceptionable, and the character of the fair friend finely preserved; but she seems to understand the method of attaching such a man as my father, and, I fear, will reverse the fable of the Turtle and Ring Dove,[†] having got the clue from him to his heart, by making herself as necessary to his peace, as she must be pleasing to his sensibility.

Now, Arabella, am I about to play the woman in a most unworthy degree. I have never beheld Mrs D———'s son, or even heard of him until this visit; yet am I armed, at all points, to refuse an offer I may never receive.—What unpardonable prejudgment! May he not have his mother's graces, his mother's understanding, which is much celebrated?—He may; but take my word for it, he is not the man I shall ever unite myself to; for your made-up matches are, of all things, the most odious to me. Let the man have eyes to chuse me, on whom I am ever prevailed upon to bestow my hand, that I may not suppose the question is coolly canvassed whether I shall be accepted by him, aye or no. I am neither a vain nor an ambitious woman; but I own I am not able to stand the idea of being pointed out by the maternal finger to a booby heir, that would never otherwise have thought of me. I would not thus be disposed of, even to the Nabob himself. Jerry Blackacre† (for so my mind would perversely call this unknown young man) never once, however, made his appearance; nor did Mamma glance the way I apprehended.—May I find myself alarmed without a cause!

Mrs D——— is a woman of taste and good education, and has a menagery, as you call it in England, of the feathered tribes peculiar to this country; beautiful cockatoos, and minhos† without number; lories—but she gave five-and-twenty gold mohrs for three of them; they are natives of Batavia, and in high esteem here for their articulation: she has also a bird with buff-coloured wings and a white breast, of the Bilo species, that has a million of worshippers among the Gentoos, and named by them the Bramine kite.

She has presented me with one of each, if Mrs Hartly can forgive my introduction of them into her family; but I am certain, if they prove inconvenient inmates at Calcutta, she will have them accommodated at Hartly bungilo, and my little friends will be kind to them for my sake.

There are, besides the Bramine kite, very many birds that enjoy high privileges; the Indian raven, for example, (a bird known in Europe by the name of the Rhinoceros bird) which

draw themselves up in curious ranks in the most populous streets
of this town without interruption, and are called by the sailors
Jerry Daw's soldiers.[†]

Mrs D——— is to return our visit in a few days. I am but
a novice in these matters; but it appears very extraordinary to
me, that, after what has passed between her and Mrs Hartly,
(and that she cannot flatter herself my father's refusal of her can
be a secret, as it speaks herself) she should chuse to mix with
such heterogeneous parties: but she carries off the affair with
an admirable grace, in which my father assists her in a manner
peculiar to himself, and, I believe, without her perception of it.
It is well for the world at large, and happy for me, that all his
arts are honest ones, and all his frauds pious; for, had a bad
man his endowments, his collected mind, his command of face,
who would be able to stand against him?—I will teach myself to
be a more dutiful daughter, and less capricious member of the
community, that I may merit the partiality I know you feel for

Your's, &c.

S. G.

LETTER XVIII

No wonder lawyers return from this country rolling in wealth;[†]
their fees are enormous; if you ask a single question on any
affair, you pay down your gold mohr, Arabella, (two pounds)!
and if he writes a letter of only three lines, twenty-eight rupees
(four pounds)! I tremble at the idea of coming into their hands;
for what must be the recoveries, to answer such immense
charges!—You must, however, be informed, that the number
of acting attornies on the court roll is restricted to twelve; who
serve an articled clerkship of three years only, instead of five, as
in England. These twelve regular-bred gentlemen, nevertheless,
from motives of friendship, or for certain *douceurs*,[†] best known

to themselves, lend their names, on manifold occasions, to the great extension of practice.

The style of living, if you wish to be deemed genteel, is indeed such as demands an ample revenue; but the custom of the country is so much in favour of improving your fortune at all points, that it is not considered in the smallest degree derogatory for gentlemen of whatever denomination to merchandise, or, as I have already mentioned, to provide lodgings or lodging-houses for the East India Company's servants, who are only temporary residents.

The fee for making a will is in proportion to its length, from five gold mohrs upwards; and as to marriage articles, I should imagine they would half ruin a man, and a process at law be the destruction of both parties. A man of abilities and good address in this line, if he has the firmness to resist the fashionable contagion, gambling, need only pass one seven years of his life at Calcutta, to return home in affluent circumstances; but the very nature of their profession leads them into gay connections, and, having for a time complied with the humour of their company from prudential motives, they become tainted, and prosecute their bane from the impulses of inclination.

My father's Sekar has obliged me with the introduction of his relation, the young Bramin, at Hartly House. He has not left the Gentoo university at Benares,† which is remarkable for its sanctity, above three years. He made us, however, but a very short visit; as it was near our tea-hour, and he could not, by the laws of his religion, partake of any refreshment; but promised by his interpreter to see us again soon. My vanity will not let me suppress one compliment that was paid me by a Moor of great dignity: 'Such,' said he, 'are the daughters of Paradise.'†—I would have given more than I shall mention to have known my Bramin had distinguished me from the rest of the company; but was not so happy. We will, nevertheless, if you please, talk of him in his absence, or at least of the people to which he belongs.

The Gentoos, Arabella, are divided into five tribes;† the first of which is the most highly esteemed, and the only one (like the tribe of Levi among the Jews) from whence the priests are taken: I need not therefore add, it is called Bramins.

The second is the Sittris, whose profession ought to be the military alone; but they are not so strict as the preceding, and frequently engage in other employments.

The third are called the Beisa tribe, which consists chiefly of merchants, bankers, and banias or shopkeepers; the sekars are, I believe, of this tribe.

The fourth are called the Sudder tribe, who, by their original institution, are the meanest servants; nor can they ever rise higher. And the fifth are called Atarris, which is a tribe deserted by, and formed of the refuse of, all the others; the travelling palanquin-bearers, the most inferior and laborious of all offices, are taken from thence. And I will in this place inform you, that the travelling palanquins are so constructed, that you repose, as in Revel's machine,[†] on a couch—are served with your loll shrub, or other favourite refreshments—and thus, with incredible expedition, are conveyed to the distance of five hundred, or any other number of miles, up the country; and there is no other mode of travelling by land whatever.

By water, you have bugeros of so large a size[†] as to accommodate whole families; and, being provided with live and other suitable stock to your fortune, &c. you shorten or lengthen your voyage at pleasure, and have your state-room cooled by verandas, as in your own houses. You will therefore perceive, that our pleasures are not so local as might be imagined; and, in these nautical excursions, it is common for several bugeros to set out in company, interchange their visits, and have their little concerts, as agreeably as may be. A party of this sort is planned for my participation, and I suppose Mrs D——— will be added to the list: be it so; but, if she would give me a favourable impression of her prudence, she will decline being in the same bugero with my father.

She has, however, told me some interesting things; and I begin to have confidence in her friendship.

Her father and mother were both English, but she was born at Calcutta; they conspired, Arabella, at a tender age, to sacrifice their child for wealth. A marriage (if it could be so called, that was a violence on the heart) was agreed to by them, when Mrs D——— was only twelve years old, with a great military character, whose manners were ferocious, and his person deformed. Nine years did he live, the tyrant and the oppressor of all who knew him. A library was the sole support of her spirits, and the sole relaxation she was permitted to enjoy. She bore all without complaint; for she was sensible complaint would be unavailing. Her father and mother were little benefited by their conduct; the man of war forbad them all intercourse with his wife—he would not have her taught the sin of opposition to his will; she was his property,[†] and as such he would guard her from the approach of persons who had, to his knowledge, private views to gratify: and at length, in order to deliver himself from their reproaches, he offered them an annuity for life, on condition they resided in England; for England they embarked, without being allowed a parting interview with their child, but were lost in their passage, on the Malabar coast;[†] which piece of news her husband abruptly communicated to her, and laughed at the tears it occasioned her.—'You could not love them,' said he, 'it is impossible; the matrimonial sale they made of you renders it impossible;—to enrich themselves, they were wholly regardless of your fate; and, had you not married a man of honour, you must have been miserable.' He died, however, at the end of nine years, and she has remained nine years a widow.

Her fortune, it seems, has only a short time been clear of litigation; and her health, during that whole period, was in a very indifferent state. The first is now ascertained to her utmost satisfaction, and the second happily re-established; when, unluckily, Arabella, she has created a new grievance for herself, that nothing but her own death, in all probability, can deliver her mind from smarting under.—But I will return to the Gentoos.

The Bramins pretend,[†] that Brumma,[†] who was their legislator both in politics and religion, was inferior only to God. He was, possibly, some great and good genius, that, in like manner with Confucius of the Chinese, regulated their manners, and promoted their happiness; and is therefore rendered, by gratitude and superstition, the object of their adoration.

The Bramins, however, affirm, that he bequeathed them a book called the Vidam,[†] containing all his doctrines and institutions; and that, though the original is lost, they are still possessed of a commentary upon it, which they name the Shahstah,[†] written in the Shanscrita language; a dead language at this time, and known only to the priests who study it. The foundation of Brumma's doctrine consisted, it is said, in the belief of a Supreme Being, who created a regular gradation of beings, some superior, and some inferior to man;—in the immortality of the soul;—and a future state of rewards and punishments, to be bestowed and received in a transmigration into different bodies, according to the lives they had led in their pre-existent state. From which it appears most likely, that the Pythagorean metempsychosis[†] took its rise in India;—but that the necessity of inculcating this sublime, but otherwise complicated doctrine, into the lower ranks, induced the priests, who are by no means (the case in most religions under the sun) unanimous in their doctrines, to have recourse to sensible representations of the Deity and his attributes: so that the original doctrines of Brumma have degenerated into downright and ridiculous idolatry, in the worship of divers animals, of a variety of images, and some of the most hideous figures, either delineated or carved;[†] and they have holidays to the number of twenty annually, in honour of each;—a kind of religious jubilee, during which public processions and festivals take place; which I shall not fail to describe to you on becoming a spectator of them.

All their other pleasures are confined to visiting their pagodas or temples, which are stupendous but disgusting[†] buildings, and to the satisfactions of domestic life; and they assuredly are, as I have already observed to you, the most tranquil and temperate people on earth.—But, besides the tribes I have set before you— their ancient mode of arranging their precedence, and their numbers of casts or classes, divisions of those tribes, I shall have occasion to observe to you hereafter.—Water is their drink; but such, Arabella, is their strict adherence to what they deem their religious duties, that, though expiring with thirst, they would not taste the water of their sacred rivers,[†] the Indus, called by them *Sindah*, the Kisna, and the Ganges; the tanks or fish-ponds, fed by the heavens, or by natural springs, being alone their liquor on all occasions. But they never fail to wash themselves in the Ganges, or to oil their bodies, before they break their fast. In a word, their manners are highly interesting, from their simplicity and liberal-mindedness; and I blush to feel how superior to all that Christianity can boast, of peace and good-will towards men.—But, my dear Arabella, I have one caution to give you, which is, not to set me down for a plagiarist,[†] though you should even stumble upon the likeness, verbatim, of my descriptions of the Eastern world in print; or once presume to consider such printed accounts as other than honourable testimonies of my faithful relations: and certain it is, that true and genuine relations of objects and events admit of very little variation of language. This premised, I shall not doubt of informing or entertaining you (and perhaps both the one and the other) in repeated instances; and ill requited be the busy individual that attempts to lessen the consequence, or impeach the originality of my reports.

This doctrine of the metempsychosis is to me the religion of humanity;[†] for it is apparent, that no other tenet, temporal or divine, could have so effectually restrained the sons and daughters of this Eastern world from committing the wantonest acts of cruelty towards the brute creation, as the apprehension of being exposed, by the chances of transmigration, to similar evils;—apparent from the marking effect it has on the conduct of the Gentoos, in contra-distinction to all other species of natives; for, instead of the arrogance and ferocity daily manifested by the several nations around them, their hearts are softened into a tender concern for the kind treatment of every creature living—a concern which so powerfully regulates their feeling, that, in the very bosom of voluptuousness, they will feed on no delicacies but such as the vegetable kingdom present them with, except the nectareous juices obtainable from animals with relief to them-

selves, and salubrity to their owners—a very elegant manner, I
expect you to allow, of telling you that milk is a favourite article
of the Gentoo diet. How unlike the degenerate posterity of Adam

(Of half that live, the butcher and the tomb)[†]

is this order of beings! and how easy the transition into angelic
natures !

But enough of the Gentoos for the present, and of every other
subject, except the last and first that occupies my thoughts,
namely, with what affection I am

Your unalterable friend, &c. &c.

S.G.

LETTER XIX

Physic, as well as law, is a gold mine to its professors, to work it
at will. The medical gentlemen at Calcutta, Arabella, make their
visits in palanquins, and receive a gold mohr each patient, for
every common attendance—extras are enormous.

Medicines are also rated so high,[†] that it is shocking to think
of: in order to soften which public evil as much as possible, an
apothecary's shop is opened at the Old Fort, by the Company,
in the nature of your London Dispensaries, where drugs are
vended upon reasonable terms. The following charges are a
specimen of the expences those Europeans incur, who sacrifice
to appearances.

An ounce of bark,[†] three rupees, seven and six pence—an
ounce of salts, one rupee, half a crown—a bolus,[†] one rupee—a
blister,[†] two rupees, five shillings—and so on in proportion; so
that, literally speaking, you may ruin your fortune to preserve
your life.

But then, to balance this formidable account, every profession has its amazing advantages: accordingly, as I am told, it is

no uncommon thing to clear a hundred and forty per cent. by merchandize, on many European articles, and particularly the ornamental for ladies, and on men's hats.

Moreover, from the high demands at taverns and coffee-houses, you may conclude provisions[†] are brought to market at a high price: on the contrary, even during the time the East-India Company's ships are lying off Calcutta, and so abundantly increase the consumption, six fine ducks are sold for a rupee, two and sixpence. Bread is also good and cheap; fish both excellent and cheap. Likewise, fowls, eggs, and milk, very cheap; butter dear—geese cheap—turkies dear; and, Arabella, half a sheep is often bought for one rupee. Vegetables are plentiful and very fine—the potatoes are better tasted, in my opinion, though much smaller, than in their native soil—we have salads in great quantities, and within every one's purchase—and French beans and green pease, are, I am told, in as high perfection at Christmas, as in the meridian of your summer season, and with this advantage, that they have them in your summer also. Fruit of every kind is delightful—oranges, lemons, limes, pomegranates, ananas, pommelos[†] (which are brought to table stript of their outside coat), plantains, &c. &c. the product of their own soil; with apples, as a rarity, currants, raspberries, &c. &c. from my native country, and raised here with much care and attention. Thus you will perceive wine is the heaviest family article; for, whether it is taken fashionably or medicinally, every lady, even to your humble servant, drinks at least a bottle *per diem*, and the gentlemen four times that quantity—a fine number of twelve and sixpences in the course of the year! Their domestic animals are the same as in England—and, in like manner with England, dogs of various kinds, and cats, are great favourites—the ladies have also parrots, squirrels, minhos, lories, &c. &c. as pets.

They have elephants, camels, horses (Arabian and Armenian),[†] oxen, buffaloes, sheep, deer, lions, and

> Tigers darting fierce
> Impetuous on the prey their glance has doom'd,[†]

as Thomson tells you; with many I have not enabled myself to mention.—Nor must you be uninformed, that to hunt this terrific creature,[†] is one of the polite amusements of the East; on which occasion the gentlemen set forth with all imaginable magnificence, with bands of music, and dogs, and spears, and sometimes give fatal displays of their courage. I am happy to know my father will never make one in such wild parties; for surely there is much more of madness than folly, in thus sporting with their personal safety, and braving the Author of their existence.—I know very well, Arabella, that hunting these rapacious and powerful animals, can boast both ancient and regal origin; but what is wrong in itself, can never be rendered right, because some illustrious brute or blockhead has made it his practice.

The farmers, who supply the Calcutta markets, reside chiefly about creeks and little bays formed by the artificial meanders of the Ganges—and have a Beisar day once a week, for the sale of their commodities—especially up Tomluek river,[†] as high as eight miles, which, though shallow, is navigable for all Bugeros; and it is fashionable to visit the dairies, &c. &c. in its neighbourhood.

Confectionary shops are kept both by French and English men;[†] but the latter are most approved, and their profits are far from inconsiderable—nor is it unreasonable it should be so, when it is remembered they have their wishes to revisit the country of their birth, in common with their superiors; and are willing to purchase that felicity by dint of toil, in the service of those who choose to employ them: they have large imports in this way, as, I believe, I have already mentioned, from England. You will perceive I am not unobserving or unenquiring.—But to proceed to other matters.

His Majesty's Coronation[†] would have been ushered in with ringing of bells (the constant herald of joy in England) but for one little impediment, viz. Arabella, that there is but one church bell at present in all Calcutta, and that a deep melancholy-toned one, for the sole purpose of telling the public some one of their fellow individuals is no more. All funeral processions are however concealed as much as possible from the sight of the ladies, that the vivacity of their tempers may not be wounded.

Funerals are indeed solemn and affecting things at Calcutta, no hearses being here introduced, or hired mourners employed: for, as it often happens in the gay circles, that a friend is dined with one day, and the next in eternity—the feelings are interested, the sensations awful, and the mental question, for the period of interment at least, Which will be to-morrow's victim?—The departed one, of whatever rank, is carried on men's shoulders (like your walking funerals in England) and a procession of gentlemen equally numerous, and respectable from the extent of genteel connexions, following—the well-situated and the worthy being universally esteemed and caressed whilst living, and lamented when dead.

The Padra, however, has his ample profits; who performs this last pious act with the greatest propriety: but, such is the elasticity of European minds, that, the ensuing day, the tavern is again visited by those very gentlemen, who know, and acknowledge it to have been the bane of their lost friend—excesses of this kind being only suicide in a different form, than the pistol or sword, by which many of my countrymen in England precipitate themselves into the mansion of spirits, with how much confusion of heart and of face, no one has yet been permitted to return and declare;—but they have reason and morality for their guide, and when those are unattended to, it is not probable they would be made sensible of the first law and duty of existence, self-preservation, though one rose from the dead.

As a relieving subject, however, both for you and myself, I will mention to you, on this opportunity, somewhat of christenings:—five gold mohrs is the smallest fee thought of for the Padra's trouble in this instance—with the participation, moreover, of an entertainment that would put a lord-mayor's festival out of countenance: his Reverence must therefore have a fine time of it;—but gold mohrs are dealt about at Calcutta, as half crowns in England; and I leave you to determine with how good a grace a family of fortune or title could offer a clerical man, of respectable character, half a crown for his baptismal benediction.

The Gentoo holidays[†] begin tomorrow—when I suppose I shall have news for you; and you may assure yourself, I shall be on the look out to do you pleasure.

I have seen the opening procession, and am much entertained by it. A certain number of Bramins, dressed after their peculiar manner, with countenances such as Guido[†] would have bestowed on a heavenly saint, led the way, a prodigious multitude of people following, with an idol superbly dressed with silver, gold, pearls, and the richest manufactures—which is carried about from street to street, till sufficiently exhibited, with drums, flutes, &c. &c. to the manifest delight of all parties, and then lodged in one of their pagodas, as a sacred, though temporary deposit; for it seems, Arabella, that on the last day of these religious raree-shews,[†] all the idols are collected into a body, and, in a kind of pious frenzy, plunged into the Ganges,[†] with thirty or forty persons swimming round them, until the noble act of sinking them to the bottom is effected, when they return with inconceivable satisfaction to their respective homes—and then proper persons are set to work to furnish them with new ones; the poor deluded creatures endangering their lives, though most expert swimmers; for the contest is, who shall be the happy one to perform this ceremony, conceiving it the highest honour of mortality to be aiding and assisting in drowning these divine works of their own hands.

It is, indeed, one of the grand articles of the Gentoo faith, that the waters of the rivers Ganges, Kisna, and Indus,[†] have the sacred virtue of purifying those who bathe therein, from all pollutions and sins—they are therefore commanded by Brumma, (in his book of pious instructions, the Vidam) to dwell solely in the neighbourhood of some one of them—a tenet that is founded in good policy, by its prohibition of their migrating into distant countries; for it is remarkable, that the sacred rivers are so sit-uated, that there is no part of India where the inhabitants have not an opportunity of freeing themselves from their sins by this mode of purgation;—the Ganges flowing through the kingdom of Bengal—the Kisna dividing the Carnatic from Golconda—and the Sindale, or Indus, washing Gugurate, and all the parts bordering upon Persia.†—But they do not want any thing from abroad, having neither vanity nor ambition to gratify.

They are subject to early old-age, as I have mentioned on a former occasion; and have so little passion for vigorous exertions, that it is a favourite maxim with them, That it is better to sit than to walk,† to lie down than to sit, to sleep than to wake, and that death is best of all.

So soon as these holidays are over, the races will take place, and I am preparing to appear with *eclat*† as my father's daughter.—I cost him large sums; but we cannot have the purchase without the price; and, I promise you, he has the full credit of his generosity to me.—He calls me his second self—I think he miscalls me, for I verily believe I am the first object of his care and kindness; nay more, that he is attentive to his own health and accommodation, chiefly on my account—and I wish very many young women, more deserving than myself, could say the same.

I have as yet given you only a very inadequate idea of the wealth, the numerous dependents, the power, and the importance of the Company on this commercial spot.—However, before I advance one step further, let me set before you the rapid progress they have made in all these acquisitions.

In the year 1600, their stock consisted of only £70,000—they nevertheless had the spirit to fit out four ships, which being successful, their prosperity augmented annually.

East-India stock† sold from 360 to 500 per cent. in 1680—and a new Company was established in 1689—the old one re-established, and the two united, in 1700—and they agreed to give Government £400,000 a year, for four years, to remain uninterrupted, in 1769.

Such are the prosperous flights of commerce, when wisdom and justice holds the regulating rein;—but there are Phaetons every where;† and no wonder, therefore, that this chariot of the sun has had its wheels taken off at certain periods. Temptation is the fiery ordeal of virtue, and eastern bribes so portable, that it is almost a miracle to escape unhurt in some tender part—our fame or our conscience;—and let him that is qualified stand forth, and prove he is not included under this description of men.

I enquire every day about the arrival of ships, and find many do arrive; whence comes it then, Arabella, that you remember me not?

Mrs Hartly has looked in upon me, and most severely condemns my close application to my pen.—I shall blind myself, she says, and tear my nerves to pieces.—She found me not only incorrigible, but I set such good and sufficient reasons before her, for the practice she impeached, that she left me, (having given me the information, that the races commence in three days) confessing it could not be discontinued. In three days, therefore, my dear Arabella, you attend me to the turf, where, if I do not break forth on the public eye with unusual spirit, I greatly fear the celebrity I can now boast, will attain its utmost meridian, and rapidly decline: the preparation is important, and my friends must be consulted in every instance—I therefore beg leave to devote this whole day, at least, to the advancement of so great and necessary a design, without writing another word.

Here you have me again, beyond my own promise or intention, engaged in your service;—but, you must know, I have met with a little surprise of a singular nature—an addition, Arabella, to our usual visitants.—I therefore said not a word respecting my appearance, but waited in quiet expectation of the young man's being announced to me, (as is the custom), previous to every notice I could condescend to take of him.

The morning passed away, and he was not announced!—strange this—but true;—if he is deemed worthy admission to our parties, why should he not have the usual passport to conversation?— But it is idle for me to mention such a circumstance—and yet, as he appeared a stranger, and has a face of promise (for it is only doing him justice to say, understanding and good-nature are apparent in his countenance), I must think it wrong to leave me in my awkward situation respecting him.—If Mrs Hartly thinks I shall make him of so much consequence as to enquire after him, she is mistaken; for I am too well aware of the inference, as it is the first thing of the kind that could be charged upon me.—I will order my palanquin, and steal a visit to the children I so much admire—their kind and innocent endearments will be doubly agreeable to me, now that I am in an absolute fit of dishumour with myself, and all the world—you, Arabella, alone excepted; my father, on this occasion, having shewn no more attention to my feelings, than the rest of my friends in this house.

So said, and so done—for, Arabella, before a single creature had an idea of such a thing, was I arrived at Hartly Bungilo, and as happy as a princess. Mrs Rider, the children's *governante*, received me in a most pleasing manner; and I, for the first time, had leisure to observe a custom, with which I am delighted—it is the compliment paid to my country, in the taste at Calcutta in statuary;[†] for, instead of Neptune, his lady wife, and whole train of aquatic attendants, saluting your eye, out of their natural element, these Bungilo gardens are adorned by a Thomson, a Johnson, &c. &c.; in a word, all the literary characters, to which the British empire has given birth; and a very useful effect those objects have upon the mind—for, by a natural and instantaneous combination of ideas, the Seasons were opened on my view; with Rasselas[†] and his friends I traversed the Ethiopian regions; and so of the rest: nor did I ever, until that moment, know the fund of literary knowledge I am mistress of: and the utility must be general to the beholders;—for in youth it excites enquiry, in maturity, recollection: and it is my fixt and firm resolve, whenever I revisit England, (a nabobess, you will observe) to constitute my gardens an equal source of entertainment and instruction to all who are permitted to frequent them.——Mrs Rider, perceiving how enthusiastic I was become, (for I absolutely answered her kind and polite questions in heroics) said she was tempted to shew me Mrs Hartly's closet.[†]—'Your visits, Madam,' continued she, 'have been so short, that I conceived there was not time to introduce you, where you would doubtless wish to spend some hours—for it is a cabinet of no less elegant than rational curiosities, and I have the honour to be trusted with the key, for the purpose of improving the minds of my young pupils, as occasion requires, with little lectures upon its contents.'—I was impatient to be admitted; and the obliging Mrs Rider led the way, without further preface or preparation.

I will never forgive Mrs Hartly, for so long keeping me unacquainted with this proof of her fine taste, liberality of temper, admirable judgment, and elegant mode of spending her leisure time. The walls are covered with a pink paper from China, of the softest tint, as a ground to the portraits arranged around.—Here, Arabella, the poor Marchioness of Tavistock,[†] from the hands of one of your first artists, sheds her unavailing tears, the tears of conjugal affection, and wounded peace, never more to be healed on this side the mansions of eternity. And here also the lovely and royal victim[†] of female ambition, is drawn in her state of disconsolation, robbed of her crown, her fame, her children, of all that is dear and estimable in existence, except her beauty—but that is pourtrayed in a style of languor and softness, that relieves the feelings, by intimating her sufferings are near their termination.—Ah! my Arabella, who lost more, or had more to lose, than this sweet child of sorrow—transplanted from the nursery to a throne, and surrounded by dangers, against which she had never been taught to guard—the malign dangers of self-interest in a high-reaching and daring breast!—But I shall take an opportunity of speaking more largely on the subject, as also of giving you the names of the other fair and amiable personages, selected by my distinguishing friend from all others, to ornament and embellish this invaluable apartment. One more, however, I must place before you—a whole length;[†] a highly-finished piece— inscribed, Arabella, thus,

'Whose nice discernment, Virgil-like, is such,
Never to say too little, or too much.'[†]

The drapery is well executed, the attitude happily chosen, the likeness masterly; the commentary on the *Genius of Shakespear*,[†] which lies on a table in the back ground, a very pleasing termination of the whole.

I own, I feel myself proud, when my mind tells me this lady is my countrywoman; for to her literary endowments are superadded gifts, that bespeak her one of the first favourites of Heaven[†]—a heart replete with benevolence, and a hand prompt to bestow; in a word, she is an equal honour and blessing to the age in which she lives. Mrs Rider hinted to me (with great deference) that I should make my friends uneasy by my elopement; and, my father having a right to my unremitting attention; however I might choose to fancy he neglected me, I hesitated not to return;—where I found the family in amazement, and the young gentleman seemed to have adopted their feelings. I laughed the matter off with a good grace, and professing myself infinitely obliged to Mrs Rider, for her entertainment of me, retired, and was not again visible till supper.

At supper the races was the universal topic—and I find English jockies are well rewarded, if they visit Calcutta. There will be a ball on the evening of the first day, given by the Company, at the Court-house, to which all the Company's servants are entitled to free admission. So that, at least, there will be men enough; and, as the weather is remarkably favourable, fine sport is expected. Thus, you find, we Asiatics can contrive to vary our pleasures; and must be the envy of the European ladies, were they to read, that we of Calcutta live only to be adored, and that our gentlemen ask no higher happiness than permission to pay us their unending adoration.—You shall hear of me again in a few hours—at five o'clock in the afternoon we take our phaetons.—The race-ground[†] is three miles in circuit, and, I imagine, is found a laborious heat in this country, for once round is all that is attempted.—But I will not prejudge an exhibition, of which I shall so soon become a glad spectator:—the horses are bred and attended at a great expence[†], as with you in England.—But I have done—adieu.

❧

Letter XX

Four in the morning

I am so delighted, and so fatigued—have so much to communicate, but, unlike your heroines in romance, am so unable to keep myself awake—that the moment my musketto curtains are ready, I must slide into repose; and may the dreams of the morning only equal the pleasures of the evening, and I shall not, except in your absence, have a wish ungratified.

I promised to address you again on paper, yesterday; but I little foresaw what business was in store for me.—Mrs D———, as I imagined, goes with us, and came last night, at a late hour, to solicit Mr Hartly's company in her phaeton—I looked at my father—who, turning to Mrs Hartly, said, 'I hope you understand, Madam, that I rely upon the honour of being your attendant beau on every public pleasurable occasion.'—Mrs Hartly bowed, and smiled assent.

There sat the stranger speechless, though animated—and, until I had refused several gay offers, spoke not; when, in a half whisper, the spirit at length moved him to ask, if he might aspire—and a look of meaning was left to finish the sentence.

My father said he should be most happy, and Mrs Hartly was warm in his recommendation—I, therefore, could not decline an offer, I nevertheless scarcely knew how to accept, as he remained the John in the cloud,[†] every body is deemed until they are introduced. Having opened his mouth for the first time, in my presence, with success, he began to take a part in the conversation; and I soon discovered two things—yes, Arabella, two, unless I am greatly deceived, namely, that he is a well-bred youth, and not without the secret desire of becoming one of my most obedient humble servants.—But my obedient humble servants are already so numerous, that I do not believe I have room for one more upon the list.—I nevertheless think you would plead in his behalf, if you was to see him: he is—so in fact like yourself in his person, has so agreeable a voice, so happy a manner, and fifty other valuable accomplishments, that, was I in a land where love was of longer duration before it terminates in matrimony, I will not say but I might be in some danger of listening to him;—but such is the custom at Calcutta, that, before I shall be certain my affections are really engaged, or that I am likely to be able to prevail on myself to fix for life, he will be snapped up, if he has brought an unengaged heart among us, (which is to me, however, a doubtful point) by some female or other, who regulates both her feelings and her conduct by the established standard. I shall, therefore, enter into nothing more than a very slight acquaintance with him.—But the races, perhaps, you ask—when are you to hear of the races?

In the first place, Arabella, allow me to tell you, (for it is a proper prelude to what follows) not a phaeton on the turf was more noticed than mine—my horses are Armenian, well trained and bitted—my reins elegant—my own dress becoming—the dress of my Seapoys† magnificent—my attendant beau the envy of the men, and the admiration of the women:—and could any happiness be more complete than mine?

My father, however, played the renegade, and exchanged his place in the phaeton, with a gentleman on horseback:—he generally kept near us—his eyes, what paternal approbation did they not sparkle with! though he seemed to forbid their saying too much; and my beau had a dignity in his visible satisfaction, that proved him to be of European birth and education—of taste and sentiment. For, however little he said, he was to me the best male companion I have met with at Calcutta, the Governor and Mr Hartly excepted. The spectators were numerous—many of which were Moors; and observe, Arabella, (though that piece of information is in no degree connected with my present subject) that the Moors of Indostan, often called Mongols,† are of the faith of Omar,† the Turkish Mahometans of the faith of Hali.

The horses were led to the starting chair, four in number; and the jockies, distinguished by the colour of their turbans, prepared themselves for the word of command—the word, Arabella, was given, and they went off full speed—my eyes followed them, not wholly impartially, for my father had declared his wishes, and his wishes were adopted by me. Our favourite was the successful adventurer; but, between ourselves, such are the disadvantages of climate, that one good English post-horse[†] would infallibly have borne off the prize.—We were refreshed at the Governor's, in our return, with tea, coffee, &c. and from thence went home to sleep, and to adorn ourselves for the ball.

Now do not suspect me of minding such a thing, for I only mention it for its singularity—for to me it was beyond measure singular, that the handsome insensible I had honoured so abundantly, in the face of all my admirers, should not have the politeness to ask the favour of my hand for the evening—insomuch that I resolved, if he attempted it on my appearing in the ball-room, I would refuse him.

Note, Arabella, if you take it in your head to wish to know the dresses of the company, either male or female, I shall refer you to the fashions in England in their highest and most expensive state of ornament and decoration. For, except in the article of mourning, (which is chiefly the beautiful cassemires,[†] which are the produce and manufactures of the East) there is little difference between the appearance of a fine lady at Bengal, and a fine lady in London—for fine ladies in London have found out the elegance of enwrapping themselves in shawls; and those treasures of the mine, and of the ocean, diamonds and pearls, are well known in England, though not in such profusion; for those displayed at the ball-room would, moderately speaking, have purchased half a dozen principalities.

I can, however, at length justify the propriety of Doyly's[†] behaviour (the name of my new acquaintance) from finding he knew, though I did not, the etiquette of balls at Calcutta; for you must know the Eastern ladies, in order to preserve the peace and good order of society, as well as to promote the felicity of the evening, never dance above two country dances with one and the same gentleman—accordingly, you will perceive, had Doyly taken advantage of my want of information, the trees of destruction would, the ensuing morn, have been witness to the bloodshed, of which I should have been the innocent, he the guilty cause.

The youth, however, kept close to my father the whole evening, (on which account, I doubt not, it was that I was taken in a soft moment) when, with a diffidence and respect the Eastern air will soon cure him of, he besought the honour of going down *one* dance with me—though, on recollection, he did not arrive at this high point of courage, until my father had sanctioned his presumption by one of his speaking smiles. He approached me, bowed, and bowed again—when, (could you have supposed it?) my hand, without the concurrence of my heart, was delivered up to him, and he had conducted me to my seat, before I was sensible of my breach of resolution respecting him.

In short, my sweet friend, if nabobism was not the stumbling block of my ambition, and flattery here the daily incense of the sex, there is no saying what might happen; for Doyly's flattery is of a most insinuating kind—his eyes are full of expression, and the language of good sense flows from his lips;—but, I have a vow, that stares my conscience in the face, on the bare mention of Doyly's winning talents—and it is well I have: for, instead of the ceremony of appointing a distant day, and all the dangling visits paid in consequence thereof, you are liable, at Calcutta, to be plundered of your consent any evening of your life; and, without time to collect yourself, much less to retract—by the Padra's being one of the company, may be induced to give him a claim to twenty gold mohrs, before he takes his leave; and so; my good Arabella, being married in haste, be left to repent at leisure.

The only remedy for which evil is, that, instead of the mortification so often experienced in England, on the matrimonial disenchantment, you have innumerable methods of filling up your time agreeably, and are not less beloved by the world, for loving your husband no longer.

After what I have already written of magnificent entertainments, it must be unnecessary to mention, that our supper and sideboard were magnificent.

The ball-room, at the Court-house,† is spacious, and finely illuminated—the attendance princely—and the ladies angels.

> Amongst the rest young Edwin bow'd,
> But never talk'd of love:†

of which picture, Edmund Doyly is the original, as you will discover in the course of my epistles.

Watson's Works†, a place for building bugeros and small sloops, (the road to which lies across the esplanade, to the river, in an oblique direction) is some miles from Calcutta—and to Watson's Works, in order to see the launching of a large bugero, built on a new construction, we repaired yesterday, after taking our tea; and do but conceive the *eclat* of half a dozen, or more, of these Eastern barges, all freighted with elegant parties, gliding down the stream together, the oars beating time to the notes of the clarinets and oboes.†

Music has charms,† says the poet, to soothe a savage breast—what power must it then have over a humanised one, and especially in an elegant bugero!—the heavens the most glorious canopy I ever beheld, and the surface of the water crystalline beyond all imagination—the zephyrs!—but I will trust myself with no further description of it, for there is fascination in the recollection of the scene—nor have you any thing in England to help you to the faintest idea of it.

Doyly must, moreover, be brought into the fore-ground—his person is so pastoral, and his sensibility so oriental†—had he the Mogul's diadem, he would place it, I am confident, upon my head, and, though entitled to all the privileges of a Mussulman, live for me alone.

But, poor youth! he has, it seems, his fortune to make; and most precarious, of course, are his prospects of advancement; the arrow of disease can impede the accomplishment of the best-conceived designs, arrest the arm of skill, and bring on almost instantaneous dissolution.—I enter, Arabella, into all his delicacies—I feel the fetters with which he is bound, and am sorry my father is so encouraging to him, lest a hope should receive birth therefrom—only to expire.

The Works are admirable, and the launch gave universal satisfaction—and so profusely were we entertained on the occasion with loll shrub, and every desirable article, that we returned applauding the spirit and politeness of our entertainer.

An accident, however, took place, which will render water parties ineligible to me in future. The beauty of the evening drew all the company upon deck—and a gentleman in the next bugero to ours, having drank too freely, was noisy and troublesome in his compliments, and so abundantly did he warm with his subject, that, regardless of all danger, he advanced to the unrailed part, and insisted upon the honour of kissing my fair hand. I was not inclined to comply; for though the rowers are dexterous, I could not help apprehending it would bring the bugeros too close together for our perfect safety:—the company were, however, of a different opinion; and, ashamed to persist in fears that were peculiar to myself, I leaned forward, supported by poor Doyly, to gratify him—when, to the equal surprise and offence of the whole party, he attempted to salute me. Fired at this boldness, Doyly repulsed him with indignation, and in the same instant was pulled overboard—and your valiant friend most opportunely fainted away.

He fell not, however, unrevenged—for the Bacchanalian,[†] a man of large fortune, had his arm somehow entangled, so that they went souse together, and were both fished up by the dexterous Gentoos, (the water being, as it were, from their diurnal immersions, their natural element) before I was restored to life.

I looked anxiously around me, and, from my then feelings, should certainly have relapsed, if I had not beheld my half-drowned champion at a distance. The company, as soon as it appeared no real harm had been done, very sensibly interposed, and a general reconciliation succeeded.

Mr Doyly having changed his dress, joined us at supper.—'I think, Sophia,' said my father, when he entered the saloon, 'I have not heard you thank this knight for his stroke of Quixotism[†] in your defence—he was near paying very dear for it—What reward, my young friend, shall we bestow upon you?'

'The honour,' replied the gallant Doyly, 'of kissing the hand I preserved from outrage.'

I could not forbear telling him, so unusual was his vivacity, on this honour being granted him, that he appeared much benefited by his plunge into the holy river—the waters of the Ganges being affirmed by the Gentoos to possess, as I have already mentioned, wonderful virtues.

I expect horrible visions, in consequence of an incident, that has however gone off with astonishing happiness to all parties—for let me not attempt to sleep, until I inform you, that at one o'clock, a chit-bearer arrived post with a letter to Doyly, consisting only of these words:—'If the enclosed is accepted, I shall then, and then only, have the courage to behold Miss and Mr Goldborne again.' And the peace-offering, Arabella, was no less than an appointment to a private secretaryship, he had instantly obtained him; an introduction, of all others, the most promising for making a fortune. And may every promise it is fraught with be fulfilled, though I should never live to know it!

You may be sure this handsome action met with due commendation—and Mr Hartly said, that if Mrs D———— would permit him to choose for her, Mr M.[†] should be the man: for, as an antidote to intoxication, he must observe, that when he was sober, his heart was liberal, and his manners pleasing. I felt for Mrs D————; but I might have spared my feelings—she received Mr Hartly's speech with great good-humour, as a friendly jest—and begged he would give her leave to choose for herself. Doyly is much pleased with this lady; and the fact is, she wins unspeakably on the approbation of us all—and, in every thing but one, I sincerely wish her merit may be rewarded.

❧

Letter XXI

Mrs D——— has new merit in my sight: our phaetons drew
up close to each other on the race-ground, and we had chatted
together for a few minutes, when a young fellow, superbly
mounted, saluted her with his hat, and asked where he should
find her son—she directed him to a distant spot, where I perceived a youth with a plain person, but apparently well satisfied
with himself, that put a period to all my nonsensical apprehensions, for he could not be much more than fifteen: an age so
unsuitable to mine, as to be alone sufficient security against my
father's forming the design I had suspected.

'Is that gentleman your son,' said I, 'Madam?' with an emotion
that marked, I am afraid, a rather uncivil surprise. 'It is Mr.
D———'s son,' replied she, 'and as such I acknowledge him—
for though his father, on some trifling offence, forgot he was his
child, by the fortune he left me, I shall always conceive myself
bound to provide for him.'—Perceiving I was about to compliment her upon so generous a way of thinking, she added, 'there
are duties, my dear young lady, I need not inform you, which it
is a reproach to us not to comply with, though no positive institution.—I am only the agent of Providence in this business—and
should ill deserve the blessings I enjoy (she sighed, Arabella,
as if some blessing, nevertheless, was unattained) if I forgot his
orphan claims to my protection.'

If this is not greatness of soul, it is something vastly like it,
according to my ideas. What claims could this child have to
Mrs D———'s favour—when his father was the enemy of her
peace, and the tyrant of her existence? It is a sweet feature in her
character, and shall be revered by me.

Doyly's eyes sparkled with approbation, whilst she uttered the
words I have written for your perusal; and I shall only observe
upon the occasion, the different conduct of the world, in different instances—for, had Mrs D——— acted as thousands would

have done, towards this miserable-looking boy, the story of her unkindness would have been in every one's mouth—and they would have doubled her fortune in their report, for the pleasure of doubling her guilt. But when her liberality of mind has so honourably displayed itself, even at Calcutta no one was found forward, on the mention of her name, to give her such well-earned praise.

The gentlemen pronounced this day's sport much superior to yesterday's; but I cannot say I discovered any such thing: however, Arabella, I discovered, what gave me great concern, that with the amusement of the turf, the spirit of betting has been imported at Bengal, and the madness is, who shall be first undone.

We passed the night a second time at the Court-house; but the ball was a compliment of the Governor's, and well conducted:— and thus our races ended.

The next amusement is the theatre—which would have opened sooner, but from some necessary repairs in the scenery, which were not known to be wanting, until it was too late to accomplish them in the desired time.

My Bramin has been here this morning, and shakes his head at the gay life I lead;—and, to own the truth to you, Arabella, I am not quite clear, but I have at this moment the seeds of some alarming disease about me:—may you never experience the misery of unstrung nerves! or your charming spirits become the victim of burning suns, or baneful dews!—My heart dies within me, from the apprehension of what my dear father will suffer, if the mementos of my mortality, which now hang about me, should increase. Shattered constitutions, expiring friends, last adieus, and melancholy regrets, I cannot tell wherefore, wholly occupy my thoughts—it may be only fatigue; or, perhaps, this letter will contain the ultimate levities of my pen. Be assured, however, I shall depart, if my hour is now come, in the true faith of an European—the faith confirmed by all around me—that there is no climate more salubrious than Britain—no people more blessed—no days more pleasurable, or nights more tranquil, than her temperate air bestows.—Farewell, my Arabella!—Rapid is the progress of disease in India. I now have just sufficient remaining strength to bid you farewell—and it is not improbable, that by this hour to-morrow morning I may be in eternity.

Farewell!

I must write on while I have the power.—Mrs Hartly, as is her never-failing kind custom, opened my door to wish me a good night. I exerted myself to the utmost, that the repose of her and her family might not be interrupted—it will be time enough in the morning, to make my friends wretched.

Friendly attachments, Arabella, are great obstacles to piety: the passage to eternity is, I grant you, an awful one; but the thoughts, I am convinced, linger on temporal ground, much more from the ties of affection, than the dread of our future condition. Those whose lives have been upright, and who have, in repeated instances, been the care of Providence, dare not doubt of blessedness hereafter; and those who have a just sense of the efficacy of repentance, will have confidence therein, and, of course, due resignation.

My father! how will he learn to survive me? O could I recall my error in one respect, a most intolerable weight would be taken off my heart. Doyly I can point out a comforter for, and a successor in his tenderness; a sister of Mrs Hartly's, who, with twenty times my mental merit, is every way my superior in person also; but I am well aware it will be some time before the young man will behold her with my eyes. My father, my dearest father! (wicked creature as I have been) who shall comfort him?—I grow worse and worse, and must, I fear, submit to medical regulation.

Letter XXII

How fortunate it is for us both, that the East-India packets arrive not every day; for my last letter would have wounded your mind, without any benefit to me.—But I will tell you all that has happened, in my usual narrative manner.

Doyly, I am told, has behaved himself very well during my illness, which, Arabella, was short, but most severe, and has left me so totally emaciated, that this is the first time, for three weeks, that I have been able to resume my pen. He waited whole hours in an anti-chamber, for the purpose of enabling himself to worry my physicians with enquiries how I went on; which is considered as a high compliment to the patient: and passed his nights in supporting my father. Thank Heaven, I am restored to their wishes, and that Hartly House is delivered from an absolute nuisance of friendly salams, on my account.

My dear Mrs D———, (for dear I shall evermore hold her) from a knowledge of Mrs Hartly's condition, which rendered her unfit for so fatiguing a task, was my regulating nurse. 'O fly, Madam,' said I to her, when she first presented herself, 'fly; this is assuredly the chamber of death!'

'I would not knowingly rush upon destruction,' said she, 'or hazard my life in a common cause—but I love you better than a life of dishonour, which mine would be, if I forsook my friend in her hour of need:—commit yourself, therefore, as an obligation I will ever acknowledge, to my care and kindness, and know this is not the first service of friendship I have successfully engaged in—Is it not a double life I am anxious to preserve?'

'O Madam,' cried I, "are we alone?'—'We are,' replied Mrs D———: 'then, if you can divest yourself of apprehensions from my breath, kneel by me, and compose my mind by one solemn promise.'—'I kneel, Miss Goldborne,' said she, 'in the presence of him, I trust, will preserve you, and pledge myself to perform whatever you ask of me, if in my power.'—'My father, Madam, if he survives me, will you be the sustaining friend of my father?—O dearest Madam, I deserve your hate—your severest displeasure, instead of the affection you bear me;—for I have dreaded an event, as an evil, that will alone enable me to die in peace.—Wedded to my mother's memory, his heart is for ever in her coffin—and in this state has he been left hours, by the girl, whose felicity was his sole object, to tender melancholy and una-vailing lamentation.—What dire enemy of his peace and mine, suggested the idea to me, that it was meritorious in him to be miserable, and filial virtue in me to rejoice in his misery!'—'You must not agitate yourself, in this manner,' said the amiable Mrs D———: 'nor shall you be dissembled with on this occa-sion;—doubt not my good-will to relieve your father's mind; for, perhaps, that good-will has great share in my present conduct. Perhaps, Sophia, all amiable as you are, you would never have been dear to my heart, had you not been Mr Goldborne's child. Be composed, therefore, and rest assured, that Providence will not forsake so worthy a man—he will be consoled, though, both you and I were no more.'

'Let me have pen and ink,' said I, eagerly, 'before my reason is impaired—I will write but three words, and you shall then do as you please by me:' a pen and ink was brought me by a poor Gentoo girl I had been kind to, who weeping, took Mrs D———'s place at my bedside, to give me her best assistance. I wrote as follows,

'Pardon, dear Sir, pardon your child, who, with the prospect of danger before her, is most solicitous for your welfare.—You are alone in the world, and who shall administer consolation to you when I am no more? The blessed spirit of my mother (if the dead are conscious of the actions of the living) is interested in the cause I have at heart:—prove your resignation to Heaven, by withdrawing your affections from the ashes of her you have so long survived, and make atonement for the worst sin of my life (wishing an union, between you and the only woman on earth capable of soothing your sorrows, might never take place): and reconcile me, dearest Sir, to myself, by promising me you will solicit her acceptance of you;—and be, in my last moment, what I have ever found you, the kindest of fathers to Sophia Goldborne.'

'Take this,' said I, to the poor Gentoo girl, 'take it instantly to my father, and tell him I shall not sleep, until I receive his answer.' She flew back, with these words, hastily inscribed with a pencil: 'Sleep, my beloved child, thy afflicted father conjures thee to sleep in peace:—he will observe your request, he will religiously observe it, as he would a voice from Heaven. But if you wish him happiness, endeavour to live; for his happiness most essentially depends upon the life of his Sophia—who, living or dead, shall regulate his future conduct by her wishes.'

Mrs D——— was a silent spectator of this scene, and appeared alone anxious for my composure:—she gave me my medicines with her own hand; and for eight and forty hours my condition was deemed hopeless—a crisis then took place—and I will exhaust my strength no more on this occasion, for have I not told you I am restored?

Mrs Hartly and Doyly have oppressed Mrs D——— with thanks—my father has alone thanked her, in the happiness he displays on my recovery—I feel for her a daughter's tenderness, a daughter's gratitude, and look forward with rapture to the period, that will give me the name also—for, Arabella, if preserving my life (which, under Providence, she has done) at the hazard of her own, is not a maternal act, I know not what deserves that name;—and I will love her, dearly love her, for her mental resemblance of her

> ——— whose worth and charms
> Must never more return.[†]

I cannot write longer at present,

So adieu!

S.G.

❀

Letter XXIII

But love, the disturber of high and of low.

My father and Mrs D———, without speaking a single word to
each other on the subject, are certain, from the train into which
I have brought things, of their intentions. But Doyly, though he
dances round me on my recovery, with ardent delight, breathes
not a syllable to me of the state of his affections, or the colour
of his wishes:—teizing creature! I will, Arabella, think (that is,
write) no more of him.

You have heard of alligators[†] (a pretty contrast for the gentle
Doyly!) and their depredations—but it seems, unless you throw
yourself in their way, in their natural element, the human species
have nothing to fear from them, whilst living.

But when the Gentoos, as is-one of their pious customs, lay
their dead (or, what is more shocking, their dying friends) at
low-water mark, that the flowing tide of the sacred Ganges may
bury, and purify them from all their sins—the alligators make,
together with vultures, and other animals of prey, their feast on
them.

The tide, in general, does its office—but not till after the
above-described circumstance has taken place—a nuisance, and
outrage upon the feelings, I wonder the police[†] do not correct—
for besides the appearance, so dreadful to humanity, of mangled
limbs and headless trunks, which are daily seen by all who pass
that way, impurities must impregnate the air, to augment its
native putridity at certain periods, and endanger the lives of the
inhabitants of this place.

This disposition of the dead, is a practice confined to a certain
number of casts or classes only—for there are other casts, as
you may read in the European newspapers, that burn the bodies
of their departed friends or relatives, and preserve their ashes

with great piety. And of this number are those wives, who, with a degree of heroism, that, if properly directed, would do honour to the female world, make an affectionate and voluntary sacrifice† of themselves upon the funeral pile of their departed husbands:—it is true, there have been instances of their shewing reluctance—but those instances seldom occur.

No bride ever decked herself out with more alacrity or elegance, than the women about to give this last great proof of their conjugal attachment—and they are, no doubt, sanctified to all intents and purposes by the priest's fiat, and pass immediately into the presence of Brumma, to receive their reward. This mode of sacrifice, is, however, attended with much expence, or human bonfires would be unending exhibitions; and hence the custom, it is presumable, of burying them in the water;—and so eager are they to obtain this sacred purification, for those who are past recovery (and, by the way, their superstition forbids their trying the means, in many instances, for their recovery, under the idea of opposing the will of Providence) that they are conveyed with all imaginable piety, and often with their own consent, to the banks of the river, and there fitted, by its rising waves, for their translation from earth to heaven.

You have also read of the barbarous exhibition of men, suspended from heights, by hooks run through† the fleshy part of their shoulders, and stuck on machines barbed with spikes:—these acts are acts of choice, in order to restore a poor excommunicated wretch to the privileges of his cast, or class—for, on flagrant misbehaviour, they are excluded, such as eating forbidden things, or other similar breaches of their religious duties. And those who survive this display of what they will do and suffer to atone for their faults, are reinstated in all their forfeited claims, and their sins are not only forgiven, but forgotten for ever.

I asked my Bramin, on his making me his congratulation on my recovery, to tell me what transmigrations (according to the best of his opinion) would have been my fate, if I had died, as was expected, in my illness.—He smiled—blushed, I think—and gave me to understand, that I should never have lost the power of pleasing, because I have not exercised that power unworthily in my human shape.—'I suppose then,' said I, 'I may conclude, from your complaisance, that I should have figured away as a cockatoo, or sung myself into somebody's good graces in the form of a minho—or, perhaps, have been honoured with the person (if I may so call it) of a Bramine kite.'—He shook his head, and made me believe it very probable, that, as I had so long been worshipped as a lady, I might be favoured with divine honours,[†] when I commenced one of the feathered race.—I am amused by these little sallies—for well does my Bramin know, I respect his religious tenets, though I do not subscribe to them; and can never think myself entitled to laugh at any faith that is seriously adopted, and piously adhered to.

I, in the conclusion, however, told him, that, unless I lost my consciousness with my form, I should be happy to know myself under his protection—for I really think so highly of you, said I, that you are deemed by me, one of the kindest of the kind people to which you belong. He promised me to observe every *lovely* creature, (that was his word) if he survived me, in order to accomplish my wish, and render himself happy by being useful to me.

Doyly absented himself suddenly this morning—the dinner and tea have passed away, and no Mr Doyly:—it is very well—but if he supposes these unaccounted for withdrawings are the way to try my heart, he will soon discover he is mistaken.

I find, to speak the truth, no principles so steady, or manners so uniform, in all India, as Mrs D———'s. She has subdued pride, vanity, and affectation, or she could not be the woman she is. And, from the happy effects of my indisposition, I shall ever rejoice in the recollection of it; for it was the only means on earth of opening my eyes to my duty, or of teaching my heart to perform it.

Doyly, with a face of despair, presented himself at supper. And was rallied, I thought (notwithstanding all my private wrath) unopportunely, upon having been an absentee, contrary to his usual custom.—His reply died on his lips, and I did not dare to meet his eyes, from misgivings of which I could not divine the cause.

What, Arabella, can have befallen him?—Has some nabobess made overtures to him, he is compelled from pre-engagement to decline?—Can he be sentenced to forego the height of heaven, and toil out his existence in the diamond mines?—Has he blighted his little rising prospects at the gaming-table, that bane of prosperity to thousands?—O Doyly, softly let me speak it—could my fortune repair the breaches in your's, how immediately, if I was mistress of it, should peace be restored to your breast! And fatal experience, your own natural good-nature and good sense, would secure you in future from falling.—In vain did I seek to read the cause of his sorrows, in both his own and my father's countenance; I am retired to my chamber, agitated by conjectures.—Surely, common friendship might have induced them to deliver me from the pangs of suspence, and the creations of a disturbed imagination.—Mrs Hartly taps at my door—she will relieve me from doubts that torture me, and fears that threaten I know not what.

The only misfortune I was unsuspicious of, has befallen me.— Doyly sails for Europe to-morrow, with some important dispatches, which, from the nature of his new appointment, are entrusted to his care.

Alas, Arabella, who shall hereafter venture to say an event is prosperous! when that most apparently so, thus proves, in the person of poor Doyly, the cause of his greatest mortification. The honour, or the danger, of his voyage, which shall I teach my mind to dwell upon?—I can anticipate, though I cannot follow, your advice.—But what says Shakespear, that great master of human nature?

Let no one judge of love but those who feel it.[†]

Beware then, my dear girl! how you dictate decisively in a case, that never was, and perhaps never can be your own.

> What medicine can soften the bosom's keen smart,
> What Lethe can banish the pain?[†]

Good night,—I will no longer expose myself.

He breakfasted with us, and my father desired Mrs Hartly to tell me to bid him adieu, on his embarkation for England—But what adieu can I bid the poor fellow, that will not betray my tenderness for him?—His looks, during the whole period we were together, spoke a language my heart too well understood.—Youth of my best approbation!—companion of my pleasantest hours! whose congenial taste and sentiment has afforded me so much delight!—worthy young man!—farewell!—for ever farewell!—Tell my Arabella all my imputed consequence—paint your own partial estimate of my little merits in their strongest colourings—tell her I possess wealth, fame, admiration—every thing that is desirable, but—happiness—and that I alone labour to support existence, for the repose of my father.—This was, however, my mental soliloquy, not my address.—I shall alarm you, Arabella, by this avowal of my regret, but censure me not, even in your most private thoughts. A friend of either sex, at Calcutta, that is a native of England, and of English education, who can be grave without solemnity, and gay without levity, is a treasure beyond all Golconda can bestow. I will, however, shake off this ill-timed softness, and learn to submit myself with a good grace to all the changes and chances of my destiny;—but we can bear our wants much better than our losses, which is a cutting, because an applicable remark on my own situation.—Our last hour, however, is not yet come, for he will drink tea with us.

He is gone, Arabella—and silence was the only language of adieu between us. He eat not—he drank not—he sighed not—but suddenly looking on his watch, and finding he must depart—he kissed both Mrs Hartly's hands, touched one of mine, barely touched it, with his lips, and left us—never more, perhaps, to return!

The good-natured Mrs Hartly's eyes were suffused by tears. 'There is not,' said she, 'his equal, for his age, in all the East. He has all the promise about him of being a great man; but for my part, well as I wish him, I could not have prevailed upon myself to advise him, as your father did, to cross the ocean, and deprive us of his agreeable society.'

Every thing but this I supported with fortitude—but the mention of my father's name, as the author of my distress—there was no concealing my feelings! 'And, did my father, Madam'—I stopped, sensible of my error. Mrs Hartly, however, as perfectly understood me, as if I had wrote a volume upon the occasion—and said every soothing, every possible word, that benevolence and friendship could suggest—and led me to my apartment.— My best prayers, Arabella, will attend him, but I will mention him no more.

Your's,

S. G.

LETTER XXIV

My Bramin—how sweet is religion, as described by him!—the love of the Deity, and the love of our fellow-creatures, its fundamentals—and peace and charity the superstructure.

For love, this young priest affirms, refines the sentiment, softens the sensibility, expands our natural virtues, extinguishes every idea of jealousy or competitorship, and unites all created beings in one great chain of affection and friendship.

'So far,' replied I, 'so far, my good Sir, for the happy side of the prospect;—but what cure have you for the wounds your sensibility must receive by the dissolution of the tenderest, ties of friendship, the survival of your dearest connections?'

'We resolve every event,' said the amiable Bramin, 'into the divine appointment, and dare not repine.'[†]

'This is very delightful doctrine in theory, Sir,' returned I.—'And salutary in practice, Madam,' replied he, 'as the man before you is a living testimony;—for that he was born a Bramin, he submits to, as the will of Heaven—and that you are the loveliest of women, he acknowledges with pious resignation.'[†]

I was astonished—Mrs Hartly was silent—and the Bramin retired, with more emotion than quite accorded with his corrected temper, as if he felt he had said too much.

Wretch that I am, Arabella! this confession, which I shall ever remember with pain, did I, in the idle gaiety of my heart, ardently aspire after.—O, how I lament, that young men and women (with few exceptions, I am afraid) cannot form a friendship of the tranquil and liberal kind, a friendship that ends not in an exclusion of all other attachments, I mean as to precedence!—A life of voluntary celibacy,[†] an unsocial state, which nature revolts at, is the life of a Bramin—for the joys of conversation surpass all other joys, they are the peculiar blessing of the human race. And you find, Arabella, the mental claims are the same in all—for, that I am a conversible being, is the attraction with this Gentoo devotee.—I therefore at length see, and subscribe to, the wisdom of confining their amusements to their pagodas, and their public shews; for they have hearts made for society, and, having once tasted the pleasures social intercourse gives, must pass their days in secretly condemning, what they openly profess to approve, the misconceived tenets of Brumma—for I am clear, the wonderful and enchanting gift of speech was not bestowed upon us, to be sons and daughters of solitude.

Doyly's departure has only been a prelude to the loss of our Governor,[†] and every creature is plunged into disconsolation. Not a bugero will be unoccupied—it is the last proof of their heart-felt respect they can shew him; and you may judge of the preparation, when I tell you, it is an absolute voyage they have resolved upon, to do him honour.

The Company, it is affirmed by those who appear well informed, will, by this event, be deprived of a faithful and able servant; the poor, of a compassionate and generous friend; the genteel circles, of their best ornament; and Hartly House of a revered guest.

He has three times, it seems, stood forth, in his late public station, the worthy character I found him—and his plans of government have procured him the repeated thanks and plaudits of the Company.—But,

Envy will merit, as its shade, pursue.[†]

A more uniform good man, or so competent a judge of the advantages of the people, he will not leave behind him; nor possibly can a successor be transmitted, of equal information and abilities. For, Arabella, he has made himself master of the Persian language,[†] that key to the knowledge of all that ought to constitute the British conduct in India, or can truly advance the British interests.—But I am getting upon political ground; and will only add, as the friends of this gentleman observe, that, as the sun is often obscured, without lessening its brightness, so the clouds, which have so unaccountably gathered around his fame, *may* I say, (*will* they say) be one day universally and ultimately dispelled.

The whole place is engaged in adieus, and Mrs H——[†] will be accompanied to England (for the Governor sails in a different ship) by a Mrs M——, who has been presented with 500 gold mohrs (a thousand pounds) in return for her complaisance in making the voyage with her. Two black girls, and a steward, are Mrs H——'s attendants; and the state cabin and round-house will be entirely devoted to her use.

My father wishes me to make one in Mrs D——'s bugero; but I think it impossible I can comply with that wish—so recently as poor Doyley has quitted us, and so distressing as all bidding adieu is to the feelings of your

S.G.

✤

Letter XXV

It is over, and we behold our Governor no more.—He would have taken leave of his friends at Diamond Point, but they would not hear of such a thing—their bugeros were well stored with provisions, and every requisite, &c. so with pendants flying, and bands of music, to the last man and instrument to be found in Calcutta, they attended him to Sawger, the extremity of the river.

He was, moreover, saluted by nineteen guns from every Indiaman at Bengal, and the general voice, in all quarters, continues to be, they ne'er shall look upon his like again.

They returned not, Arabella, until they beheld the packet and Indiaman sail out of soundings; in the former of which was the Governor, and in the latter his wife: and then slowly, and with solemn music made for Diamond Point, where palanquins, to an incredible number, were in waiting to convey them to their respective homes.

I passed the period of their absence at Hartly Bungilo—my father not only consenting to my declining the party, from a hint of Mrs Hartly's, that the fatigue would be too much for me, but laying his injunctions upon me, not to think of going;—and Mrs Rider, and the children, were unremitting in their endeavours to amuse me, and keep up my spirits.

But I found time for meditation; and the result is, that I shudder at the narrowness and illiberality of my past conduct—For what but narrowness and illiberality of heart, could for a moment have incited me to suppose, that my father's union with an amiable and accomplished woman, would weaken his affection for me, or throw his conjugal faith and tenderness into shade?

O Arabella, Arabella, admirably does Rochefoucault[†] distinguish, when he affirms, 'that there is much more of self-love, than love for the object, in jealousy;'—for, if we love truly (I am now convinced) in the character of either husband, wife, child, or friend, the *happiness* of those we love will infallibly be the first-rate consideration with us;—and that I was not aware of the benefits that must accrue, from having an assisting and relieving partner in the business of promoting my father's tranquillity, is a crime of my nature I will not easily pardon.

I intreat you will be very particular in transmitting me all that passes in your interview with poor Doyly: this request originates solely from common good wishes towards him—for would it not be an impeachment of the friendship I bear his *friends*, to be unmindful of his fate?—not that I bar your conclusions, be they what they may, so you only do me the justice to believe I am,

Your's most affectionately,

S. G.

END OF THE SECOND VOLUME

Volume III

Hartly House – III

Letter XXVI

Henceforth, Arabella, you are to consider me in a new point of view.—Ashamed of the manners of modern Christianity, (amongst the professors of which acts of devotion are subjects of ridicule, and charity, in all its amiable branches, a polite jest) I am become a convert to the Gentoo faith, and have my Bramin to instruct me *per diem.*

What a sweet picture would the pen of Sterne[†] have drawn of this young man's person! But such is the European narrowness of sentiment, that if I was to attempt to do it, you would instantly conclude,

> I love the precepts for the teacher's sake.[†]

But love, I can assure you, is not so spontaneous an effect (in general) of a friendship between the sexes, in India as in England; the object of admiration being mental charms, which bid defiance to decay.

The Mahometans have their public processions as well as the Gentoos; but the colour of their minds, so unlike that amiable people,[†] is displayed therein—for the Gentoos dance, sing, and pay their enraptured homage to their idols with benevolent aspects—whereas the custom of the sons of Omar is to exhibit sham-fights,[†] as they are called, though often productive of very fatal and barbarous consequences—insomuch that, on my first knowledge of the light and darkness these religious shews are to each other, I felt myself in danger of becoming a *Braminate,*[†] though all the wealth of Indostan could not bribe me to become a Mahometan.

And striking, indeed, are the opposite tenets of these opposite people—for the Gentoos, with a liberality of temper for which I shall ever honour them, bestow souls without number, and existence without end, on both sexes;—the proud Mussulmen make a monopoly of immortality[†] in their own persons—for which piece of unauthorized daring, I am unable to restrain my indignation towards them, nor would I honour even the nabob himself with an exception, but that I have hopes of his apostacy—for, Arabella, whenever the time shall arrive, when either your charms or mine are destined to convince him he has a heart to fall a victim thereto, he will not, he cannot persist in refusing us a soul also.—Then his wealth pleads so powerfully for him, and his high-sounding title, and his magnificence altogether—that one has very little to say in his disfavour.—If you have made the observation, that the wicked tyrant Surajah Dowla,[†] the destroyer of the English at Calcutta, is styled a Soubah, you may perhaps wish to understand the difference between a Soubah and a Nabob.—The Moors, or Mahometan princes, are said to have introduced the division of India into provinces, or, as they are called in their language, soubahs; which provinces, being of such immense extent as to form whole empires, were subdivided into nabobships, every nabob of course being immediately accountable to his soubah for his conduct and government. But in process of time, from internal commotions and irrepressible invasions, both soubahs and nabobs became almost independent[†] of the Mogul himself, or at least held their dominions under him by the sole tenure of an annual tribute. The rajahs, or kings, as you will find, in the history of Indostan, are the unconquered Black Monarchs, who possess the Northern provinces, and furnish the Mogul emperor, or any other prince, with troops of their own complexion, called Rajapoots,[†] from their royal descent; who fight like the Swiss for pay, without any curiosity or principle respecting the cause of contest. But a droll practice of theirs is, that on beholding their leader slain, they instantly deem themselves absolved from every engagement, and, openly laying down their arms, run out of the field—and this without incurring the slightest impeachment of their courage.

The great military officers of the Mogul are called Omrahs,[†] and if they have been generals, they are called Mirzas. But though the Pagan rajahs and nobility inherit the honours and estates of their ancestors, there no such things as hereditary honours or estates amongst the Moors or Mahometans; but, on their decease, all their possessions, real and personal, are seized by the sovereign, as in Turkey.[†] And, Arabella, you have heard much in England of jaghires,[†] which I can inform you are neither more or less than these lands, which revert; on the death of a Mahometan chief, &c. to the emperor; by whom they are sometimes bestowed on those who occupy them, and sometimes are their personal acquisitions: some of which our countrymen have obtained as *douceurs* on certain great occasions; their merits on those occasions, however, are not always either obvious or satisfactory to the higher powers in England.

Politics again!—but I am on the point of being furnished with a far more agreeable subject—for the theatre opens to-morrow, with *Love in a Village*—it opens, Arabella, when Doyly is absent—when your friend's heart is—and why should not your friend's heart be occupied by soft sentiments?—for, in a country where so large a number of its inhabitants dare to deny her a soul, sure she may amuse herself with feeling she has a heart. O how I at this moment wish myself in England!—I am fascinated, to write so much about such wicked unbelievers.

Adieu.

S.G.

Letter XXVII

The theatre, Arabella, is opened, and to-night will be honoured with my presence. The door-keepers are, I am told, Europeans;

for the black people, in an office of that nature, would have no authority with the public.

The doors will be opened at eight o'clock; but the performance seldom terminates, I am told, till twelve or one in the morning.

Mrs D———, Mrs and Mr Hartly, my father, the country-born lady I have so often mentioned, and Miss Hartly, (mentioned by only in a melancholy mood, previous to my illness) accompany me; but alas! Arabella, I have not the requisites about me, I had promised myself, for participating this, my nevertheless favourite amusement; for what says the poet?

> —— Not of themselves the gay beauties can please,
> We only can taste; when the heart is at ease.[†]

We go in palanquins, and shall make a fine illumination with our flambeaux; nor can you imagine a sight more extraordinary, than the contrast of the Gentoo complexion with their white dresses, or the advantage I am well aware it is to us Europeans, in general, to have them about us; for who does not know the alternate and striking effects of black and white?[†] The artillery officers will also, I suppose, figure away in the boxes, and their uniform is elegant—blue, trimmed with silver—smart fellows, I can assure you; besides the recommendation of being men of taste and sensibility,[†] as I could, if this was one of my vain moments, give you some undeniable proofs that they are.

Few things are more uncommon (or, let me tell you, more exemplary) than Mrs D——— and my father's behaviour to each other; she having the good sense not to be *obtrusive*—he the good principle not to be a hypocrite:—they meet, without the folly of appointment, wherever they go—and are certain of speaking each other's sentiments in all conversations. I have observed my father pensive, without knowing the cause, until he has looked around and perceived Mrs D——— absent; when he has mechanically (so natural has been the action to his feelings) enquired if she was not expected—and twice, Arabella, on hearing she was confined at home with a cold—giving me a look of gentle reproach, he ordered his palanquin, to make her a visit. If I ask his opinion, he refers me to Mrs D——; and on his applying to me for my choice in any instance, I always beg him to consult that lady. 'Her eye,' I said to him this morning, 'my dear Sir, is become my law—my oracle, her tongue.'[†] 'Grateful, winning girl,' he called me, 'child of his tenderest affection;' and, pausing a moment, 'in return for your open, your liberal-mindedness, you shall know all that has passed in your father's heart.'

'Mrs Hartly has a thousand perfections; of one fault, my Sophia, you must therefore permit me to accuse her: she did not do justice to Mrs D——, in her manner of communicating, either to me or you, the approbation with which that lady honoured me; in consequence of which, the first impression you received of Mrs D—— was not a favourable one.'

'But I was well acquainted with Mrs D——'s noble disposition, and numberless accomplishments; and was therefore happy, since I could not offer her my hand, to soften my seeming neglect of her, and ungentlemanly return for her singular kindness, by soliciting her friendship for my Sophia.'

'For, Sophia, at that period it was my fixed resolution to end my days in the East. I will not wound you by the mention of my motives; but my whole soul was in the desire of your establishment in England. Mrs D——'s fortune enabled her to live under whatever meridian she liked best; and, from my knowledge of the female mind, I was persuaded no event could be more likely to take place, on her meeting with a little disappointment in India, than that she should make England her place of residence; and to whose care could I have so satisfactorily intrusted my Sophia as Mrs D——'s, whose generous way of thinking has made her a parent to the son of her cruel husband?'

'I told her my resolution respecting myself, with circumstances that melted her into tears you would have honoured, for your deceased parent was the object of them; and she assured me she would be all that dear departed one herself could wish to render her, in your service. Your attachment to her, your filial anxiety for me, have produced a most unforeseen alteration in the sentiments of us all. I remain not at Bengal, when she and you determine to quit it; but, by Mrs D———'s request, I mention no change of condition to her in India. We meet with pleasure, we part with friendship; and, in a word, our manner of considering each other here, is an implied prelude to our living together in England; and this is a victory over my feeling, the view, as I believed, of your approaching dissolution, could alone have effected:—but I am now convinced we both acted wrong. Your mother can never indeed be forgot by us, however wisely or piously we may bring ourselves to accept happiness at the hands of Providence, let it assume what shape it may.

Mrs Hartly broke up our *tête-à-tête*, by telling us we should not be ready for dinner, if I did not make dispatch at my toilet.

I am, therefore, in great haste,

Your's, &c.

S.G.

Letter XXVIII

Miss Hartly and Miss Rolle,[†] the country-born lady I introduced to your knowledge, with her hooka before her, are only occasionally our visitants; for, in order to finish their education in a few particulars, they are, it seems, placed at a boarding-school, the only one in Calcutta[†], in much esteem with the Europeans.

The stipend, you may be assured, is considerable, but I have not yet qualified myself to announce it. There masters in every polite science attend, and there are public days for the friends of the children to see them dance, in like manner as in England; and at this school both the young ladies are to remain, until proposals may be received for their change of condition. Their fortunes are small (for Calcutta fortunes) twenty thousand rupees, only; but I think there can be little doubt of Miss Hartly's marrying well, from her own great merit, and her brother's good connections.—Had young D. been a better figure, and his mind such as I could wish it, I would have tried my hand, for the first time, at match-making. I might have thought, you will perhaps say, of Doyly; but Doyly, I have already told you, is poor, and consequently such a union would ruin them both: besides, Arabella, why should you be so provoking, as to suggest him, when you know he is gone to England.

Morn. 4 o'clock.

I have been greatly entertained—the company, Arabella, was brilliant; and a birth-night[†] could alone have eclipsed us.

The house is about the size of the Bath Theatre, and consists, as I was informed on my first arrival, of pit and boxes only: the first, an area in the center; the second, a range of commodious enclosed, or rather separated seats round it, from one corner of the stage to the other. No expence has, Arabella, been spared to gratify either the eye or the ear—a very pleasing band of music saluted the present Governor[†] on his entrance—and the pit was crowded with spectators. It is lighted up upon the English plan, with lamps at the bottom of the stage, and girandoles at proper distances, with wax candles, covered with glass shades, as in the verandas, to prevent their extinction; the windows being Venetian blinds, and the free circulation of air delightfully promoted by their situation.

The character of Young Meadows was very agreeably supported by one of the Company's writers, a young gentleman that visits at Mr Hartly's, and is in a rising way. Moreover, if I have any skill in physiognomy, he does not behold the sister of that house with unfavourable eyes, and I must mention as much to Mrs Hartly. Hawthorn was performed by an adjutant in the artillery; Deborah Woodcock, by poor Doyly's patron, who has much pleasantry; Rosetta, by a young gentleman in the law department; Lucinda, by the son of an East India captain; and in like manner were the other characters filled up: and I do declare upon my word and honour, that I was as well entertained as if the female parts had been sustained by females—and again wish, in the cause of morality, the custom could be re-established in England. The scenery was beautiful, and the dresses superb. Here Golconda's wealth in all its genuine lustre astonished the beholder, and a profusion of ornamental pearls were disposed with good taste; in a word, whether it was the poet, or the performers, or the diamonds, or the air of enchantment they all together certainly wore, I know not; but so pleasing an effect had the whole upon my mind, that I forgot Doyly, my native country, my Arabella, and my mother, and, for the only period of my residence at Bengal, was completely happy.

Several country-born ladies figured away in the boxes, and by candle-light had absolutely the advantage of the Europeans; for their dark complexions and sparkling eyes gave them an appearance of animation and health, the Europeans had no pretensions to; and their persons are genteel, and their dress magnificent. Whereas, on the other hand (speaking for myself at least) paleness and languor told the country of my birth, and were not to be concealed or compensated by all that polite negligence, or accomplished manners, could do.

The pit was full of gentlemen of every denomination, which gentlemen paid their compliments, at convenient pauses, to the ladies; who, by the aids of perfumes and verandas, of fruit and of flattery, went through the fatigue of the evening with a good grace, and were conveyed home, as they were conveyed there, in their palanquins, in very tolerable spirits.

As for myself, my attention was so engaged by the piece, that my heart several times asked, if it could be possible I was at the distance of 4,000 miles from the British metropolis?

Lionel and Clarissa[†] is to be the next performance.

The gentlemen to whom we were indebted for our evening's entertainment, were soon at our supper-table; and the evening would have been concluded with a rational degree of chearfulness, beyond all one can hope for in large companies, but for a little incident I shall mention:—Doyly's patron was so generous (having dispatched him, poor fellow, across the ocean on an embassy) to declare himself his rival. I was almost sorry the Gentoos had taken so much pains to fish him up on the Bugero disaster, and could alone consider him as the enemy of a youth, whose life he had most cruelly a second time endangered—for who knows not the precarious safety of him who rides upon the waves? This declaration was laughed off; but having swallowed his complement of claret, he no less suddenly than forcibly seated himself between Mrs D—— and me; and, calling every power to witness that he would have one of us, boisterously kissed Mrs D——'s cheek. I trembled for my father's feelings; nor was she, I believe, without her tender alarms. However, with a command of temper that astonished me, so present was she to the occasion, that she told him, on condition he gave up his chair to Mr Hartly, she would be glad to hear how handsomely he could make love to her the next morning; and handsomely she was convinced, (by the abilities he had displayed in the character he had performed) he could acquit himself in every instance. This had the desired effect; and Mr Hartly exchanging seats with him, universal harmony was restored. Mr Hartly, however, whispered us, that he must give him a civil hint, such freedoms were not to be repeated in his house.

How I rejoiced in the circumstance, which, but a moment before, was no soothing recollection! for the winds and the waves, in their utmost wrath and violence, could alone rob Doyly of his existence; whereas, had he died in a quarrel, of which I was the cause, could I have attempted to survive him?—I would not be this bold man's wife, was he the Great Mogul himself.

My opinion was then asked by the gentlemen, my genuine opinion (as being a competent judge, from my acquaintance with the London theatres) of the Calcutta candidates for fame on theatrical ground; and it was with pleasure I could, and did sincerely assure them, that I found good sense was sufficient to make a gentleman a player, though all the professional excellence on earth, without good-breeding and liberal connections, could not make a player a gentleman.

My father and Mrs Hartly exchanged a look (for I did not perceive their lips move) that was perfectly intelligent to each other, and Mrs D—— left us not, nor is she to leave us until to-morrow evening; so it is plain my father was not an unmoved spectator of the rough scene.—I shall dream, Arabella, of those horrible trees of destruction—and most heartily do I wish myself in England.

Yours,

S. G.

❋

Letter XXIX

Half a word of Doyly, and I have done.—Should he arrive safe, Arabella, and deliver into your hands the *chit* with which I have intrusted him, treat him kindly, for he has a truly valuable heart.

My father was in the breakfast-room before me—not so Mrs D———; for she had slept little, she said, and complained of the head-ach.

My father's eyes met mine; he was greatly alarmed—'If we should lose you, Madam,' said he, in a low voice, walking up to her, 'how ardently shall I wish my Sophia had never known you!'

'I shall do very well,' replied she, smiling, 'I hope, notwithstanding the endeavours of all your friendly countenances to terrify me. Bear witness, Mr Hartly, if I die, I pronounce myself the victim of the dismal faces around me.' We all made an awkward attempt to smile, in return to this lively sally; but Mrs D——— protested it was a vile imitation, and begged us to desist. 'However,' said she, 'though I am unwilling to prolong so melancholy a scene, (having beheld disease in various forms, and well knowing that the most severe attack must have its commencement) I think I should be unpardonable, not to set my house in some little order. Is there any one in this company so weak,' cried she, looking around her, 'as to suppose the idea of making a will a bad omen? if so, let them be turned out, for they are a disgrace to good sense, and an insult to piety.' We were all silent. 'Have you, Mr Goldborne, never made your will?'—'Yes,

Madam,' replied my father. 'within these last three weeks of my life—and have presumed to appoint you, without either your knowledge or consent, my executrix, in one instance.'

'I will be more polite than you then,' said she, 'and solicit permission to encumber you with the care of a young man, who, if he survives me, will not have a friend on earth to guide him aright.—His temper is not without faults,' continued she, 'but I do hope his heart is in the right place; and your friendship will awe him into the adoption of your example.—Sophia, my gentle, Sophia, take your pencil, and, before the lawyer arrives, commit what I shall tell you to paper.' I obeyed; but my hand shook in such a manner, I was fearful I could not form a letter. 'To Sophia Goldborne,' said she, 'I bequeath my firmness of mind, that she may never more be found incapable of assisting a friend in need.—But I think I am better; and so, Miss Sophia, put up your pencil with your trembling hand, and let me be left alone with Mr Hartly, who is the only person present that does not wear the features of my executioner; and yet I am confident he takes as kind an interest in my health and safety, as the best of you all.'

'Mrs D——— can be insincere,' said I, 'which is a sin of the heart; whereas the offence I committed against her, was the sin of my constitution.'

'I deny it,' said she—'your heart was equally guilty with mine; for virtues are vices, when productive of baneful consequences.'

My father arose, bowed, and was withdrawing. 'Why, Mr Goldborne,' said Mrs D———, 'if I was not afraid of your opposing my last will and testament, I should not have the least objection to your being present, when the gentleman I have sent for arrives. Do you allow it is lawful for a woman to dispose of her property to her wishes? or would you recommend the delicacies and romantic fancies of her friends for her rule of conduct?—I have (but do let us all sit quietly down) a good deal of wealth. Young D——— shall receive from me as much as he can spend with a good grace.—And now, Mr Goldborne, I ask your advice, who shall I leave the remainder to? relations I never heard of (if such relations are upon the earth). To the patron of poor Doyly, in return for kindnesses received? Or do you allow it to be reasonable I should bestow it upon one I love, though that one should happen to be your own daughter? I will lay a thousand pounds you give judgment against my inclination.'

'You do me injustice, Madam,' replied my father;—'may you long live to enjoy your fortune! but, should my daughter be fated to survive you, I hope I can answer for her being grateful to your memory, for every mark of your affection you may be pleased to confer upon her.'

'You surprise me,' said Mrs D———, 'you most agreeably surprise me.'

'Then have I done more by you, Madam, than your utmost generosity to my daughter will do by me. However, since we have been led so far upon the subject of wills, I must beg you will do me the favour to read mine;' and, taking out his pocket-book, he broke the seals of a small packet, and put it into her hands.

'It is very concise,' said she; 'but I hope there is some mention of Mrs D———, that will prove to her, that her friendship for this company does not so far outstrip the friendship entertained for her as she may imagine.'—Many were the changes of countenance she exhibited, whilst she perused it. 'You have made me quite vain,' said she, 'Sir, by intrusting me with the contents of this paper; am I not, then, in danger of becoming less worthy of your good opinion?' I felt my curiosity interested, but would not shew it; and my father returned it into the pocket-book from whence he had taken it.

The lawyer now arrived, and young D——— came soon after. The business was, however, soon over; and Mrs D———, with great kindness, called to tell me she was not worse, and waited to introduce her son. I made all possible haste to dress, and hurried into her apartment; but fancying she looked very ill, all the vivacity, the lively assurance of her not being ill, had given birth to in my breast, forsook me, and I could only say, 'Is this, Madam, the young gentleman?'

Mr D——— (for, early days as it is with him, he assumes that title) made me a very decent bow; and, upon the whole, appeared much less disagreeable in his person, than on my first view of him; and I could perceive she was pleased that I paid him some attention.

He did not, however, stay long with us; and she told me, as soon as we were alone, I should greatly oblige her, by saying what I really thought of a plan she had formed, in her own mind, for his establishment. 'In the first place, observe, my Sophia, I mean to give him a good fortune, and, of course, enable him to chuse a woman less amply provided for, if her connections and her character are recommendatory. Miss Hartly is an agreeable girl; and, I think, comes in every respect under my description. She is too happy, nevertheless, with all her merit, to be troubled with your nicety of temper; and will not disdain to hear a generous matrimonial proposal, from a young man, though his person may not be the most unexceptionable in the world. He is not ill-tempered, though a coxcomb; and she will only have to humour his foibles, to do what she pleases with him.—Is my scheme good or bad?'

'We do not,' said I, 'Madam, behold Miss Hartly with the same eyes. To me, she is elegant in her person, and lovely in her manners.' And, Arabella, as from the abundance of the heart (you know the proverb) we are apt to speak, I was within a hair's breadth of telling her my scheme for Doyly; but, checking myself, 'Madam,' said I, 'is not the gentleman very young?'—'He is turned of twenty,' said she. (I was amazed; for on the course I did not suppose it possible he could be more than sixteen, at the utmost.) 'Eighteen years of which,' continued Mrs D———, 'I have had him under my care, if I may so express myself, when the fact is, that half the time, I scarcely ever beheld him, and he was not encouraged to bear me much respect. He is one of those that improve upon acquaintance; and, though no genius, does not want for sense. His coxcombry is his only great fault; and time, and a discreet wife, I think, will do much towards extinguishing that folly.'

Every body went to *Lionel and Clarissa*, except Mrs D———, my father, and myself, who played a short pool at tradrille.[†] It was not, however, to be concealed, that though Mrs D——— did her best to make us happy, she was indisposed, and I prevailed with her to retire early.

I will only take upon me to answer for myself; but certain it is, I passed the night in great anxiety, and self-condemnation. Had I not been the illiberal girl I have been, it is most probable we should have avoided the present threatening evil. Let no one hereafter, who would escape self-reproach—escape self-condemnation—fail to improve every possible opportunity of promoting the happiness of their friends; for, ultimately, that conduct will be to promote their own. What was it I feared? that my dear father, to love his wife, must cease to love his child? and thence, in the moment I was professing the warmest filial affection for him, prefer a situation for him that must, on any change of condition I might turn my thoughts to, leave him comfortless and companionless! Nay, how could I find the pleasure I did in Mr Doyly's conversation, without remembering, how many melancholy hours the conversation of such a woman as Mrs D———, could preserve my father from experiencing?

I, to the disobedience of every injunction I had received, and the breach of every promise I had made, was in Mrs D———'s chamber at seven o'clock, and had the grief to find her unable to sit up. She confessed to me, that Mr Emson (Doyly's patron) had frightened her; and imputed her indisposition solely to that cause. 'But this is a piece of information,' said she, 'we must not give your father. The quarrels of men are so alarming, that whoever wishes to prevent mischief, must be cautious how they breathe inflammatory complaints before the sex, lest some idle or fatal point of honour should make them conceive themselves bound to resent, or even remonstrate with the offending party.'

I went down to breakfast with the most chearful look I could assume; and, as we were only a family set, this morning, by way of amusing my friends, I mentioned Mrs D———'s wishes respecting Miss Hartly; and, contrary to my expectations, found her perfectly right. Mr Hartly said, 'The offer was equal to whatever his sister had a right to expect; and that the kind intentions

of such a mother as Mrs D———, were full security for the
felicity and provision of the woman she was so generous as to
make the object of her choice, and honour with her friendship
and protection.' This had the desired effect, and filled up the
breakfast hour; but, on my acknowledging that Mrs D——— did
not think of dining with them, a cloud of discontent hung on every
brow. Mr Hartly was so good as not to leave my father; and I, with
a heavy heart, revisited Mrs D———. In the evening, however, her
physician assured us, she was not in the smallest danger; and so
we were all convinced, and, therefore, very freely forgave him
the *prudent* attention, it was evident, he meant to pay to his own
interest; nor did he pronounce his visits unnecessary, until he
had pocketed two hundred gold mohrs. Who then shall complain,
that the sons of Esculapius[†], in England, understand a little
manoeuvring; or, when occasion fairly presents itself, contrive to
reimburse some of the great expence of time and fortune, which
is inevitable, before they can obtain their diploma? I protest
it would be for the good of society at large, in Britain, if some
characters, I could mention, were to smart for one twelve months
under the exactions, from which there is no defence in India, for
the man or woman of wealth, except flying the country; nor do I
conceive, if Mrs D——— would tell the truth, that the law and
medicine, she has so recently stood in need of, has cost her less
than five hundred pounds sterling, in so short a period as four
days.

Mrs D——— is gone home—and it is reported, that Mr
Emson sails next month for Europe—two circumstances that
have had so agreeable an operation on our feelings, that we go
to the play tomorrow evening (*The Conscious Lovers*); and I shall,
the next morning, resume my custom of telling you all I learn of
this country and its inhabitants. For, so numerous are the people
of England connected with the East, that I am well satisfied I
shall enable you to figure away, to the delight of three-fifths of
the company into which you will circulate, in consequence of my
equally *entertaining* and *intelligent* correspondence. Nor is there
any impropriety or indelicacy, Arabella, in saying a handsome

thing of ourselves, when we are so situated, (which, at the present writing, is the case with me) that it must otherwise be *unknown*.

Congratulate us, I charge you, on our cause for rejoicing respecting Mrs D————; and, if Doyly is with you, when this letter arrives, communicate the contents, and he will truly rejoice also; for he has the most sincere and abundant good-will for her of any one I am acquainted with, my father excepted.

I am your's, &c. &c.

S.G.

LETTER XXX

The natives of Bengal no dirty customs, like the Europeans.[†] For example, if a snuff-taker is mentioned, you know he, or she, is an European; insomuch that, partial as I am to my native country, I must wish that it would take a lesson from hence, and reprobate several propensities I could name, that are altogether incompatible with the virtue of cleanliness. Your own observation will suggest the points of indecorum, not to say indecency, which I allude to.

I was startled, within this half hour, by the discharge of guns; for, though the affair of the Black Hole is but little remembered, at this distant period, at Calcutta, I myself am unable to forget it. Accordingly, with emotions I will not stop to describe, I sent to enquire the cause of the firing at the Fort, &c. &c.

The funeral of one of the Company's officers, was the answer I received; and the minute guns were continued for some time, with a solemn effect on my feelings; nor could I suppress a wish to see the procession—but that was negatived by all my friends; and yet, Arabella, to me, this kind prohibition heightened the concern I took in the affair.—Death again!—It is a subject that insensibly forces itself upon my notice, and tinges my most brilliant efforts at agreeable description, with a gloom, I fear, you must find contagious.

The tide of the Ganges[†] (for I will change my subject) for three successive months flows one way; so that though ships can at all seasons (as far as that article is accommodating) leave Calcutta, no ship, on any extremity whatever, for three months, can effect its navigation thereto; a circumstance that accounts for what you may often hear mentioned, of India-men losing their passage to this coast, and being obliged to defer it, until the sacred river becomes propitious.

I own I was much disappointed by my view of the banks of the Ganges, for I expected to have seen them ornamented with every beauty of the vegetable world, the spontaneous product of the soil; instead of which, its borders are unfavoured by nature, and uncultivated by art; and alone exhibit a sameness of prospect, wholly uninteresting to the beholder.

The immediate shores of Culpee and Cudjeree, where, as I have already mentioned, the Indiamen are stationed (though not so heretofore, for some of them come up as high as Diamond Point) are visited by both officers and sailors—who, having made a fire, sit fearless around it, in the very face of enemies that would chill my blood with horror—for tigers, I am assured, approach so near, as to be within a bound or two of the spot they occupy; though no instance has ever yet occurred, in which the fire has not proved their infallible security. Would one conceive it possible, Arabella, that any of the human species could sit with tranquillity amidst the howlings of formidable brutes, prompt to devour?—All the sea forms are served, on entering the mouth of the Ganges, of hoisting a pendant for pilots,[†] and receiving the salutes of the ships previously arrived, in their passage to the Hughley, the name under which a branch of this celebrated river runs for above fifty miles, and on the most western part of which the New Fort is erected.

And now I mention the Fort, I recollect I have not yet told you that the public prison is within its walls; and few things, Arabella, are more curious or striking, than the machines which convey the prisoners from thence to the Court-House to take their trials. The wheels of this machine[†] are fourteen feet at least high, and under the axle-tree is suspended a wooden cage, sufficiently large to contain a couple of culprits, perforated with air-holes to preserve them from suffocation; and in this miserable plight, guarded both before and behind by seapoys, they are exhibited to the eyes of the populace—the whole of which has to me a very distressing appearance. There is but one Court for civil and criminal causes, though the judges are three in number; and an Armenian always attends, as interpreter between the Court and the plaintiff, or defendant, on all occasions. Moreover, the Company have a linguist† entertained in their service, who is a Baronet, and receives a liberal gratuity for the exercise of his knowledge of those languages, so essential to their commercial interests. The Esplanade, like those several royal parks, St. James's, the Green, and Hyde Park, answers manifold purposes of convenience and pleasure to the Europeans.

For the Esplanade contains, besides the race-ground, many shady and delightful spots; the roads also to the Fort, to Watson's Works, &c. &c. lie through it; and it is often frequented by moon-light, by elegant walking parties, notwithstanding both the Company's and the Governor's gardens are always open for polite resort, and contain articles of vegetation of the first beauty and value, and every other mark of taste and happy cultivation.

You will naturally suppose, that statuary is a species of garden ornament the Governor and Company are not unmindful of; but to give you a lift of the characters introduced, is a task I shall not undertake.—I had, indeed, a scheme for immortalizing you and Doyly, could I have only brought you together on this spot; for, superadded to a Milton, who

Into the heaven of heavens, &c. &c.†

your figure should have represented the Allegro, his the Penseroso, of that sublime poet. But I thank Mr Emson's tyranny, and your want of affection for Sophia Goldborne, that so happy a thought must remain unexecuted.—I trifle, Arabella, with my pen, when my heart is dejected;—but I beg you will consider that dejection as one of those many follies human nature is surprised into, when pleasure, by too long enjoyment, has lost the power to please; and that, like another Alexander,[†] weeping for the discovery of unconquered worlds, we weep for want of some new amusement.

Landscapes, ruins, and every rural, every interesting *et caetera*, are much admired at Calcutta, as garden decorations; and I visit a lady who is mistress of a spot, that is a close copy of Mrs Southgate's beautiful lawns,[†] parterres, and displays of agriculture, which meet the eye at her villa in the neighbourhood of Chertsey.

Did I ever yet tell you, that dreams and omens are much attended to by the natives of Calcutta—and that they have their lucky and unlucky days, which they observe with the same religious deference, as the most superstitious European of us all?

The well-bred and well-informed, affect to ridicule these attentions; but I can clearly perceive, that there are few minds uninfluenced by them—and, if you would do me strict justice, separate me not from the number—for when I dream of my father, or you in particular, I am either animated or depressed, according to the agreeable or terrific sensations with which I awake. Is this a proof of affection or weakness?—I own to you, I wish to be flattered by you on the subject; and let me not be disappointed.

I have told you, the outside of the houses are white—but I find, bricks[†] are made at Calcutta;—and therefore, unless washed by the composition called Chinam, I have been too hasty in my conclusions; for it was my idea, that the walls consisted merely of a clayey kind of substance, or of lath and plaster; so little defence is necessary against the climate.

When the hot winds are abroad, the angel of death, Arabella, is busy in all quarters; and, though numbers survive, the devastations are awful. Then is existence only supportable in the morning and evening; and the whole European people droop the head, and dissolution solely occupies their thoughts.—I shall infect you—unless I hasten to tell you, I am,

Your's, &c.

S. G.

❋

Letter XXXI

Moorshedabad[†] is the place at which the nabob of Bengal formerly kept his court, and which I, on that account, have a strange curiosity to visit. Our late Governor resided there, in the bosom of esteem and respect, even at the time when contests were deciding between the Company's servants and his *Mightiness* on the sword's point; and near this city is the Gentoo university I have already mentioned.[†]—I find myself very dull—but opiates are sometimes as salutary as cordials, and common life does not unremittingly supply us with great or astonishing incidents.

It is rather *mal-a-propos*[†]—but no matter—I will, while it is fresh in my memory, tell you, that the natives wear arm-bracelets; and, as a proof of my remembrance of you, I have enabled myself, on my return, to present you with a pair of no contemptible value.

It is my intention (though perhaps it may surprise you) on my return to England, to visit all places of polite resort in such magnificent apparel, as may bespeak the splendor and the dignity of my Eastern connections, and obtain me first-rate consequence in my native country. For, unless I bear the marks of travelled knowledge about me, who will be inclined to give me the superiority I am so justly entitled to, over those who have never travelled at all?

The Conscious Lovers is a piece I read with displeasure (at least some scenes of it) and behold represented with disgust:—Sir Richard Steele is in general both a chaste and a moral writer;—and how such a character could be capable of drawing a Cimberton, with all his *outré* licentiousness about him, is to me a problem beyond the power of the present age to resolve.

However, to spare the author, I will advert to the performers of this comedy. The Rosetta of *Love in a Village*, with elegance and propriety sustained the part of Indiana; and in Beville,[†] a young gentleman recently arrived from China, did himself great credit.

Mrs D——— was so pleased with him, that she invited him to
her house, as did also the Hartlys; and my father honoured him
with so much notice, that I began to fear he would outstrip poor
Doyly in his approbation;—but let him do his best, I will not
be found an unfaithful friend to the absent. Should he chuse to
admire me, he has my consent; but for a serious attachment he
must excuse me.

You complain, Arabella, that instead of enabling you, in fancy,
to trace out my voyage to India, step by step, and enter into my
amusements and surprises—that the first of my letters is dated
Bengal Bay, and all my succeeding ones are filled with anecdotes
and descriptions of Calcutta. I assure you, it is not my fault that
you are not better informed; for I wrote you every particular, I
could suppose would amuse you, from Madras, and did believe it
would be safely transmitted to you. However, since you so much
desire it, I will endeavour to recollect the few observations I had
an opportunity of making, and adventures I met with, before I
reached this land of gallantry and politeness.

The first port we touched at on our passage, was the Madeiras[†],
which I need not tell you, is an African island, in the hands of the
Portuguese. It consists, chiefly of a wonderful rock, the surface of
which is a continuation of vineyards, fruitful beyond credibility;
and though our stay was short, we made a visit to the Governor,
whose house is situated on such an eminence, that we laboured
hard to attain it: but, the eminence attained, our reception and
entertainment well rewarded our trouble.

The principal town is Funchall: but so much has already been
said of this place by other voyagers, that I will only mention a
dexterous and critical manoeuvre, performed by the Portuguese;
for, by means of the surf, on your quitting the island, boats are
shot to a distance from the shore, that is like enchantment; and
though dangerous, is seldom known to be fatal, these people
being so perfectly acquainted with the business. Here we took in
some pipes of that wine, which receives its name from the Island;
and it is not improbable, on their return to England, (having
twice doubled the Cape, and acquired the perfection believed

derivable from that circumstance) but you may drink my health in some part of it, when circulated thro' your metropolis, by the wine-merchant to whom it is consigned.

From the starting of some of our water casks, we brought to in the harbour of St. Johanne,[†] a small island, inhabited by black people only; who, from a species of whimsical pride, are ambitious of being employed, though in the meanest offices, by the English.

Amused with the singularity of their humour, I suppose, some of the ship's crews, that have visited them, have made them understand the dignity and consequence of Dukes and Marquisses,[†] &c. &c. in the British empire; for, ludicrous as you may conceive it, our water casks were filled and rolled, to and from the shore, by a Lord Duke, and three Earls, of the first titles you are acquainted with; together with a whole illustrious progeny of sons and daughters around, soliciting equal honours in our service.

At St. Helena,[†] I was much struck by the transparency of the water at the mouth of the harbour, to the depth of upwards of thirty fathoms, which flows over black rocks, that are as visible to the eye, as if barely beneath the surface.

At Bombay, the Company have a dock, and a most capacious harbour; to which place of safety the India ships make their periodical return; for, though the mountains Balagant[†] (which run the length of the peninsula, within the Ganges) are so high as to check the western monsoons, yet is the Coromandel coast in no degree fitted to be the station of ships, beyond a certain time.

I was ashore at Madras[†]—the Governor's boat being sent off for our conveyance, which is well built and manned. But the boats are, all of them, merely boards lashed together by a kind of thongs, made of some vegetable substances; the thongs passing thro' holes bored for that purpose, and stopped by chinam.

Their appearance is unwieldy; nor are they so well calculated to bear the sea, having flat bottoms, as those of a different construction; on which account, it is no unfrequent thing for them to be swamped, that is, filled by water, and sunk, with all on board, to the utmost depth of the harbour.—They are manned by six Blacks, one of whom steers, and one watches the waves; for, to speak in the nautical language, what they have successively to encounter, are, the surfs, and a lull; and, during the last calm moment, they pull with all their might, and then prepare themselves to combat the violence of the former. The passengers, however, when acquainted with the laws of the place, take a sousing with great composure; for, should one single European be lost by a swamp, all the poor Blacks belonging to the boat are put to death; they are, therefore, certain of being fished up with safety and dexterity, with no worse consequence than spoiling their cloaths†, and, of course, preventing their figuring away on the island.

The Governor's house is a handsome building, and his entertainment of strangers liberal. The island consists of two towns, called, from the complexion of their inhabitants, the White and Black Towns.† The name of Fort St. George is so seldom used, that it is almost forgot—it is under the civil, and every other regulation of Calcutta.—Of the Cape I shall not speak—though I was regaled with some of the wine so called, whilst we lay off Table Bay†—so much has been written, by persons of taste and information, respecting the beauty of the country.—We were treated with an illumination, very surprising in its appearance, from fire insects, which overspread the surface of the water; and, though prepared for it by report, I did not marvel the less on beholding it.—The Line,† I need not tell you, is twice crossed in an East India voyage and many phenomena are encountered;— such as its raining on each side of the ship, without one drop falling upon deck; of which I, your friend, was a spectator, with alternate squalls and calms, that startle a fresh-water sailor; and this is all I can remember, uninserted in a multitude of authors, who have either been eye-witnesses of what they relate, or received their accounts from good authority.—The tempests off the Cape, are, in general, frightful; but so prosperous were our gales, that Neptune's domain has no terrors for my recollection, experienced in my own person—tho' I tremble at every breeze, on account of those to which my perhaps less fortunate friends may be exposed.

Mrs Hartly has sent to inform me, by Miss Rolle, that a resolution has just now been carried, *nem. con.*† by the company, assembled in the saloon, with my father's highest approbation, to deprive me of the use of pen, ink, and paper, during my future residence at Bengal. Which will they punish most, Arabella, you or me? I leave you to decide, (as you best know how far my literary labours are pleasing, and imagine yourself competent to declare the degree of pleasure I receive therefrom) whilst I attend this tribunal; where I am certain of creating more friends by a gracious smile or two, than I shall find malecontents from any article of conduct in your

S.G.

✣

LETTER XXXII

It is a common observation, Arabella, with moral writers, and the fact is literally true at Calcutta—that life is a chequered scene.†—The last ships that take their departure this season, are gone, and my levees are sensibly affected by the returns to Europe. But I am told the rule at Calcutta is, to balance the regrets of absence by the pleasures of reunion.

'Do but conceive,' says Mrs Hartly, 'what delight it will give you to renew these intermitted connections—to hear all the news from England—to receive fresh supplies of fashion—and, perhaps,' added she, with an agreeable look of meaning, 'see Edmund Doyly again.'

I felt myself blush, to a painful degree, as we were not alone; for, if we had, I should not have attempted concealments, that would have been an insult on her penetration. She, however, kindly relieved me, by instantly changing the subject, and appearing unconscious of her triumph over my former reserves;—yet would

it be much the wisest part in me, to appoint a successor in my
partiality—for my mind, Arabella, tells me, I shall see Doyly no
more.

Young D—— improves every hour, and mixes in all our
parties;—which is a proof of one of Chesterfield's tenets, however
apocryphal I hold them in general; for, that we rise or sink with
our company[†], is undeniable. Example—precept—a sense of
shame—and a desire to please, are great, I had almost said
infallible, polishers of the manners; and we become very decent
copies of first-rate originals, unless incorrigible beings indeed,
and incapable of feeling, and of distinguishing.

I am plunged into the utmost concern;—my amiable Bramin,
Arabella, died last night; and died, I am assured, blessing me.
It seems he took a fever, a few days ago, but my friends were so
kind, they kept it from my knowledge; and, on my father's Sekar
presenting himself this afternoon, with a woe-begone aspect, Mr
Hartly drew him aside, as if on particular business and received
from him the account I have set before you.—Gentle and benevolent spirit!—if it is permitted for mortal beings to exercise thy
care, and to be constituted objects of thy kindness, deign to bestow
a thought on me!—O! he was all that Heaven has ever condescended to make human nature—and I will raise a pagoda to his
memory in my heart, that shall endure till that heart beats no more.

How will they dispose of his worthy remains? No funeral
pile will, I hope, consume them to ashes—Yet wherefore that
wish?—for then will they be secure from every possibility of
insult, or danger of mingling with dust less pure than their own.

I have, by my father, begged the Sekar to procure, if that
indulgence is not incompatible with the Gentoo customs, a lock
of his hair, for the purpose, my dear girl, of making it a mental
talisman, like the poor monk's box[†] and Yorick, against all the
irregularities to which we Christians are subject. You want such
a shield the least of any person I do or ever did know; yet,
Arabella, you shall have a locket set with pearls, with some
device suitable to the occasion, and wear it near your heart, for
its virtues will be abundant.

My sensibility was, however, too much interested by this unexpected event, for raillery to be seasonable, or good advice well timed; I therefore retired to my chamber, not, I fear, to sleep, but to reflect upon the transient gift of existence.—Doyly will feel for me, if you mention this news to him, for much did he honour and prize my Bramin, and court his favour. Doyly may, nevertheless, even whilst I am writing his name, have reached the confines of eternity, and found the ocean as merciless, as the cruel disease to which our favourite has fallen a victim. Peace, unending peace, be with his shade!—and, take notice, that should time and chance restore me to my country, I will erect a pagoda in Britain, to perpetuate the remembrance to *my*, or, what will be exactly the same thing, *your* posterity, that so exemplary a character was on the list of my Bengal acquaintance; and that I doubt not but I shall meet him, where parting is an evil no longer to be apprehended; and sin and sorrow have no place. I would not, Arabella, believe, at this moment, that any attachment he felt for me, was the cause of the slightest pain to him, for the world—and henceforth be all my vanity subdued.—Tyrants of every kind, are the terror and disgrace of their species; but the victories of vanity, like those of the grand enemy of mankind, are marked by devastation, and enjoyed without other delight, than the delight of a malign and baneful soul. I will, however, try to be chearful.

Did I ever tell you, that the Calcutta ladies are passionately fond of jessamine and roses?—but such is the fact; and moreover, if my recollection deceives me not, I called their bowers, *recesses*, for fear you should not understand so obsolete a term, at this refined period, in England. It was an absurdity of my own creation—for the celebrated bower of the celebrated Rosamond, at Woodstock,† will give you some proper idea of the Eastern taste, in this respect; some of them being wholly impervious to the sun-beam, and a most relieving situation, you may suppose, in such a climate as Bengal—at the same time that they are diffusing the most grateful odours around, and feasting the eye with an intermixture of the loveliest productions of nature;—and these bowers also, it is a settled point in my breast, will be introduced by me, at my British villa;—not as an improvement, but a revolution in the ornamentals of gardens[†]—and a proof, that when good sense bade adieu to my fair countrywomen, she fled on the wings of the winds to this Eastern shore;—and, should you, or your friends, be inclined to engage in her pursuit, you will find her, much at her ease, at Hartly Bungilo.

These are flights of fancy, I grant you—mere creatures of the air I breathe; but let me once find myself set down safely on the banks of the Thames, and I will endeavour to convert them into realities, of which you would, I trust, become a glad spectator.

We are all of us oddly situated.—Mrs D——— is tired of India—but Mrs D——— cannot declare as much, without implying that she is desirous of being a bride, the determined consequence of her arrival there.—I sigh for my Arabella's company, and would advance the secret wish of Mrs D———'s heart; but that it is very probable poor Doyly and I should then meet on the high seas, and have the power only of exchanging a passing look.—My father has affairs to settle, he cannot so suddenly bring to bear as he imagined—and is so fettered and so entangled by his own sublime ideas, and the sublimity of his bride elect's sentiments, that he knows not which way to turn himself.—Moreover, should fate and fortune send Doyly back—have I not a vow, like a wall of brass, thrown up between us?—I will only say thus much on the occasion—that sentiment leads us frail and narrow-sighted beings into more follies and perplexities, than any other rule of conduct whatever. We must not, for example, make ourselves happy, if not altogether consistent with sentiment;—we must not be sincere to those we love, unless that sincerity can be reconciled to sentiment;—nor, on detecting ourselves guilty of an egregious absurdity, dare to renounce it, unless duly authorised by sentiment:—so that sentiment, which is a thing amiable in itself, is rendered the most pernicious of all things in its effects; and we live and die in the act of sacrificing all that is truly valuable or amiable in life, to a chimera of our own brain; which we, like lunatics, dress up in the likeness of sentiment. We laugh at the Gentoos, and their plurality of gods—but truly ridiculous our wisdom must appear, which, instead of being exerted in the cause of happiness, its whole end and aim is to teach us to be miserable with a good grace,[†] and undo the benevolent work of Providence with our own prophane hands;—for, to be happy, not miserable, were we, most undoubtedly, created.

I will change my subject a second time—for I can make nothing to my satisfaction, or my reputation, of the one I am now engaged in.

I am called by the natives, Belate Be Bee[†]—the English Lady;—for, however low rated in England, I am a sovereign princess here; and, was I so inclined, could wring the hearts of my dependents. But, in like manner with yourself, Arabella, I love to see the human countenance dressed in smiles of content, of gratitude, of innocent pleasure. It is a reproach of the severest kind, to a feeling temper, to have interrupted the felicity of others.

Belate Sab,[†] is an Englishman; Chookalo Calalo, is a lighted candle:—but I am forming a vocabulary, with which I mean to present you, that I may at least find one in England able to understand the words I so much pains to acquire.

Beville, (for so he is universally called, in honour of his excellent performance of that character) visits much at Hartly House; and those who profess the art of analysing, place those visits to my account. If my conversation was half as agreeable to him as his is to me, there might be danger at Calcutta; but he has many connections that can supply my place to him, though his well-stored mind has no counter-part under this meridian.—I therefore measure time by the long minutes till his return.

My father observes me more than usual, as if he would read my most secret thoughts—I shrink not from his penetrating eye; I know he is too generous to constrain me, and too well read in his daughter's thoughts, to mistake her wishes in any instance beyond the present moment.

I am courting Beville for *you*; and he has already taught himself to dwell upon your praises. Is the picture you draw of your friend, Madam, a real or a flattered likeness?—Why do oceans roll between us?—Your letters of recommendation, what a high point of favour would they not procure for me!—I would make an immediate voyage to England, if I was possessed of such credentials, and to such a lady. Where it will end, I do not take upon me to say; but the marks are at present strong about him, that whenever within the reach of you, he will make you a visit.—Young D———, I perceive it, likes him not.—I honour him for it, because it is not natural for us to love those who eclipse us; and at dissembling, in this respect, he is a novice.—When my Bramin was alive,[†] I had a strange wild desire to outshine all my female acquaintance; the desire was unworthy of me, and as such has been reprobated by me. I set my understanding no longer out to shew—I spend no idle hours at my toilet; and am an uninterested participater of all the gay scenes which I behold others enjoying with rapture. You will be, perhaps, for placing this change in my taste, temper, and conduct, to a wrong cause; but I protest to you, Doyly's absence or presence is no part of the question, at this precise period, in the deranged breast of,

Your

S.G.

Letter XXXIII

The Sekars, or Brokers, to whom the sale of all kinds of merchandize is intrusted, have an Ana, I understand, in every Rupee; keep three writers each; and are, many of them, masters of much wealth:—but there is no doing without them, and they generally preserve a fair reputation. My father is, however, so well satisfied with his Sekar, that he intends making him a handsome present on his leaving India.

I was last night at *The Tragedy of Zara*,[†] and shed abundance of tears. The poet has indeed created a distressing conflict for a youthful heart, that has a powerful effect on the feelings; and I think, Arabella, the constitution of my mind is such, that I should have fell a victim to the parental injunction. What abundant reason have I not, therefore, to be thankful for my happy condition! for I am not more anxious for my freedom of choice in the article that must determine the colour of my future life (I mean, the choice either of a single or a married situation) than my father is anxious in all things for my felicity; and I am as little desirous of bestowing myself contrary to my father's approbation, as I should be reluctant to do violence to my own inclination; which I indeed consider as the natural rights of existence.—I have sat for my picture, to oblige Mrs Hartly, but have enjoined her to let it remain in Calcutta, and not suffer her friendship to lead her into the error of believing, because I may hold a tolerable first-rate place in her heart, that she is entitled to introduce my resemblance into her closet at Hartly Bungilo, where I should disgrace her collection.

It requires no small talents, Arabella, to prevent our heads being the dupe of our hearts. We esteem an object, and we will, for argument's sake, allow the object to be estimable; but, the character is a private one, and its beauties and its virtues have neither influence or operation beyond the small circle of friendship; and consequently, though to us very striking and great, would become ridiculous by being brought forward to universal admiration, like a taper in the sun-beam. And, I pray you, who am I, Sophia Goldborne, that I should be found amongst the most perfect and the most accomplished of my sex—who want not the aid of a foil to palliate the folly of my obtaining a niche?—I should die with confusion at such a violation of common sense and common decorum.

I have made an acquaintance with a Mrs Savage, the gentlewoman who keeps a boarding-school at Calcutta, and find her very well qualified for so arduous an undertaking; for her morals are good, and her understanding cultivated. She sighs, however, she confesses, like myself, for her native country; and will, I doubt not, as soon as she is able, return to England. The loss Calcutta must sustain on such an event taking place, has made me cast about for a successor: and I hoped Mrs Rider might have been prevailed upon; but she modestly declines, saying, there is a great difference between the education of children under the parental roof, and in a situation that renders you answerable at all points for their safety and welfare; an undertaking no abilities are equal to; for, in such a situation, you must depend upon others, who may either abuse or betray their trust, and defeat the best-formed, and the honest-executed plan, as far as respects the superior on earth.

There are, however, in England, my good girl, many accomplished and slenderly provided for women, with more courage than Mrs Rider possesses, that might be induced, by the knowledge of the great advantages derivable from the exercise of their talents at Calcutta, to make the voyage. Will you put the knowledge, therefore, into circulation? for no one article of female provision or accommodation can be of half the importance as the happy direction of the mind and manners, at the period when impressions are most lively and indelible. For I would challenge my whole sex, by an appeal to their own experience, to disprove this assertion, so well understood by Pope, and so worn in the public eye by quotation—

For as the twig is bent, the tree's inclin'd.[†]

And so much has the worthy and amiable Mrs D——— her good wishes in this cause, that she has offered to be a subscriber to any established fund, for making it an object with an accomplished Englishwoman to spend one seven years of her life at Calcutta, and to ensure a valuable candidate for the vacancies as they may occur.

My father has purchased a spot for a Bungilo. I was low-spirited at the information, it seemed so strongly to imply our prolonged residence in India. Mrs D——— has had the goodness, however, to let me into a secret; for my father intends it as a compliment to Miss Hartly on her becoming Mrs D———, with the permission, nevertheless, of him and his friends to visit it, whilst he is within the reach of such visitation.

How variable is human opinion!—this intelligence constituted that very act a pleasure, which, while its motives were unascertained, excited much pain—and here am I, entering, with my whole powers, into its decoration and embellishment.—Adieu, my Arabella! I do not at this moment despair of our re-union.

S. G.

Letter XXXIV*

I have exposed myself, Arabella, and every tongue in Calcutta is now employed in telling it. My father presented himself somewhat hastily, I thought, because unexpectedly, just as we were this day seated at dinner; and standing behind my chair, without the least preparation, said, 'Poor Doyly is'—and on some account, I did not observe what, stopped.

'Is what?' cried I, with an emotion that surprised all the company—'O what, Sir, is poor Mr Doyly?'—'Only,' replied my dear father, pressing my hand, 'only arrived, within this ten minutes, safe at Calcutta.'

What a mortifying discovery has the interest I took in his safety occasioned!—Mrs Hartly endeavours to sooth me into self-reconcilement, but, I think, it can never more take place. Infatuated girl!—but first impulses, I find, are not to be guarded against; and the secret of my heart, which I have so long treasured up, has escaped me, irrecoverably escaped me!—'Where is the good gentleman,' said Mrs Hartly, with a provoking turn of countenance, 'shall we not be favoured with his company?'—'He is following me,' replied my father, 'with dispatches for Sophia, from her old friend and school-fellow; the honour of presenting which he refused making a transfer of, or I should have had the delivering of them.'

---

* The date of which is six months after the preceding one. [Author's note.]

Doyly now entered, and with his usual grace bowed to the company; who with one voice congratulated him on his return, except the foolish weak creature I need not name. His dress improved his appearance—I never saw any body—abstracted from all superabundant partiality—look so well in deep mourning. An uncle, who stood between him and the possession of a fine estate, and who, with an unkindness that forbids all regret for his decease, had compelled him to quit his native country a mere adventurer, did not live to reproach him, on his return to England, with the madness (as he called it) of his East India voyage, though solely resulting from the narrowness of his finances, and the consequential unfavourableness of his prospects in life. And (could you have supposed such a thing, Arabella?) the young man's head, on this change of fortune, became instantly giddy, insomuch that, having got rid of his commission the first possible moment, he forgot every earthly creature, and every earthly spot, except Calcutta, and some few friends there that shall be nameless, and accordingly embarked, with a heart I had marked down for some other female's prize, in the first packet, in order to lay that no less faithful than affectionate heart at my feet; and, delivering me back my own packet, made every imaginable apology for his sin of omission, &c. &c. on the occasion.

And this wild act my father considers as a token of violent regard, forbidding me, by his looks and example, to shew any displeasure. An exclamation, however, escaped me, that sufficiently spoke my feelings:—'Not seen my Arabella!—not given her the satisfaction of knowing I am alive! or enabled yourself to tell me a thousand pleasing particulars where her welfare is concerned!—O Mr Doyly, is it possible?'—'Yes,' replied my father, in an accent that mortified me not a little, 'it is, my dear Sophia, possible, that *poor* Mr Doyly is safe arrived at Calcutta.'

Wonderful all this!—nor do I foresee when my wonder will cease.—Now am I convinced of the power of my charms, and shall want no farther support in my own good opinion for ever.

Mrs D———'s reception of Doyly was like herself, engaging beyond what I can describe. 'Our parties,' said she, 'have been

incomplete without you, and my *petits soupers*[†] devoid of animation. Remember, we never lose you again at Calcutta; nor will I
open my doors, unless you are to be one of the company.'

Young D—— stared, and I enjoyed the alarms this
address visibly gave rise to in his breast; for at Calcutta, as
I have repeatedly told you, the idea of matrimony is insep-
arable from the knowledge of an acquaintance between the
sexes—and he seemed to anticipate his downfall, should his
mother-in-law take a husband to herself, not much more than
his own age.

Mrs D——— saw the effect her good-humour and friendship
for Doyly had produced in the selfish mind of her son; and, to
the entertainment of all present (for all present were soon aware
of her motive) coquetted with the young man, until the hour for
retirement arrived; but then thought proper to undeceive him,
lest any mischief between them should ensue;—for Mr D———
wears a sword—and who will not grant, that a rival in interest,
is as severe a provocation, with some tempers, as a rival in
love?—A pretty winding up, indeed, it would have proved of
Mr Doyly's romantic voyage, to have had his throat cut, from an
innocent frolic, in the hour of self-congratulation and imagined
security!—but that, Arabella, is frequently found the hour of our
worst danger—and, of course, it is our duty to be evermore on
our guard.

But let me do Doyly justice, before I go to sleep.—He did,
I find, enquire for you, agreeably to the superscription of my
letters, but you was gone into the country. He waited your return,
while patience, in his situation, was a virtue—and did *intend*,
but forgot to fulfil his intention, to leave them in the care of your
servant, with a note of lamentation for the disappointment he had
met with, in not meeting with your fair self;—and so the whole
matter is rather more decently accounted for than in the first
instant;—for, let me bear witness, when the heart is occupied
by such fluctuating subjects as the winds and the waves, it is not
extraordinary the memory should be absorbed, and the conduct
vague and inconsistent. His return would have given me tenfold

pleasure, if he had brought me news of my Arabella;—but, from this state of the case, I think he must be forgiven—What say you?—Aye or No!

Adieu!

O talk not to me of the wealth she possesses[†]—

it seems, was the language of Doyly, on my father's attempting to make a long speech relative to what he intended to give me:—and thus you find me on the edge of the matrimonial precipice;—for, though tender distress, and delicate embarrassment, are very pretty decorations for *painted* scenes—the realities of life need receive no such colourings from the pencil—for the sensible head, and the sympathising heart, feels them all;—I shall, therefore, say not one word how I looked, or how I replied, when solicited by the man of my choice, on the one hand, to accept him, and commanded by my father, on the other hand, to follow my own inclinations. Generous, indulgent command!—for well was he acquainted with the bent of my inclinations, before such command was issued;—the Padra, therefore, stands a good chance of obtaining some twenty gold mohrs, at least, on my account—but I will have the whole affair as private as possible, let my friends remonstrate as they may.

Lord Cornwallis[†] is on his way to Calcutta, to assume the reins of government. That he is a man of fashion, we hear without emotion;—but that we hear he is a man of abilities and honour, we rejoice. He will be received with every mark of distinction, in honour of his and our Sovereign; but his hour of departure, alone, will evince the advance he has made in our approbation and attachment.—I stand impartial, and will give his claims due weight:—but, if it should be required of me to forget the Governor I have known, and sink his fame in the celebrity of any new-comer, I shall beg to be excused. Hereditary advantages, however brilliant their effects, are but secondary recommenda-tions;—the self-ennobled individual,[†] and him who disgraces not the memory of his illustrious forefathers, being the only highly-revered characters in this land of commerce and plain understanding.

I am, &c. &c.

Your's,

S.G.

LETTER XXXV

Amazement!—so this same little winning Mr Doyly, is the godson of my beloved mother, and your near relation.—A pretty plot, this!—and may I lose my pretensions to the privileges of a Christian female, if I pardon your share in it—or, what is tantamount, be compelled to embrace the narrow and illiberal faith of the sons of Omar;[†] which, by the way, I have now some thoughts of doing—for I shall, at least, be of consequence whilst living, if annihilation (in the opinion of my adorers) must be my portion when dead;—and that is more than my professed friends, though of the race of Believers, have chose to give me, in this instance.—The following is the confession the offending parties in the East have been brought to make; nor shall I fail to add your's thereto, the first opportunity by which it can be obtained.

My father, perceiving me disinclined to marry in the East, for wealth, &c. with men old enough to make me guilty, in so doing, of a breach of the canonical articles, which positively forbid your marrying your grandfather;—and anxious to unbend *tête-à-tête* with a son-in-law likely to make his daughter happy—writes off to England for Doyly, telling him, if his prospects were not improved, he believed he could promise to be serviceable to him in India. Doyly embarks, and, being arrived, receives the offer, point-blank, of his friend's daughter, with all her emoluments and endowments, provided her consent could be obtained; in which attempt he was to have all lawful aid and assistance.

Doyly (as who would not) snaps at the offer. A young damsel of my claims and appearance might, Arabella, have been carried with success to a much higher market;—but every man in his humour, say I—and, being my father's property, he had a right to indulge his fancy, as far as it was reconcileable to my wishes.

Doyly began his manoeuvrings, I suppose, nothing doubting; for where is there a young man in this age to be found, that thinks humbly of himself—person or mind?—when lo! what should come to pass, but his imbibing so exalted an idea of the height and depth of my deservings, that he falls into the state of boobyism, which caused all my suspence, folly, &c. &c.—for, though his respect for my mental merits was abundant, from repeated conversations with you, our common friend, thereon—yet, not having seen me, within my remembrance, my personal graces (which were to be superadded to the account) were so dazzling and so dismaying, that he very childishly gives away his heart, without seeking a return in kind;—and no less childishly resolves never to disclose his tender absurdity, until some change, or chance, had lifted him a few degrees nearer an equality with me in pecuniary matters;—a resolution that locked up his lips, not only in all the intercourse he enjoyed with me (and encouragement to speak out, I fear, was legible in my countenance, had translating looks been his talent) but, in the moment also of bidding adieu, when presumption is so excusable, because so natural in a lover—who knows not what he does or says, until his offended Dulcinea recalls him, by her anger, to a sense of his crime, and he begs pardon, and offends—and offends, and begs pardon, to the last point of the last interview between them.

But, to shew you the metamorphosis riches can produce—this timid, humble Doyly, is become the most ardent and precipitate of lovers—and would have seized my hand, *nolens volens,*[†] the first evening of his arrival at Calcutta; in consequence, however, I should add, of the universal opinion (with my father at the head of that opinion) that I entertained a secret *tendre* for him.— Secret, do I call it?—that ever falsehood and deceit should look so well upon paper!—but, bound by the laws of decorum to preserve such secrets inviolate, that should, Arabella, by the courtesy of our friends, be deemed a secret, which has not been confessedly revealed, whatever presumptive evidence is producible of the contrary.

And yet, there is something premature in the business;—for who knows what friends Lord Cornwallis may bring over with him—to make one repent one's yieldingness of temper?—I have, however, placed the emblems of tranquil feelings before me (the devices I mentioned to you, wrought with the hair of my departed Bramin) in order to extinguish the embers of vanity, now re-kindling in my heart:—yet what have I to ask of quiet-mindedness, more than I possess?—for, Arabella, I am content to leave Calcutta, without occasioning one scene of blood and slaughter in my name, under the spreading branches of the trees of destruction (which might have been so reasonably expected from my charms) in contest for the honour of my hand; and am preparing myself (with my own consent) to domesticate in Britain, to the very confines of oblivion—which is carrying the virtue of humility to a most unprecedented height, in a damsel of my complexion and turn of sentiment.

The same round of amusements is about to take place, as at this time last year.—The Gentoo holidays begin first—the races succeed—and the theatre will open some weeks sooner than at that period;—all things being thus early in a proper train, out of compliment, I suppose, to the expected Governor—so that we shall not want amusement;—and I have it in contemplation to point out a few dramatic characters to Doyly, which, I persuade myself, he would fill in a manner far from disgraceful to either me or himself. Calcutta once more looks like itself;—men, Arabella, in other words, abound;—and I am beheld, by all my old acquaintance, as if I had horns on my head, because I have not renounced my maiden state;—but the mystery will soon be unravelled, and they will find, that tho' wealth could not tempt me, modest merit, noble-mindedness, and a long list of matrimonial requisites, could prevail, even over a vow—a vow you can produce against me, to the impeachment of my morals, and the discolouring of my lily-white fame;—for, amongst my other articles of celebrity, my sincerity of heart, and the sincerity of my lips (or, as you would call it, veracity) have a distinguished place.—I thank you for your kind remembrance of me, and shall conceive every cause lost, in which you may chuse to accept a brief—so prevailing are the reasons you have set before me, in excuse for Doyly's conduct—not to mention a word of the force of example for you, Arabella, forgive him neglects, I could not hope you to pardon.

I am your's, &c.

S. G.

Letter XXXVI

Lord Cornwallis is hourly expected, and bugeros are in readiness to fall down the Hughley, on its being announced he has made the mouth of the Ganges.

Mrs D———, with an ardour I did not think her capable of, has fitted herself and friends out at all points, to do this great man honour—at least, by adding one more bugero to his train; and my father says, our company cannot be dispensed with.

What can I say?—my spirits are in unison with the occasion;—

My shepherd is kind, and my heart is at ease.†

But I shall not be without my apprehensions;—for, did I not see the time, when Doyly's life was in imminent danger, though on a party of pleasure:—but Doyly promises to be discreet, and Mr Emson has taken himself to England;—I will, therefore, speak peace to my fears, and gratify Mrs D———'s desire of exhibiting me.—But of Mrs D——— I have somewhat to mention, not quite so much in the style of friendship as I had expected; she can have her concealments, as well as a certain young Lady, when she pleases—for (could you have thought it) my father's

will, which he put into her hands to peruse, when she was about
to make her own, contained his approbation of Doyly for a son-
in-law—his act of sending for him from England, for the purpose
of gaining my favour—and a solemn request, that she would
finish what he had begun, provided it was discovered to be my
inclination.—A pretty business, truly!—and thus, it is probable,
she will be often employed by him, in secret services respecting
his child, that will be preconcerted between them.—I would
be angry, if I could resist being pleased—but, next to yourself,
Arabella, she is the wisest and the best creature on earth.—Mrs
Hartly is not forgot by me—nor her sweet disposition unremembered. She has, however, a family to share her attentions and
kindness; whereas Mrs D——— is ours entirely, and without
alloy.

One of our visiting friends has taken a French leave[†] of us. I
believe I have told you, that one side of the river Hughley is priv-
ileged ground, the opposite shore to Calcutta, to which place this
young spark is fled. He spent his evening, I find, in the tavern,
at the gaming-table, where, having lost considerable sums, he
was pushed on from one act of desperation to another, until, not
being worth a shilling, he was compelled to become a fugitive
among fugitives (for no one of good prospects or good connections
resides there) the fatal and frequent consequence of this dreadful
infatuation. Card-playing was designed for amusement only, to
unbend the mind from too intense studies, and to dissipate too
intense reflection. It has, however, been perverted into an engine
of destruction—a calamity without a mitigation—for what
resources has a wretch in his hour of self-created affliction, when
the whole world, and his own heart, are united in his condem-
nation? The gamester, moreover, seldom falls alone; an amiable
wife, a lovely offspring, are too often involved in the crushing
misfortune; and such is the nature of his profession, that even
success ought to wound his feelings, for he must, Arabella, undo,
if he is not undone. I am, nevertheless, so much interested in
the fate of this young sinner, that I have besought Doyly to serve
him if he can—for he is the victim of premature, of unbounded

prosperity;—had he been less, he would have been much more fortunate. We shall therefore make a point of procuring him some moderate re-establishment, which, we trust, he will be smarted into a knowledge of the value of, and game no more.

Lord C———— is arrived,[†] and professed himself much pleased with his reception.

Every creature is flying to his house to pay their *baise-mains*;[†] and it is said, that as soon as the bustle is over, the Nabob will make him a public visit. There will be a sight, Arabella, for an European gentlewoman!—How lucky it is, my hour for embarking did not arrive previous to this grand raree-show!

Our voyage was a pleasant and delightful one—for when the surface is smooth, I am fond of water excursions—and, by what you London people experience in your parties to and from Vauxhall, &c. &c. you may judge how musical accompaniments must increase the pleasure of the Eastern voyaging.

Young D———— has a good voice, and, what I should never have suspected him of, sings with much taste. We had an awning of kittesaws, and did our best to be noticed when the Bugero of bugeros passed us; but, mortifying so ever as the confession may be, it shall be confessed that I verily believe we were confounded with the multitude.

My father has furnished himself with large assortments of Eastern manufactures,[†] by much the largest part of which is intended for a present to my friend, so that you stand a chance of eclipsing all the Misses of your acquaintance—a most sentimental gratification: but as for my part, *simplex munditiis*[†] shall be my motto, which requires as much skill to hit off, without being under or over dressed in a single article, as any female etiquette I know. Moreover, so altered am I in my views and wishes, that I have, settled with myself to affect the Gentoo air, which is an assemblage of all the soft and winning graces priests or poets have yet devised a name for, and Doyly shall figure away as my Bramin; and so well have I instructed him[†] in every humane tenet of that humane religion, that he will not hurt a butterfly, nor can he dispatch even a troublesome musketto without a correspondent pang—and habit, you know, is said to give us a kind of second nature;—but it is to do Mr Doyly barely justice to say, that no savage climate, not even the climate of his, mine, or your ancestors, has power to render him aught but the friend of all created nature, and the universal admirer of all Nature's productions;—but, as Sterne says, I am not celebrating the man, but the sentiment.

We are to have a fishing party next week, for the participation of which amusement, nature has disqualified me by a painful degree of sensibility; for I cannot call by the name of pleasure, what must be purchased at the high price of the suffering or death of any thing that exists. This was the first attaching feature my still-lamented Bramin discovered in my mental character. 'You are,' said he, 'Madam, a Christian by profession, but a Gentoo by nature; you would have done honour to the religion of Brumma.'—They refused me not, as I apprehended, a lock of this saint's hair, and I have had it elegantly set for his sake. He merited no less a compliment, in return for his unfeigned approbation of me.

It is got abroad, that we mean soon to leave Bengal; and here I have it, under the hand and seal of one of my adorers, that broken constitutions, and broken hearts, will be the consequence of my departure; for that those who do not die of grief, will send themselves speedily to their graves by libations to Neptune[†] for my safety. This, in your sober judgment, may be deemed carrying gallantry to excess; but there have been instances of facts to the full as extravagant, some years ago;—the Eastern world is, however, much improved, and their errors corrected.

A generation of European children (if you will give such an Irishism your passport,[†] when you observe that I mean chil-dren born in the Eastern world) grow up daily, whose natural endowments are excellent, and their education wonderful for this distant land; so that, instead of languishing, as formerly, for European ladies, and receiving with rapture the hands of such as have the courage to brave all the perils of the ocean to

obtain them a husband, and arrive with their credentials from
the Company in their hands;—wives are now chosen, by men
of nice feeling, from among these India-born ladies,[†] (through
natural intimacies, and a knowledge of their tempers, manners,
and conduct) in preference to these adventurers. Yet is there no
rule without an exception—so that if you will be prevailed upon,
Arabella, to make an East India voyage, I will engage a genius
of my acquaintance, who has repeatedly celebrated my small
merits, both in prose and verse, to present you a congratulatory
address upon your arrival, and will ensure you a host of admirers.

You will, I fancy, be convinced by my trifling, I am no love-sick
nymph—no, Arabella! so far from it, that though it is not unlikely
I may marry Doyly, in obedience to my father's commands, you
must do me the justice to acknowledge I bore his absence like
a heroine, and seldom or ever made him the subject-matter of
my letters to England. I have managed, however, to my father's
satisfaction, and have taught myself to despise your malicious
smiles;—yet, on recollection, before it is given me to embrace
my Arabella, by being made the young man's lawful wife, it may
be more for my credit to confess, than deny the tender sentiments
with which he inspired me.

In Calcutta, I believe, Hymen[†] is seldom known to be attended
at the nuptial ceremony by Cupid (for it is who bids most that
wins the prize); and whilst the fair lady's person appertains to
one happy man alone, her conversation is at the service of all
those who have sufficient interest to get themselves introduced
to her; and the husband is so complaisant as to ask no questions.

Your's, &c.

S. G.

❧

Letter XXXVII

Alas, Arabella, I am undone!—I have beheld so brilliant, so divine a spectacle—am so dazzled, and so captivated, and, like Gulliver in the land of Lilliput, find all the objects around me so diminutive and so mean, that I overlook and disregard them at every point. You will perceive, by this exordium, the Nabob has made his intended visit to the new Governor, and has carried off the heart of your unfortunate friend;—but I will endeavour to conquer and regulate my feelings.

From Chitpore (the Nabob's palace) to Calcutta, I have already told you is four miles; from whence such a procession as I must never hope to behold again, proceeded to the Esplanade, and that at a very early hour in the morning.

His guards, on the occasion, were no less in number than his whole battalion of black troops, fine-looking fellows—and their complexions gave a grandeur to the scene. Their uniform and their turbans were new, and their fire-arms glittering bright; and I would have given the world on the instant to have been a Nabobess,[†] and entitled to so magnificent a train.

I whispered Doyly, and asked him, what he thought of the London sights in such a moment? He shook his head with due contempt, but made no reply, as we were surrounded by those who would have taken umbrage[†] at the most distant reflection (though in the voice of truth) on England.

Seven elephants of the first magnitude were led by their keepers, in like manner as our sumpter-horses[†]; seated on the back of one of which, on a throne of indescribable splendor, was his Nabobship, with a man behind him, holding a superb fan, in the very act of collecting the breezes in his service.

The throne was composed of gold, pearls, and brilliants, and the nabob's dress worth a sovereignty; nor was ever animal more grandly caparisoned than the no less honoured than exalting elephant on which he rode.

His state-palanquin followed, and was by much the most desirable object my eyes ever encountered, and differently built to those used by the Europeans. Four pillars of massy silver supporting the top, which was actually encrusted by pearls and diamonds; and, instead of verandas, fine glass plates[†] on every side, as well as the back and front, to shew his Mightiness's person, I suppose, to the greatest advantage.

I was stationed nearly on a level with the throne as it passed along;—and judge, Arabella, if you can, of the ambitious throbs my heart experienced, when I saw the Nabob's eyes, sparkling with admiration, fixed on my face!—Doyly turned pale, and the procession advanced—yet were my charms unforgotten by him; for he twice or thrice looked back, and constituted me the envy of the women, and the torture of the men; in a word, my conquest was as evident as the noon-day sun: and who could dream of a mortal female's refusing an enthroned adorer, with the wealth of the Indies at his feet?

Down knelt the half-reasoning animal,[†] at the entrance of the Governor's house, for his illustrious master to alight;[†]— so powerful, yet so docile!—so gentle, yet so terrific in their appearance!—I am dying, Arabella, to have one of these very Elephants at my command.

Breakfast was prepared for this princely guest, at the Governor's;—from whence he was conducted across the Esplanade, to the New Fort, where the troops were drawn out, to compliment him with an exhibition of their martial manoeuvrings;—and he was shewn, with apparent astonishment, to how great a distance bombshells[†] can be thrown.—He was accompanied by the Governor's Aid-de-camp,[†] the whole day—expressed much delight on viewing the camp at Bugee Bugee—but returned to Chitpore to dinner, the peculiar customs of his religion not admitting of his mixing with the Europeans, on that occasion. Many of the officers were invited to his palace, and sumptuously entertained, in an adjoining apartment; and in the evening, some beautiful fire-works were played off in the garden of Chitpore—and the company returned much satisfied with his liberal and courteous demeanour.

I thought of Lady Wortley Montagu's[†] account of her being noticed by the Grand Seignior, when spectator of a Turkish procession, on the Nabob's observation of me;—but there was this difference between the circumstances—namely, that the attention the Sultan paid that Lady was merely *en passant*; whereas this Nabob of Nabobs proved, in the face of all the people, how long he bore me in mind—that is, how deeply he was wounded—and I hold myself in expectance of hearing more of him.

The return of the procession was with the same ceremonies—and I have dreamed alone of state palanquins, thrones, elephants, and seapoys, ever since.

My friends, who visited the Fort, and traced the Nabob's steps wherever he went, tell me, a ship now on the stocks, at Watson's Works, of three decks[†] (the first ever built at Calcutta) will be launched in a few days, and receive the name of the Earl Cornwallis, in honour of our Governor.—It will, no doubt, be a brilliant day;—but whether it will be thought safe to trust me to be a spectator, or not, lest the Nabob should form plans for carrying me off, is uncertain, until I have heard the opinion of my male friends. That Doyly was frightened, is most certain;—but an Englishwoman was not born to fear giant knights, or enchanted castles; and the more especially, where an army would stand forth in her protection and defence. It would flatter my vanity to find them alarmed.—Ha! ha! ha! Arabella—did you ever imagine your friend would make so magnificent a conquest?—Poor Doyly, how small he has felt himself ever since!—Forgive my folly—I recollect my Bramin, and am myself again.

I am affectionately,

Your's,

S.G.

❀

LETTER XXXVIII

Bless me, Arabella, how different objects can appear to different optics!—My father talks of nothing but going to England, or Doyly but of becoming a bridegroom.—'Softly, my dear Sir,' said I to him, 'for there are a few preliminary articles to be adjusted, before that great event can take place.—If my father marries not in India, I will follow his example; and so, if you chuse to make it a concern of yours, get him to appoint his day, and that, I promise you, shall be mine.'

We shall be a fine party of us, in crossing the ocean;—for, Mr and Mrs Hartly, the children, Mrs Rider, and young Mr and Mrs D———, will accompany us;—letters having arrived, that require Mr Hartly's personal attendance in England, and he will not leave his family behind.

Mrs D——— has been reproaching me, in the severest terms, for my treatment of Doyly.—Unkind Mrs D———! I never thought it possible for you to chide in so serious a manner.—She says I shall distress my father beyond measure, by requiring what cannot be complied with.

'And why not, Mrs D———,' said I, interrupting her, 'why not, I beseech you?—If a union *is* to take place between my father and you, wherefore should you embark for England previous thereto?—or, if it can be necessary to observe such delay, why should you set yourself in array against a compliment I propose making you, of delaying my nuptials also, until the air of my native country gives me sufficient resolution to constitute Mr Doyly my sovereign lord?—Me thinks he shews great impatience to assume the husband.'

Mrs D——— walked off in great state—the first fit of the pouts I have ever seen her fall into; and who will give the second lecture on the subject, I am at a loss to conjecture.—Perhaps your eloquent little friend, my intended—you understand me,

Arabella—but I shall not allow it lawful for him to plead in his
own cause.—His reports will be so partial, his representations
so——Ah, Arabella, I hear my father ask for me!—what will
become of me?

I have great powers, my good girl—and I stood in need of their
utmost exertion, when opposed, as they have been, to Mrs
D——'s best performance. I acknowledge her to be a great
actress, and only inferior to your friend, who has carried her
point, to all intents and purposes; and not a word more is to
be mentioned—until the Padra receives his instructions to fill
his purse in our service.—I do not suppose, Arabella, that the
evening will be worth less to him than 500 gold mohrs.

You will, perhaps, think I treat the subject very gayly.—I
do—in order to keep my mind clear of melancholy thoughts. The
dear woman, that is now a saint in heaven, approves the work I
have accomplished; and I am teaching myself to forget the grave,
and look for her only in the bright regions of eternity.[†]

On which account, it has been determined, no one of us shall
visit the spot where her earthly remains are lodged. Mrs Hartly
affirms, it is flying in the face of Providence, to neglect the practice of resignation; and Mrs D——'s speaking silence seems
to claim that respect from us, no language could have engaged
for her.—Sentimental sorrow,[†] as Dr. Johnson calls it, is, I am
now satisfied, the bane of happiness, in a wider degree than the
worst evil under the sun, which that refinement is prompted to
resist; insomuch, that I hope you will find we have benefited by
our voyage.

There are monsters, Arabella, in human shapes, and the Eastern
world is (what I should have returned without conceiving it to be,
but for the incident of this morning) the scene of tragedies that
dishonour mankind.—I have, within the passing hour, beheld
one of these wretches conveyed to prison—and may condign[†]
punishment be his portion!

He is, my dear, an officer in the army[†]—who having, in some of his country rides, discovered an old man's daughter to be lovely beyond whatever this country has produced, cruelly and basely resolved to rob him of her. To her father's house he went, on this diabolical design, and was received by its innocent and unsuspecting inhabitants with the utmost kindness;—in consequence of which reception, he changed his plan of outrage—and instead of bearing her off, as he had intended, he settled it to violate the laws of hospitality—of God and of man—and accomplish his work of darkness under the paternal roof!

To win her, he found impossible—he therefore had recourse to violence; and, when the poor old man, terrified by his daughter's cries, advanced to her assistance, he shot him dead before his child's eyes; and then proceeded to fill up the measure of his iniquity. Yes! Arabella! the man whose profession it was to protect, thus brutally and barbarously destroyed!—May his name be branded with infamy!—and his death be equally unpitied and ignominious.—I now rejoice, more than ever, that I am about to leave a country, where fiend-like acts are, I fear, much oftener perpetrated than detected; for, the grave complains not, and gold can unnerve the arm of justice.—Lord C——— will not, however, stain his noble deeds, by suffering such a villain to escape; and the facts I have related are too well known, and too glaringly confirmed, to be palliated, or atoned by less than the life of him who could devise deeds of such turpitude; or, when even devised, could have the savage nature to carry them into effect.—I am all indignation, terror, compassion, and agitation:—the young woman survives, however, to appal the guilty wretch by her melancholy testimony.

We embark, Arabella, within the hour I am now devoting to my pen; and few evenings, I should suppose, produced more weddings, than took place, three evenings ago at Hartly House. Yes, Arabella, I have been three days a wife; and so abundantly are my family connections enlarged, that I have a mother I am proud to acknowledge, and sisters and brothers, in consequence of my change of condition; for the sister of Mrs Hartly is now Mrs

D————'s daughter, and inclination, will convert an alliance into the ties of relationship, beyond legal claims:—and, Arabella, I bring over with me the man I have chosen for your husband, the celebrated Beville of our Calcutta theatre.—Be propitious, ye gales; let not so much happiness be the prey of disaster!— But remember, Arabella, for your consolation, should we all be buried in the deep, that Providence has a right to dispose of us at will; and that, however unable mortals are to penetrate Heaven's design, every seeming misfortune is a disguised blessing, to those who possess rectitude of heart and uprightness of conduct: such are kindly sheltered by what is called a violent death, from the approaching, though unseen, miseries of existence.

A thousand times farewell!

S. D.

Letter XXXIX

Portsmouth

We are all landed safe at this place, after a tedious, though not hazardous voyage.—The addition of your company is ardently wished by every individual of the party to which I belong. Meet us then at Guildford, and, augment the happiness of your own

Sophia Doyly

Finis

Explanatory notes

Volume I

3 *debarked*: disembarked

6 *island of Sawger*: Sagar is approximately 77 miles from Calcutta. *The Annual Register, for the year 1787* (1789) reported that on 12 October 1787 at the island of Saugar a young man named Dawson, a silversmith and engraver of Calcutta, was carried off and consumed by a tiger (203). In 'Verses Written at the Island of Sagur in the Mouth of the Ganges, in 1807', John Leyden (1775–1811), the friend of Sir Walter Scott and assay-master of the Calcutta mint, depicts the island as the horrific scene of female infanticide and sacrifice to the warrior and mother goddess Durgā; see *The Poetical Remains of the late Dr. John Leyden* (London: Longman, Hurst, Rees, Orme, and Brown, 1819), pp. 174–6.

7 *Indiamen*: East Indiamen, the capacious cargo ships of the East India Company, were some of the biggest ships of the time; though heavily built and heavily armed, they were often remarkably fast.

Culpee: is, according to James Rennell, 36 miles, 3 furlongs from Calcutta; see *A Description of the Roads in Bengal and Bahar* (London: East India Company, 1778), p. 22. '[T]here is not in the whole world a more unhealthy situation than Culpee', John Clark, *Observations on the Diseases which Prevail in Long Voyages to Hot Countries, particularly on those in the East Indies*, 3rd edn. (London: Murray, 1792), p. 114. See also pp. 80–1, where Gibbes mentions the danger of tigers.

Cudgeree: '*Khijiri* or *Kijari*, a village and police station on the low lands near the mouth of the Hoogly, on the west bank, and 68 miles below Calcutta. It was formerly well known as a usual anchorage of the larger Indiamen', *Hobson-Jobson*. Gibbes's geography is faulty here as Kulpi is closer to Calcutta than Khājari. Its situation on a dry plain made it a more healthy spot than Culpee; see Clark, *Observations on the Diseases*, pp. 114–15.

bugeros: budgerows; see also p. 75. [See Henry Yule and A.C. Burnell, *Hobson-Jobson: The Anglo-Indian Dictionary* (London; Murray, 1886), under 'budgerow and 'buggalow'.] William Hodges, an artist patronized by Warren Hastings, described them as follows: 'These boats [...] may be about sixty feet in length, having very high sterns [...] in the centre they are broad, having a considerable bearing in the water, and quite sharp forward. They are steered with a large paddle or oar extending ten feet from the stern; and there is generally one mast in the center, on which is hoisted a large square sail [...] These boats are ill calculated to go near the wind, and indeed are dangerous, from the great weight abaft; they are, however, extremely commodious, having in the center a small verandah, or open portico, opening by a door into a handsome room, lighted by a range of windows on each side', *Travels in India, during the years 1780, 1781, 1782, & 1783* (1793), reprinted in *The European Discovery of India: Key Indological Sources of Romanticism*, ed. Michael J. Franklin, 6 vols (London: Ganesha Publishing/ Edition Synapse, 2001), 3: 39.

Dryden's Cydnus: 'Her Gally down the Silver *Cydnos* row'd, / The Tackling Silk, the Streamers wav'd with Gold, / The gentle Winds were lodg'd in Purple sails', John Dryden, *All for Love: or, the World Well Lost* (London : J. Tonson, 1709), p. 28.

Kittesan: [also *kittysol, kittesaw* p. 41] A sunshade or parasol, made of bamboo and either oiled paper or fabric.

8 *orientalised*: this appears to be the earliest known use of this word; *OED*'s first example of the verb 'orientalize' is from a text of 1810.

Southern's Oroonoko: Thomas Southerne, *Oroonoko: A Tragedy* (London: H. Playford, 1696). This is especially interesting as Southerne, in his dramatization of Aphra Behn's romance, *Oroonoko* (1688), rewrites the black African heroine Imoinda as a white European. The white woman, of course, in her role of repro-ducing racial purity, must always obey the patriarchal injunction against misce-genation; see Laura Brown, 'The Romance of Empire: *Oroonoko* and the Trade in Slaves', in *The New Eighteenth Century: Theory, Politics, English Literature*, ed. Felicity Nussbaum and Laura Brown (New York; London: Methuen, 1987), pp. 41–61.

Loll Shrub: 'Hind. *lāl-sharāb*, "red wine." The universal name of claret in India', *Hobson-Jobson*.

Diamond Point: 'An anchorage in the Hoogly below Calcutta, 30 m. by road, and 41 by river. It was the usual anchorage of the old Indiamen in the mercantile days of the E. I. Company. In the oldest charts we find the "Diamond Sand," on the western side of what is now called Diamond Harbour, and on some later charts, Diamond Point', *Hobson-Jobson*.

debarkation: disembarkation, landing.

palanquin: the Flemish artist Frani;ois Balthazar Solvyns (1760–1824), who lived in Calcutta from 1791 to 1803, depicts no fewer than eight separate designs of palanquin in his *A Collection of Two Hundred and Fifty Coloured Etchings* (Calcutta: Mirror Press, 1799). It would seem that Sophia is here describing a 'Chair Palanquin' as etched by Solvyns (Sec. VI, No. 6. "A Short, Palkee"); see Robert L. Hardgrave, Jr., *A Portrait of the Hindus: Balthazar Solvyns & the European Image of India 1760–1824* (Oxford: Oxford University Press and Mapin Publishing, 2004), pp. 463–4. The image, which can be viewed online at Hardgrave's superb website: http://asnic.utexas.edu/asnic/hardgrave/solvyns online/pages/Calcutta228.html displays the Venetian blinds, the bearers, and what Sophia terms a 'kittesan boy', outside an elegant European-style house.

har-carriers: a *harkara* [Hindi, Urdu] was a messenger or courier. Gibbes should have used the term *mussaulchee* (see *Hobson-Jobson* q.v) for a torch-bearer or Calcutta 'link-boy'. The European doctor, in an interesting tale by Bernardin de Saint Pierre, is furnished with a retinue which included 'a kitti-sol-gee, or umbrella-carrier, to shade him from the sun by day; and a misol-gee, or flambeau-carrier, for the night', *The Indian Cottage, or a Search after Truth* (London: William Lane, 1791), pp. 11–12.

Tok, Tok: the sound of bamboo sticks being struck together to announce their progress. It has become the popular name of motorized rickshaws.

9 *auri veni*: '"Quae" que "meos releves aestus," cantare solebat / "Accipienda sinu, mobilis aura, veni"', '"Come, fickle breeze *(Aura)*, who cools my heat," he used to sing, "be welcome to my breast"', Ovid, *Ars Amoris* 3: 697–8.

furniture was all Chinese: The fashion for Chinese furniture, facilitated by East India Company trade with Canton, was also in very much in evidence in London, since the publication of Sir William Chambers, *Designs of Chinese Buildings, Furniture, Dresses, Machines, and Utensils* (1757).

muskettos [...] bugs in London: it is characteristic of Sophia's relativism that she should juxtapose colonial and metropolitan annoyances. Cf. 'In the hospitals at London, bugs are frequently a greater evil to the patient, than the malady for which he seeks an hospital', J. G. Keysler, 'Travels', in *A New Collection of Voyages, Discoveries and Travels*, 7 vols (London: Knox, 1767), 4: 450–51.

10 *commencement of the temperate season*: Gibbes's information concerning the onset of the monsoon season is incorrect [it begins in June, not February], but from these details it can be gleaned that Sophia must have landed in Calcutta in late September of 1784, exactly a year after Sir William Jones had arrived in the *Crocodile* frigate.

11 epigraph: 'Prime cheerer, Light! / Of all material beings first, and best! / Efflux divine!' ('Summer', ll. 90–92). This is a slight misquotation from Gibbes's favourite James Thomson, *The Seasons* (London: Millar, 1746), p. 58. An anonymous poem published in the very first number of the *Bengal Gazette* (29 Jan. 1780) was entitled 'The Seasons'.

degagé: relaxed, unconstrained.

à la volonté: at one's will.

state levees: the reception of visitors by the king on rising from bed.

country-born: '"country-born" people are persons of European descent, but born in India', *Hobson-Jobson*. Despite this clear definition, some confusion continues to exist concerning this term. Sophia writes: 'a *country-born* young lady-as the phrase is, to distinguish them from the Europeans', and some readers have understandably seen this distinction as between European and 'native', rather than between, as *Hobson-Jobson* explains, what is 'imported from Europe' and what is 'produced in India'. The phrase did subsequently come to be used euphemistically of children of mixed-race marriages between British or European fathers and Indian mothers. In some respects the difficulty is related to the changing meaning of the term 'Anglo-Indian' which until the early-twentieth century simply denoted the English in India, and only later came to mean 'Eurasian'. Elizabeth Buettner's comments, albeit referring to a later period in the Raj, are useful here: 'Although domiciled Europeans were popularly known as 'country born', this distinction could also apply to most children of the highest-ranking British families if interpreted literally-as simply having been born in the subcontinent. Instead 'remaining in India' was the decisive feature distinguishing the 'domiciled', who were racially suspect, from the 'real' Europeans, who were able to pay for travels that allowed them to maintain contact with Britain', 'Problematic Spaces, Problematic Races: Defining "Europeans" in Late Colonial India', *Women's History Review*, 9:2 (2000), 277–98; 281. It is quite clear that this young lady (whose name, we learn on p. 120, is Miss Rolle), smoking her hookah while her hair is dressed, is not an Indian woman. See also the following note, and n. to p. 15 below.

hooka: Smoking the hookah was a pastime and addiction much remarked upon and much copied by Europeans. The idea of smoking *betel* (or *paan*, a leaf rather than a root) which was chewed by Indians for its mild narcotic effect, might well be an error of Gibbes. In an authentic and elaborate description of the hookah belonging to Mubarak ud-Daula, Sophia's 'Nabob of Nabobs', the attendant filled 'the silver bowl with a nice compound of musk, sugar, rose-water, and a little tobacco finely chopped, and worked up together into a kind of dough, which was dissolved into an odoriferous liquid by the heat of a little fire made of burnt rice', *The Travels of Dean Mahomet: An Eighteenth-Century Journey Through India*, ed. Michael H. Fisher (Berkeley: University of California Press, 1997), p. 62. The 'country-born' young lady might well have been based upon the lively Miss Emma Wrangham, born, not in India, but in St Helena in 1762, one of whose soubriquets in the pages of *Hicky's Bengal Gazette* was 'Hookah Turban'; see n. to p. 40 below. On James Augustus Hicky and the insights into Calcutta politics provided by this first Indian newspaper, see my '"The Hastings Circle": Writers and Writing in Calcutta in the Last Quarter of the Eighteenth Century', in *Authorship, Commerce and the Public: Scenes of Writing, 1750–1850*, ed. Emma Clery, Caroline Franklin, and Peter Garside (Basingstoke: Palgrave, 2002), pp.186–202.

12 *Hartly Mansion*: impressive imperial architecture flourished in Calcutta, soon to become known as the city of palaces. A good idea of the city in the period in which the novel is set may be gained *from Oriental Scenery. Twenty-four Views in Hindoostan, taken in the year 1792; drawn by Thomas Daniell, and engraved by himself and William Daniell* (London, 1797); images from which and a variety of other contemporary sources are available from the British Library online at: www.imagesonline.bl.uk/britishlibrary/

13 *view of the esplanade*: 'Cheringhee is situated on the east side of the Esplanade [...] The houses, which are of brick, stuccoed, and afterwards coloured, are inhabited by opulent English gentlemen', *Oriental Scenery*, p. 11.

lustre: 'A glass ball placed among artificial lights to increase the brightness of the illumination (*obs.*); also, one of the prismatic glass pendants often attached in circles to a chandelier or hung round the edge of an ornamental vase. A chandelier [the usual sense in Fr.]', *OED*.

girandole: 'A branched support for candles or other lights, either in the form of a candlestick for placing on a table, etc., or more commonly as a bracket projecting from a wall', *OED*.

chinam: chunam, cement or plaster made of shell-lime and sea-sand, which imparted a brightness to the fine buildings of Calcutta. Unlike Sophia, John Henry Grose found the effect 'very offensive to the eyes from the glare of the sun', *A Voyage to the East-Indies* (London: S. Hooper and A. Morley, 1757), p. 82.

the Governor's house: Gibbes probably means Hastings' 'Garden House' in Alipore, [then] just outside Calcutta, which was described by Eliza Fay as 'most superbly fitted up with all that unbounded affluence can display'; see *Original Letters from India (1779–1815)*, ed. E. M. Forster (London: Woolf, 1925), p. 175.

Venetian blinds (or verandas): here and elsewhere Gibbes seems to confuse the two; cf. the description of Hartly Mansion, p. 13.

14 *gold mohrs*: 'the chief gold coin of British India, Hind. from Pers. *muhr*, a (metallic) seal', *Hobson-Jobson*. They were minted in Calcutta and worth, as Sophia rightly says, 16 rupees; see Francis Gladwin, *A Compendious System of Bengal Revenue Accounts* (Calcutta: Manuel Cantopher, 1790), p. 17.

epigraph: "'Tis raging noon; and, vertical, the sun / Darts on the head direct his forceful rays. / O'er heaven and earth, far as the ranging eye / Can sweep, a dazzling deluge reigns', ('Summer', ll. 429–32), Thomson, *The Seasons*, p. 72.

All-conquering heat: 'All-conquering Heat, oh intermit thy wrath! / And on my throbbing temples potent thus / Beam not so fierce!, ('Summer', ll. 451–3), *ibid.*

15 *chuse country-born ladies for wealth*: referring to this statement, Felicity A. Nussbaum, in an otherwise sensitive and nuanced reading, incorrectly takes 'country-born' to mean 'native': [H]er [Sophia's] presence implicitly helps prevent British officers' intermarriage with Indian women [...] and ensures a pure national and racial line', *Torrid Zones: Maternity, Sexuality, and Empire in Eighteenth-Century English Narratives* (Baltimore and London: John Hopkins University Press, 1995), pp. 175–6. Later in the novel Sophia uses the term 'India-born' for ladies of European extraction born in the East; see p. 157.

dulcineas: Sophia's clear-eyed account of the Calcutta marriage-market is sharpened by her reference to Don Quixote's mistress.

matrimonial overtures: John Macfarlane cites from the *Calcutta Gazette* of 12 August 1784 some lines of a poem by a lady addressed to her 'friend in England': 'No place, where at a bolder rate, / We females bear our sovereign state. / Beauty ne'er points its arms in vain, / Each glance subdues some melting swain'; see *Hartly House, Calcutta; A Novel of the Days of Warren Hastings* (Calcutta: Thacker, Spink and Co., 1908), pp. 298–9.

Mr. and Mrs. Hartly: No prominent family of this name has been traced in Calcutta. A Bartholomew Hartley was appointed surgeon in the Company's Medical Service on 29 October 1783; *The Bengal register, containing lists of the Hon. Company's civil and military establishments, under the Presidency of Fort William. 1st December, 1787* (Calcutta: Stuart and Cooper, [1787]), p. 37. He married Elizabeth Lane on 4 October 1789 in Calcutta; see OIOC N/1/4/84. Hartley was a signatory of the 'Address of the British Inhabitants of Calcutta' of 1 February 1785 upon Hastings' departure from Calcutta, testifying to 'our general Satisfaction in the whole Tenour of your long Administration, and our lasting Sense of your many patriotic Exertions'; see *Minutes of the evidence taken at the trial of Warren Hastings Esquire, late Governor General of Bengal, at the bar of the House of Lords*, 11 vols ([London], 1788–95), 6: 2451–2. Macfarlane noted that he was 'the leading promoter of the lottery which was organized in 1784 in aid of the building fund of St. John's Church'; see *Hartly House, Calcutta; A Novel of the Days of Warren Hastings*, p. 293; and my note to 16 below.

the church: St. John's Chapel was adapted from a section of the Old Fort in 1760. 'The fort is now made a very different use of: the only apology for a church is some rooms in it, where divine service is sometimes performed', Mrs. [Jemima] Kindersley, *Letters from the Island of Teneriffe, Brazil, the Cape of Good Hope, and the East Indies* (1777), reprinted in *Women's Travel Writing: 1750–1850*, ed. Caroline Franklin, 8 vols (London: Routledge, 2006), 5: 275.

16 *a new church erecting*: in the spring of 1784 the 'Revd. Tally-ho' William Johnson, the Senior Chaplain of the Presidency, had applied to Sir William Jones for a subscription towards the building of the new Church of St. John; see *The Letters of Sir William Jones*, ed. Garland Cannon, 2 vols (Oxford: Clarendon Press, 1970), 2: 639–40. The new Church, St John's, was designed by Lt. James Agg (*c*. 1758–1828), erected and consecrated (on Sunday, 24 June 1787; see *Calcutta Gazette*, 28 June 1787) on land which had been provided by Hastings; see William Johnson, chaplain to the East India Company at Calcutta, *A Circular Letter to the Most Reverend the Archbishops and Bishops of the Church of England* ([London], [1788?]), pp. 7–8.

Padra's salary: Cannon notes that 'Padre' Johnson 'left India in 1788 with a considerable fortune', (*Letters of Sir William Jones*, 2: 639); no doubt on account of his 'perquisites', fees attached to his office, in addition to salary.

17 *virtue of cleanliness*: the 'great unwashed' of Europe marvelled at such daily immersion in the Ganges.

Gentoos: 'a corruption of the Portuguese *Gentio*, 'a gentile' or heathen, which they applied to the Hindus in contradistinction to the *Moros* or 'Moors,' *i.e.* Mahommedans', *Hobson-Jobson*.

astonishing empire: this term is used by James Rennell, *Memoir of a Map of Hindoostan; or the Mogul Empire* (London: printed for the author, 1783), p. lxiii.

sublime ideas: Sophia points to the centrality of the East in matters of religion.

18–19 *India, it is supposed, was first peopled [...] meet with hereafter*: this section is lifted almost verbatim from Thomas Salmon, *A New Geographical and Historical Grammar: . The sixth edition* (London: William Johnston, 1758), p. 456.

19 *Persian Monarch, Khouli Khan [...] properly adhered to*: Kouli Khan is Nadir Shah (1688–1747), the subject of William Jones, *The History of the Life of Nader Shah, King of Persia* (1771). This section draws very heavily upon William Guthrie, *A New Geographical, Historical, and Commercial Grammar; and Present State of the Several Kingdoms of the World*, 9th edn. (London: Charles Dilly; and G.G.J. and J. Robinson, 1785), pp. 695–6; cf. also Alexander Dow, *The History of*

Hindostan (1772), repr. in *Representing India: Indian Culture and Imperial Control in Eighteenth-Century British Orientalist Discourse*, ed. Michael J. Franklin, 9 vols (London: Routledge, 2000), 3: 39–40.

a prince [...] his power is feeble: Prince Ali Gauhar (1728–1806) became emperor Shah Alam II upon the murder of his father Alamgir II in 1759, but was soon reduced to little more than a figurehead. By the treaty of Allahabad (1765) Shah Alam granted the *Diwani* (right to collect revenue) of Bengal, Bihar, and Orissa to the East India Company in return for an annual tribute of twenty-six lakhs of Rupees. In 1788 he was humiliated and blinded by Ghulam Qadir, a Rohilla Afghan chieftain.

20 *Prince Hyder Ali*: Haidar Ali (1722–82), the energetic ruler of Mysore, expanded his kingdom at the expense of the Maratha states and Hyderabad to become, together with his son, Tipu Sultan, the fiercest Indian opponents encountered by the British. See Innes Munro, *A Narrative of the Military Operations, on the Coromandel Coast, against the Combined Forces of the French, Dutch, and Hyder Ally Cawn* (London: printed for the author, 1789).

20–7 *This Arabella [...] friendship affection*: this section was reproduced unacknowledged in the *Aberdeen Magazine, Literary Chronicle, and Review*, XXIX, (Thursday, July 2, 1789), 416–21; see Introduction, pp. xviii–xx above.

21 *stays are wholly unworn*: cf. the remarks of the Dutch Admiral Stavorinus on 'fashionable undress' in Bengal: 'The ladies affect, for coolness, to wear no covering on their necks, and leave none of the beauties of a well-formed bosom to be guessed at', Johan Splinter Stavorinus, *Voyages to the East-Indies*, 3 vols (London: G.G. and J. Robinson, 1798), 1: 524. The fact, however, that there existed a demand for such corsetry is evidenced by an advert appearing in the *Calcutta Gazette* of 27 May 1790: 'Ladies' stays, for the warm season, made by Stephen Quick, No. 161, Cossitollah. They are perfectly cool, being both outside and lining of fine Irish linen, and upon so easy a construction that a servant may with ease shift the bones from one pair to another in a few minutes, so that a lady having three or four pairs may shift her stays as often as her Linen. N.B.- Price one gold mohur each pair.'

friseur: hairdresser.

flowers of British manufacture: such authentic details, revealing a certain home-sickness, are typical of what convinced some readers that these letters were genuine.

21–2 *At three [...] the company assembled [...] no soup*: Eliza Fay places the hour for dining at two, insisting that soup was an integral part of the bill of fare; see *Original Letters*, p. 181.

22 *burnt to a clinker*: the use of charcoal, also associated with Persian cookery, was traditional in India; see 'The Ordinances of Manu', *The Works of Sir William Jones*, ed. Anna Maria Jones, 13 vols (London: Stockdale, and Walker, 1807), 5: 283.

23 *three bottles of claret*: British India had a well-earned reputation for hard drinking.

24 *domestic servants [...] are Gentoos*: by contrast, Stavorinus asserts: 'Moorish domestics are kept for the menial services of the house', *Voyages to the East-Indies*, 1: 522. Bartholomew Burges provides a detailed and fascinating account of the number and range of servants he employed upon a surveying trip; see *A Series of Indostan Letters* (New York: Ross, [1790]), pp. 38–9.

consumer: 'Consumah, Khansama, s. P. *Khansaman*; 'a house-steward.' In Anglo-Indian households in the Bengal Presidency, this is the title of the chief table servant and provider, now always a Mahommedan', *Hobson-Jobson*.

Seda-bearer: 'Sirdar, s. Hind. from Pers. *sardar*, and less correctly *sirdar*, 'leader, a commander, an officer'; a chief, or lord; the head of a set of palankin-bearers, and hence the '*sirdar-bearer*,' or elliptically 'the *Sirdar*,' is in Bengal the style of the valet or body-servant, even when he may have no others under him', *Hobson-Jobson*.

25 *secure from every possibility of contamination*: this reference to cups being exchanged supplies a somewhat unsavoury insight into the metropolitan tea ceremony; Sophia is pleased by yet another example of subcontinental attention to hygiene.

five gold mohrs (ten pounds) a corner: her reluctance to countenance such extravagance at cards allows Sophia to develop the onomastics of her surname; cf. p. ix above. Her subsequent remarks concerning 'this pernicious propensity' echo Gibbes's repeated concern about the effects of gambling; see Introduction, p. xiv. Also cf. her remarks about betting at billiards (p. 49), and the gaming-table (pp. 105, 154).

some author: 'drunkenness is ever the vice of a barbarous and gaming of a luxurious age', *Miscellaneous Works of Oliver Goldsmith* (London: Griffin, 1775), 'Essay XIX', p. 115.

26 *vocal music*: on the Calcutta Catch Club and the popularity of glee singing, especially among the Hastings circle; see Ian Woodfield, *Music of the Raj: A Social and Economic History of Music in Late Eighteenth-Century Anglo-Indian Society* (Oxford: Oxford University Press, 2000), pp. 116–42.

Calcuttonians: I have not elsewhere encountered this term for the inhabitants of Calcutta and it might well prove to be a coinage of Gibbes.

27 *silver casnets*: I have found this spelling for 'castanets' in the period, but they would hardly be made of silver or worn at the ankles. It would seem that this is an attempt to convey the bands of tiny bells which Indian dancers wear on their ankles.

notch-girls: 'Nautch, s. A kind of ballet-dance performed by women; also any kind of stage entertainment; an European ball. Hind. and Mahr. *nach*, from Skt. *nritya*, dancing and stage-playing, through Prakrit *nachcha*', *Hobson-Jobson*. A most detailed description of a nautch is provided in Burges, *A Series of Indostan Letters*, pp. 30–36.

Company's gardens: The Company's botanical gardens on the west bank of the River Hugli were founded in 1786 by Colonel Robert Kyd, who acquired plants from all over the subcontinent. He and William Roxburgh were encouraged by Sir William Jones to send seeds to Jones's friends, Sir George Yonge and Sir Joseph Banks; see *Letters of Sir William Jones*, 2: 771, 891.

28 epigraph: *Bear me, Pomona! [...] feast with Jove*: 'Summer', ll. 663–89 Thomson, *The Seasons*, p. 81.

produce of this Eastern soil: Jones, a ground-breaking botanist himself, celebrated Indian fruits in his 'The Enchanted Fruit; or, The Hindu Wife' (1784), *Sir William Jones: Selected Poetical and Prose Works*, ed. Michael J. Franklin (Cardiff: University of Wales Press, 1995), pp. 80–97.

29 *Great are the scenes, [...] double seasons pass*: ('Summer', ll. 643–5) Thomson, *The Seasons*, p. 80. Cf. 'Here, while the Sun his polar journeys takes, / His visit doubled, double seasons makes', *The Lusiad; or, the Discovery of India [...] Translated from the original Portuguese of Luis de Camoens. By William Julius Mickle* (London: Cadell *et al.*, 1776), p. 195.

Come then, expressive Silence! muse his praise: this is the concluding line of Thomson, 'A Hymn', *The Seasons*, p. 230.

wonder-working hand of Nature: cf. 'By Nature's swift and secret-working hand', 'Spring', l. 97, *The Seasons*, p. 9.

For me the mine [...] my canopy the skies: Epistle 1, ll. 133–36, Pope *An Essay on Man*, (London: printed by John Wright, for Lawton Gilliver, 1734), p. 13.

29–30 *the Mogul emperor-the camp*: the description of Mogul encampments is taken almost verbatim from Salmon, *A New Geographical and Historical Grammar*, p. 454

30 *Ornament of the Earth*: cf. *The Pupil of Adversity, an Oriental Tale*, 2 vols (London: W. Lane, 1788), 2: 164.

500 sacre rupees (£60): 'sicca a. [Pers. (Arab.) *sikkah* a die for coining, the impression on money.] *sicca rupee*, originally, a newly-coined rupee, accepted at a higher value than those worn by use', *OED*. Gibbes's unusual transliteration is also used in the *Minutes of the Evidence taken before a Committee of the House of Commons, ... appointed to Consider of the Several Articles of Charge of High Crimes and Misdemeanors ... against Warren Hastings* (London: John Stockdale, 1788).

birds of passage: It is somewhat ironic that Sophia should echo a phrase of Burke's. 'Animated with all the avarice of age and the impetuosity of youth, they roll in one after another; wave after wave; and there is nothing before the eyes of the natives but an endless, hopeless prospect of new flights of birds of prey and passage, with appetites continually renewing for a food that is continually wasting. Every rupee of profit made by an Englishman is lost forever to India', *Mr. Burke's Speech, on the 1st December 1783, upon [...] Mr. Fox's East India Bill* (London: J. Dodsley, 1784), p. 31.

astonishing rent: cf. 'That large and convenient Garden House to the south-ward of Chirengee, formerly, for several years, occupied by Sir Robert Chambers. The monthly rent is 400 Sicca Rupees', *Calcutta Gazette*, 8 September 1785.

31 beisars: Gibbes's error in using this to refer to tradesmen would seem another indication that her knowledge of India was second-hand. 'Bazaar, s. H. &c. From P. *bāzār*, a permanent market or street of shops. [...] In S. India and Ceylon the word is used for a single shop or stall kept by a native', *Hobson-Jobson*.

bada beisar: this means 'big bazaar' in Bengali.

muchee beisar: cf. 'Nikari or Machhua. Fishmonger', Solvyns, *A Collection of Two Hundred and Fifty Coloured Etchings*, p. 245.

dewdwallar: Gilchrist supplies 'doodhwalla' for milkman; see John Gilchrist, *The Anti-jargonist, or a Short Introduction to the Hindoostanee Language* (Calcutta: Ferris & Co., 1800), p. 124.

suedwallar: Gilchrist gives 'soour' for hog or boar', *ibid.*, p. 203.

chine beisar: 'Cheenee, sugar, &c. from *cheen*, China', *ibid.*, p. 120.

Europe shops: cf. 'The principal diversions of Calcutta, are balls, card parties, and what are called the Europe shops, which are literally magazines of every European article of luxury or convenience. These early in the morning are the public rendezvous of the idle and the gay, who here propagate the scandal of the day, and purchase, at an immoderate price the toys of Mr. Pinchbeck and the frippery of Tavistock-street', Philip Dormer Stanhope, *Genuine Memoirs of Asiaticus, in a Series of Letters to a Friend, during Five Years Residence in Different Parts of India* (London: Kearsley, 1784), p. 45. [On this author, 'late of the

First Regiment of Dragoons', was probably the grandson of the fourth Earl of Chesterfield (whom Gibbes also cites; see notes to pp. 59, 139); see the note of R.A. Austen-Leigh and the response of Wm. Asheton Tonge, 'Philip Dormer Stanhope, Author of *Genuine Memoirs of Asiaticus*', *Notes and Queries*, s.12–XI (1922), 165–7; 213.]

controul is not an article of matrimonial rule: cf. 'The least in rank stand in need of five or six thousand rupees annually. Most people spend twice as much, although their income does not amount to more than half of what they disburse. The dearness of provisions which are brought from Europe, contributes thereto, but perhaps the greatest cause may be traced in the excessive expense which the ladies incur, in the articles of dress and appearance. Domestic peace and tranquillity must be purchased by a shower of jewels, a wardrobe of the richest clothes, and a kingly parade of plate upon the sideboard; the husband must give all these, or, according to a vulgar phrase, "the house would be too hot to hold him," while the wife never pays the least attention to her domestic concerns, but suffers the whole to depend upon her servants or slaves', Stavorinus, *Voyages to the East-Indies*, 1: 523.

Governor's house: 'The Council House stands on the north side of the Esplanade [...] The house, with pillars, has an example of a Virandah, or open corridor, a mode of building of considerable utility in tropical climates', Thomas Daniell, *Oriental Scenery*, p. 5.

32 *An old fellow, with an incredible fortune*: cf. 'I believe an instance never was known for a young maiden of spotless character not making a brilliant fortune by a trip to Bengal', Burges, *A Series of Indostan Letters*, p. 11.

33 *ring unending changes on negative phrases*: Calcutta gives the young heroine much practice in refining her power of no-saying.

like gallantry in France [...] I trust you with my wife: it is possible that Gibbes had in mind the scandalous affair of Hastings' greatest adversary, Philip Francis, who in December 1778 was found in compromising circumstances at night in the house of the recently-married, beautiful sixteen-year-old Mme. Grand, whose furious husband, George Francis Grand, obtained damages of 50,000 rupees against him in the Supreme Court. Her maiden name was Catherine Noele Worlee (1762–1835) and she subsequently married the French Minister of Foreign Affairs, Talleyrand, becoming Princesse de Talleyrand-Perigord.

34 *I adore the customs of the East*: instead of servants speaking in broken English, Europeans learn to ask for what they require in 'Gentoo phrases', thus 'making English the vehicle only of polite conversation'. Sophia's remarkable example of language acquisition promoting exclusivity is not, perhaps, in the Jonesian spirit.

phaeton: a fashionable and sporting light four-wheeled carriage with open sides in front of the seat, often drawn by a pair of horses; see also nn. to pp. 34, 41.

Writers Buildings: the Daniells portrayed these, 'so-called from being the residence of the junior part of the Gentlemen in the service of the English East India Company', *Oriental Scenery*, p. 7.

35 *Her fairest virtues fly*: 'Her fairest virtues fly from publick sight / Domestick worth, that shuns too strong a light', 'Advice to a Lady', ll. 53–4, Baron George Lyttelton (1709–1773), *The Poetical Works* (Glasgow: Andrew Foulis, 1787), p. 55.

Indostan is the land of vivacity, rather than that of sentiment: Sophia effectively demonstrates subcontinental opportunities for both.

Calcutta Theatre: this was the theatre formerly called the New Playhouse at Lyons Range, behind the Writers' Buildings; it was established in 1775 by George Williamson, an auctioneer, and lasted until 1808. The early practice, which so interested Sophia, of female parts being played by young male actors, was soon abandoned as more adventurous young ladies arrived in Calcutta. One such young lady, Miss Emma Wrangham, who had won a certain notoriety in the pages of *Hicky's Bengal Gazette* during the 1780s, established what was later to become known as 'Mrs Bristow's Theatre' (she married John Bristow at Chinsurah on 27 May 27 1782) at Chowringhee in 1789. See Sushil Kumar Mukherjee, *The Story of the Calcutta Theatres, 1753–1980* (Calcutta: Bagchee, 1982); Mita Choudhury, 'Sheridan, Garrick, and a Colonial Gesture: *The School for Scandal* on the Calcutta Stage', *Theatre Journal*, 46 (1994), 303–21. On fictional representations of the Calcutta theatre; see Charles Dibdin, *Hannah Hewit, or, The Female Crusoe*, 3 vols (London: printed for the author, [1792]), 3: 201ff.; and Agnes Maria Bennett, *The Beggar Girl and her Benefactors*, 7 vols (London: William Lane, 1797), 1: 45–7.

eight rupees (twenty shillings): for a ticket in the pit; as Sophia reminds us, theatre at Calcutta was obviously entertainment for the affluent; see also p. 121. Her prices exactly agree with those mentioned by Hickey as being set by Francis Rundell, the theatre's actor-manager, late in 1783; see *Memoirs of William Hickey*, ed. Alfred Spencer, 4 vols (London: Hurst & Blackett, 1913–25), 3: 207.

the London Hotel: the London Tavern was south of Tank Square; Sophia warms to the topic of exorbitant prices in Calcutta. Eliza Fay informs us that subscription assemblies were held at both the London Tavern and the Harmonic Tavern in the Loll Bazaar; see *Original Letters*, p. 192.

36 *coffee-houses*: a 'dish of coffee' costs 'a rupee (half a crown)', but allows you perusal of English newspapers, together with the *[India Gazette, or] Calcutta [Public] Advertiser* (1780–1843), the *Calcutta Chronicle* (1786–98), etc. Most of the material concerning prices at the London Hotel and the coffee-houses is attributed to John Hawkesworth (Asiaticus) by W. H. Carey, *The Good Old Days of Honorable John Company, Being Curious Reminiscences Illustrating Manners & Customs of the British in India During the Rule of the East India Company, from 1600 to 1858*, 2 vols (Calcutta: R. Cambray, 1906), 116. My thanks are to Brian Schofield who brought this to my attention.

the Hospital: this was the Presidency General Hospital, originally founded in 1768. See also p. 44.

ruins of the Black Hole [...] Mhir Jaffeir: Gibbes does not use the primary source, John Zephaniah Holwell, *A Genuine Narrative of the Deplorable Deaths of the English Gentlemen and Others, who were Suffocated in the Black Hole* (1758); her description is taken virtually verbatim from Guthrie, *A New Geographical, Historical, and Commercial Grammar*, pp. 692–3.

Soubah: 'Souba, Soobah, s. Hind. from Pers. *suba*. A large Division or Province of the Mogul Empire (*e.g.* the *Subah* of the Deccan, the *Subah* of Bengal). The word is also frequently used as short for *Subadar*, The Viceroy, or Governor of a *suba'*, Hobson-Jobson.

37 *a most romantic and beautiful spot*: this was most probably Garden Reach, a suburb of Calcutta, where many wealthy Company and Crown employees built substantial 'Garden Houses' or bungalows (Hindustani *bangla*, 'belonging to Bengal') with lawns stretching down to the River Hugli.

38 *espaliers*: lattice-work upon which shrubs can be trained.

parterre: a garden with geometrically arranged flower beds.

recesses [...] queen Dido: the queen of Carthage sought such secluded groves when deserted by Aeneas.

bosom of free air: Garden Reach was seen as an airy and healthy location. Cf. Gibbes's comments on the Presidency General Hospital in note to p. 45.

jessamine and roses: the Indian jessamines or jasmines are particularly fragrant varieties; Mrs. Hartly (cf. Sophia's remark on p. 140) might be referring to the 'Málatí', or to the white or yellow 'Yut'hicà'; see Sir William Jones, 'Botanical Observations on Select Indian Plants', *Works*, 5: 62–162; 74.

39 *this golden world*: such a description would seem characteristic of the enthusiastic Miss Goldborne, but cf. Gibbes's earlier use of these words: 'changing the mild climate of Britain for the burning suns of the golden world', *Elfrida; or, Paternal Ambition*, 3 vols (London: Joseph Johnson, 1786), 2: 38.

to England for education: in employing a generously-paid governess or 'gouvernante', rather than sending her children to English boarding-schools, Mrs Hartly constitutes something of a trend-setter. See also p. 106.

Nature is here so lavish of her most beautiful productions: although this is mentioned in the context of an admirer's gift of a large bouquet, Sophia's enthusiasm for Bengal is everywhere apparent.

40 *The Nabob*: Mubarak ud-Daula (1757/8–1793), Nawab Nazim of Bengal, Bihar and Orissa; see the Introduction above, and my 'The Palanquins of State; or, Broken Leaves in a Mughal Garden', in *Romantic Representations of British India*, ed. Michael J. Franklin (London: Routledge, 2006), pp. 1–44.

his wife of wives [...] copper complexion: Sophia's tolerance concerning the Nawab's polygyny and her complete lack of racial prejudice (which she also confidently ascribes to her correspondent Arabella) seem remarkable at this period. From a male perspective and considering the comparative paucity of European women, inter-racial attraction was not at all unusual, however. Stanhope underlines 'the attractive charms of an Asiatic beauty. I have seen ladies of the Gentoo cast [...] I already begin to think the dazzling brightness of a copper-coloured face infinitely preferable to the pallid and sickly hue, which banishes the roses from the cheeks of the European fair', Stanhope, *Genuine Memoirs of Asiaticus*, p. 47.

Can wealth give happiness: Edward Young, 'Satire V: On Women', ll.393–4, *Love of Fame, the Universal Passion. In Seven Characteristical Satires* (London: J. Tonson, 1728), p. 107.

The manners of the ladies at Calcutta: the fearlessness and apparent gender trespassing so admired by Sophia is reminiscent of William Hickey's description of Miss Emma Wrangham also known as 'Turban Conquest', 'Hookah Turban', or 'Chinsurah Belle', who, it would seem, performed both on and off stage: 'a fine dashing girl, not by any means a regular beauty, but an uncommonly elegant figure and person; remarkably clever and highly intelligent. Her natural flow of spirits frequently led her into extravagancies and follies of rather too masculine a nature; instead of seating herself like other women on horseback, she rode like a man astride, would leap over any hedge or ditch that even the most zealous sportsmen were dubious of attempting. She rode several matches and succeeded against the best and most experienced jockeys. She was likewise an excellent shot, rarely missing her bird; understood the present fashionable science of pugilism and would without hesitation knock a man down if he presumed to offer her the slightest insult; in short, she stopped at nothing that met her fancy, however wild or eccentric, executing whatever she attempted with a *naivete* and ease and elegance that was irresistible', *Memoirs of William Hickey*, 3: 377.

41 *such charioteers as these*: Edward Young, 'Satire V: On Women', ll. 129–30, *Love of Fame*, p. 91. See also Introduction, n. 67.

the phaetons are English built: the combination of British workmanship and Asiatic decoration in these light sporting carriages is particularly pleasing to Gibbes's heroine.

Lady C-m-rs: Frances, Lady Chambers (1759–1839) was the daughter of the sculptor Joseph Wilton, and she had married Sir Robert Chambers (1737–1803), judge of the Bengal Supreme Court, on 8 March 1774 when she was not yet sixteen. Described by Samuel Johnson, Chambers' friend, as 'exquisitely beautiful', she was a celebrated member of Calcutta high society, who proved a most supportive 'patroness' of Eliza Fay in her marital and financial problems in Calcutta; see *The Letters of Samuel Johnson*, ed. B. Redford, 5 vols. (Oxford: Clarendon, 1992–4), 2: 127; *Original Letters*, pp. 173–4, and *passim*. The Chambers' five-year-old eldest son was lost in the wreck of the *Grosvenor* East Indiaman in 1782 while on his way to school in England; see note to p. 39 above.

Mrs. Hartly like myself is the daughter of an East India captain: i.e. captain of an East Indiaman, a most prestigious rank in the service of the Company.

42 *an offer she cannot disapprove*: Sophia remains 'unconvinced, and unconverted' by Mrs Hartly's opinion 'that esteem', rather than love, 'is the best basis for affection'.

rara avis: 'rare bird'; Sophia's father remains the exceptional 'model of him I can ever love',

43 *the New Fort*: construction began after Clive's victory at Plassey in 1757 and the fort was completed in 1780. It was of a pentagonal brick-built design, with a moat and bombproof barracks for 10,000 men; see Stavorinus,. *Voyages to the East-Indies*, 1: 496–7.

Batta-money: 'H. *bhata* or *bhata*: an extra allowance made to officers, soldiers, or other public servants, when in the field, or on other special grounds; also subsistence money to witnesses, prisoners, and the like. Military Batta, originally an occasional allowance, as defined, grew to be a constant addition to the pay of officers in India, and constituted the chief part of the excess of Indian over English military emoluments' *Hobson-Jobson*.

seven hundred pounds of his own: that a 'common soldier' might leave India with such a fortune goes some way to illustrate the attractions of the subcontinent, and not merely for Sophia.

death and dirt being synonymous in this climate: the example of the natives, not to mention texts such as James Lind, *An Essay on Diseases Incidental to Europeans in Hot Climates* (London: T. Becket, 1777), were beginning to make an impact concerning the necessity for high standards of cleanliness.

44 *Company's troops*: 'A British regiment, King's or Company's was normally posted to Fort William as part of the garrison and large numbers of white troops were temporarily stationed there in transit to postings up-country', P. J. Marshall, 'The White Town of Calcutta Under the Rule of the East India Company', *Modern Asian Studies*, 34:2 (2000), 307–31, 309. Gibbes's knowledge of the policing of Calcutta and the important positions of Town Major and Fort Major would seem to indicate that her son's letters had frequently contained most specific military detail.

These are imperial works, and worthy kings: an apposite use of the final line of Alexander Pope, *An Epistle to the Right Honourable Richard Earl of Burlington* (London: L. Gilliver, 1731), p. 14

united contributions of the Europeans: Sophia's pleasure in learning that the building of the hospital 'originates from commerce' typifies her author's pro-Company position.

45 *no harpy keepers*: Gibbes's comparative stance contrasts the efficiency and benevolence of the Presidency Hospital with the inadequacy of many such institutions in those of the metropolis; in this way she hopes 'to promote new and salutary regulations' at home. Her use of the term 'impeachment' with reference to 'the customs in my native country', and her 'extolling the country I now reside in, and sighing for the disgraces of the country I have quitted', might be seen to provide a polemical contrast between conditions under Hastings' regime and those under the regime of his accusers.

They love me the more [...] from my tongue: an adapted quotation: 'And I lov'd her the more, when I heard / Such tenderness fall from her tongue', 'A Pastoral Ballad, in Four Parts. Written 1743', ll. 87–8 in *The Poetical Works of William Shenstone* (London: G. Dilly, 1788), p. 160.

so outre should I have exhibited myself: unorthodox, eccentric. The need for a 'gentleman companion' when taking the reins herself (see p. 90), and the reluctance of her father to be driven by his daughter, lead to Sophia's taking Mr Hartly 'for my cicisbeo'. This is a little confusing as a cicisbeo is the acknowledged gallant or *cavalier servente* of a *married* woman! Sophia's praise for Mr. Hartly, however, echoes that for her own father.

46 *Hercules at the court of Omphale*: in the famous painting of this title, Hans Cranach (1605–1662) portrays Hercules surrounded by ladies, one of whom hands him a distaff. Apart from the fact that this reverses the gender imbalance both in Calcutta and at the New Fort dinner, there is a substantial irony in this representation of 'Mars in the East' when we consider subsequent events in the novel and remember that Hercules was being punished for the brutal murder of Iphitus.

Chitpore [...] Bugee Bugee: Chitpore is four miles north of Calcutta, and the garrison at Budge-Budge on the Hugli is some 15 miles south of Calcutta.

in terrorem: as a deterrent warning.

evolutions: 'Mil. [...] unfolding or opening out of a body of troops', OED.

47 *so agreeable a man*: Sophia's interest in the Fort Major is almost sufficient to defeat her resolution never to wed in Bengal, but the appearance of his wife 'save[s] my credit'.

dégagement: a favourite term of Sophia's; see Introduction, pp. xxxi–xxxii above. Her ability to conduct herself with such nonchalance is the result of living 'with a multitude of men'; superior to any 'private education' is the education of the East.

'Tis not to make me jealous: slightly inaccurate quotation of Othello's speech: "Tis not to make me jealous, / To say my wife is fair, feeds well, loves company, / Is free of speech, sings, plays, and dances well; / Where virtue is, these are more virtuous', *Othello*, III. iii. 187–90.

not correct in my quotation: an interesting excusatory ploy which enables Sophia to recommend Arabella visit her library.

48 *en militaire*: in a military manner.

woman of thirty: cf. 'A man is in the decline of life at thirty, and the beauty of the women at eighteen; but at twenty-five they have all the marks of old age', Guthrie, *A New Geographical, Historical, and Commercial Grammar*, p. 681. Sophia's Montesquieu-based conception of the effects of climate and the acclimatization of Europeans accords with her recommendation of a 'ten or twelve years' fortune-making residence in India.

Formerly his residence was at a distance from Calcutta: the Nawab's seat remained at Murshidabad, the Mughal capital of Bengal, and it here that he entertained Cornwallis in the summer of 1787; see Charles William Madan, *Two Private Letters to a Gentleman in England, from his Son who Accompanied Earl Cornwallis, on his Expedition to Lucknow in the year 1787* (Peterborough: J. Jacob, 1788), p. 9. Mubarak ud-Daula also had a residence at Chitpore 'which although a suburb of Calcutta, and full of seats and gardens is four miles from the Old Fort, the center of that city', Ghulam Husain Khan Tabatabai, *A Translation of the Seir Mutaqharin; or, View of Modern Times, being an History of India, from the Year 1118 to the Year 1195 (this year answers to the Christian year 1781–82)*, 3 vols (Calcutta: James White, 1789 [1790]), 2: 450.

dinners, fireworks [...] but always eats alone: far from being a solitary diner, Mubarak ud-Daula's hospitality at his Murshidabad palace is described by an appreciative Hickey: 'The Nabob received us with the utmost politeness and affability, giving an excellent breakfast, quite in the English taste, after which he took me round his noble suite of apartments, his gardens, menagerie, aviary' and stud of horses. Upon our departure he presented me with a pair of beautiful shawls'. A few days later, he was 'magnificently entertained by the Nawab's 'supper and display of fireworks', *Memoirs of William Hickey*, 3: 279–80.

commanding officer of the Nabob's guard: 'The Commanding Officer of His Highness's bodyguard' was the Hon. David Anstruther. According to Hickey: 'This gentleman, although accomplished in many respects, was very vulgar and brutal in his behaviour to women, especially to those of his own family', *Memoirs of William Hickey*, 3: 320, 278. Despite this, Hickey spent a 'cheerful day' at his residence, interestingly entitled 'Felicity Hall', near Murshidabad; an aquatint of this house, published by Edward Orme of New Bond Street, is in the Peabody Essex Museum.

49 *Chit*: 'Chit, Chitty, s. A letter or note; also a certificate given to a servant, or the like; a pass. H. *chitthi*; Mahr. *chitti*. [Skt. *chitra*, 'marked.']', *Hobson-Jobson*.

eight anas, or half rupees: the rupee is divided into 16 annas.

50 *written myself into the spleen*: Sophia's discussion of ruinous gambling at billiards has occasioned morose feelings.

horses are cheap at Calcutta: not necessarily. On 2 December 1783, in one of his first letters from Calcutta to his former pupil, Viscount Althorp, Sir William Jones writes: 'Anna rides a prancing steed every morning, and I have just given an hundred & twenty five pounds for a strong riding horse, and two hundred for four bay coach horses. Fine economy! you will say', *Letters*, 2: 624.

as you English feed pigeons: it is fascinating to note that, after even a short space of time in Calcutta, Sophia seems to be completely identifying with a colonialist perspective.

at the Governor's: both Mr. Hartly and her father are presented as close to Hastings.

Palanquins are, indeed, such state appendages: her interesting remark concerning Calcutta etiquette-a walking European being followed by his palanquin-leads into Sophia's description of a Gentoo marriage procession, and how palanquins themselves are gendered. Cf. Eliza Fay's description of 'the marriage procession of a rich Hindoo', *Original Letters*, p. 206. John Gilchrist is far less tolerant of native processions: 'When I observe these and similar examples of encroachment-the eagerness which overgrown rich natives betray, to jostle us with their carriages and palkees [palanquins]; to hire Europeans as coachmen; to have their grand processions and marriages graced in the open streets of Calcutta, with the attendance of military bands of music:–I cannot avoid asking my countrymen one sober question. Pray, what is the aim and end of all this?' *The Anti-jargonist*, p. xviii.

51 *most lively tunes imaginable*: while many Europeans rejected such a 'horrid noise', Sophia, characteristically open to Indian music, would endorse Jones's opinion of it as 'a happy and beautiful contrivance'; see 'On the Musical Modes of the Hindus', *The Works of Sir William Jones*, 4: 116–210, 174. On Hasting's band of Indian musicians, see Woodfield, *Music of the Raj*, pp. 160–1, 149–80.

their Pythagorean tenets: cf. 'It is then highly probable that the doctrine of the Metempsychosis, which so particularly distinguished Pythagoras, was derived from them [the Brahmans]', Grose, *A Voyage to the East-Indies*, p. 323.

They ask no angel's [...] bear them company: an adapted quotation of Pope's description of 'the poor *Indian*': 'He asks no angel's wing, nor seraph's fire, / But thinks, admitted to that equal sky, / His faithful dog shall bear him company', Pope, *An Essay on Man*, ll. 106–8, p. 12

Sekars are all Gentoos (a kind of brokers): 'Sircar, s. Hind. from Pers. *sarkar*, 'head (of) affairs.' [...] In Bengal the word is applied to a domestic servant who is a kind of house-steward, and keeps the accounts of household expenditure, and makes miscellaneous purchases for the family', *Hobson-Jobson*. (The word was also used of administrative areas, government officials, and government itself.) See also p. 143. In terms of fictional representation, it is interesting that Elizabeth Hamilton's Raja employs 'an English Sircar, who has uncontrouled disbursement of my money', Elizabeth Hamilton, *Translation of the Letters of a Hindoo Rajah; written previous to, and during the period of his residence in England* (1796), ed. Pamela Perkins and Shannon Russell (Peterborough, Ontario: Broadview Press), p. 250.

impossible to dispose of European goods without their assistance: here Gibbes appears to be describing the necessary commercial role of the banian; see Introduction, p. xxx. However we read in a publication, that capitalized upon public interest in Hastings' trial, that: 'In common usage, in Bengal, the under Banyans of European gentlemen are called Sircars', *The Indian Vocabulary. To which is Prefixed the Forms of Impeachments* (London: John Stockdale, 1788.), p. 119.

52 *walks in and out of Hartly House at pleasure*: it is, perhaps, only within such a racially tolerant context that Sophia might dream up her 'whim [...] to please a Bramin' (the highest Hindu caste), protected as she might seem by her mistaken belief that 'celibacy is their engagement'.

What a transition!: with her return to all-male casting she moves from one species of sexual/mental theatre to another.

no female performers: as she had enlisted moral reasons for flirting with a Brahman, her reasons for supporting theatrical cross-dressing are similar high-minded, in opposition to 'the polished Charles' (II), who had introduced female actors. See also p. 121. Hickey mentions 'two gentlemen, Mr. Bride and Mr. Norfar, who excelled in female parts', *Memoirs of William Hickey*, 3: 209; cf. *Original Letters*, p. 194.

53 *in blazing height [...] incessant vapours roll*: 'Summer', ll. 773–9, Thomson, *The Seasons*, p. 85.

54 *Trees of Destruction*: Hastings' duel with Philip Francis on 17 August 1780 was certainly not one of 'contending lovers', but the romantic Sophia likes to think of duelling in these terms. The site still possesses a certain legendary status: 'Somewhere in the ample grounds of Belvedere, in all probability where the Zoological Gardens are now, Hastings fought his famous duel with Philip Francis under the "trees of destruction". There are trees near the building today, so old they might have heard the shots', *Calcutta Online-Newspaper*, 28 July, 1999, at www.calonline.com/news/Jun99%5C28Jun99.html

55 *no quarrel without a woman in it*: Addison , *Tatler*, no. 10 (Tuesday May 3, 1709), *The Tatler* (London: Rivington, *et al.*, 1789), p. 103.

coquetry is practised at Calcutta in a new style: or a very old one; for in Calcutta, as in the medieval castle, a lack of unattached ladies inspired the devotions of *fin' amour*. That this seems to be the tendency of Sophia's thinking is indicated by her use of the tropes of 'tilting' and of 'throw[ing] out a lure'. Not content with simple appropriation of the male practice of duelling, she imagines raising an army to combat those Europeans who might advance Arabella's suit with the Nawab. The conceit has complex ramifications for the sex war is extended into something approximating a Calcutta civil war in which rival armies of colonists contend to further an advantageous inter-racial marriage.

cara sposas: devoted wives.

Volume II

59 *concert at the Governor's*: on the abundance of musical activity in Calcutta see Thomas Tolley, 'Music in the Circle of Sir William Jones: A Contribution to the History of Hadyn's Early Reputation', *Music and Letters*, 74: 4 (1992), 525–50; see also Woodfield, *Music of the Raj*.

sunk the emperor in the fiddler: see Philip Dormer Stanhope, Earl of Chesterfield, *Letters to his Son*, 4 vols, 5th. edn. (London: J. Dodsley, 1774.), 1: 116.

60 *very mines of Golconda*: it is, after all, a compliment to the Governor-General to display her 'diamond pins'. The products of these mines near Hyderabad were certainly of interest to Hastings; for details of his shipments of diamonds to England; see P. J. Marshall, 'The Personal Fortune of Warren Hastings', *The Economic History Review*, N S, 17: 2 (1964), 284–300.

not one of them has ever been deprived of an atom: cf. her bulky vade mecum: 'there scarcely is an instance of a robbery in all Indostan, though the diamond merchants travel without defensive weapons', Guthrie, *A New Geographical, Historical, and Commercial Grammar*, p. 680.

the blood of millions: Sophia is nor without a share of [post]colonialist guilt.

a harp presented me: a fitting gift for a young woman seeking angelic perfections; see p. 52.

61 *burying grounds*: Sophia is impressed by the carefully-maintained South Park Street Burial Grounds, contrasting the neglect of monuments in Westminster Abbey.

For many a holy text around is strewed: adapted quotation from Gray: 'And many a holy text around she strews', 'Elegy in a Country Churchyard', l. 83, Thomas Gray, *Designs by Mr. R. Bentley, for six poems by Mr. T. Gray* (London: R. Dodsley, 1753), p. 33.

Born just to bloom and fade: Isaac Bickerstaff, *Judith, a Sacred Drama* (London: W. Griffin, [1769]), p. 13.

62 *sola*: solitary.

Dryden's Timotheus [...] Arne: Sophia would have approved of the way in which Timotheus inspires Alexander with the whole gamut of human passions; see John Dryden, *Alexander's Feast: or, the Power of Musick. An Ode, written by Mr. Dryden. Set to Musick by Mr. Handel* (n.p.: n.p., 1739). The 'Coronation Anthem' might have been by George Frideric Handel (1685–1759), or by John Blow (1648?–1708). The opera *Artaxerxes*, 'that chef d'ceuvre' (masterpiece) of Thomas Augustine Arne (1710–1778) was an important Italianate *opera seria*, first performed in London on 2 February 1762. On the association between the 'ancient music' of such a composer as Handel and the bolstering of imperial values; see Woodfield, *Music of the Raj*, pp. 130–9.

63 *unoriental*: the first recorded usage of this word in *OED* is from Byron's *Don Juan* (III: xxviii); Gibbes again demonstrates a priority in new coinages; cf. 'orientalised' on p. 8.

The Governor's dress [...] His lady: Gibbes captures the juxtaposition of the 'unostentatious' and the dazzling about this devoted couple. Hodges was to stress the way in which 'all appeared struck with the simplicity of his appearance, and his ready and constant attention to prevent any injury to the meanest individual from the irascibility of his Chudars [attendant 'stick-bearers'], or other servants, who endeavoured to keep them from pressing in. They could not but contrast this appearance and conduct with that of their Nabobs, whom they had never seen except mounted on lofty elephants, and glittering in splendour with their train, followed by the soldiery to keep off the multitude from offending their arrogance and pride', *Travels in India*, in *European Discovery of India*, 3: 44. Marian Hastings (*nee* Anna Maria Apollonia Chapuset) (1747–1837) divorced the miniature portraitist, Baron Christoph Carl Adam von Imhoff, and married Hastings in Calcutta on 8 August 1777; see *Oxford DNB*. A Persian inscription upon a 'fine large ruby' presented to Marian Hastings reads in translation: 'Royal and Imperial Governess, The Elegance of the Age, The Most Exalted *Bilkiss* [Queen of Sheba], The *Zoibade* [favourite wife of Muhammad] of the Palaces', Leman Thomas Rede, *Anecdotes & Biography* (London: Myers., 1799), p. 179. The magnificent 'over-dressing of the 'Governess' was mocked by Hicky's *Bengal Gazette* within the colony, and by various metropolitan satires such as Elizabeth Ryves's *Hastiniad* (London: Debrett, 1785).

64 *Envy, malice [...] Eastern politics*: although Sophia is 'no judge of these matters', here and elsewhere she adopts a firmly pro-Hastings line.

A widow lady: Sophia's father, like Hastings when he met Baroness von Imhoff, was a widower, and the 'romantic' air of India has encouraged him to court Mrs. D—.

67 *She never told [...] &c*: Twelfth Night, II. iv. 112–13.

twenty gold mohrs: the Revd. 'Tally-ho' William Johnson's wedding fees contributed to his substantial fortune, as did his funeral and christening fees; see pp. 82, 92, 149, 162.

68 *professed botanist*: Sophia's enthusiasm for botany once more reflects Orientalist avocations; the Royal Botanic Garden in Calcutta had been founded by Colonel Robert Kyd in 1786. Seeds and flower drawings were subsequently sent to Sir Joseph Banks by William Roxburgh and Sir William Jones, whose botanical researches were deeply sensitive to Hindu culture and medicine.

69 *Who can unpitying see [...] parching beam*: 'Summer', ll. 212–15, Thomson, *The Seasons*, p. 63.

the Maid of the Mill [...] Love in a Village: these two comic operas were written by Isaac John Bickerstaff, and first produced in 1765 and 1762 respectively.

Ices: ice-making in the East Indies was based upon the production of cold through evaporation, see George Adams, *Lectures on Natural and Experimental Philosophy*, 5 vols (London: R. Hindmarsh, 1794), 1: 311–12.

London porter [...] spruce beer: the entrepreneurial publisher John Murray had little luck in his venture to export bottled beer as well as books to Bengal, but others, such as the wine merchant Benjamin Kenton, met with more success; see William Zachs, *The First John Murray and the late Eighteenth-Century London Book Trade* (Oxford: printed for the British Academy by Oxford University Press, 1998), pp.43–5. On the benefits of spruce beer; see Alexander Wilson, *Some Observations relative to the Influence of Climate* (London: Cadell, 1780), p. 209.

70 *Lo! the green serpent [...] dares approach*: 'Summer', ll. 898–907, Thomson, *The Seasons*, p. 90. The somewhat unexpected appearance of this green serpent is perhaps related to certain feelings of jealousy concerning her father's affections.

71 *the Turtle and Ring Dove*: 'There was never any such Thing under the Sun, as an *Inconsolable Widow*', Aesop, *Fables and Storyes Moralized*, 2 vols (London: Richard Sare, 1708), 2: 146.

72 *Jerry Blackacre*: this reference, to the young country-booby character, son of the litigious and petulant Widow Blackacre in William Wycherley's, *The Plain-Dealer* (1677), is not exactly complimentary to either Mrs. D— or her son.

72–3 *minhos [...] Jerry Daw's soldiers*: the Indian *Mynah* bird is known for its imitative skills. The Lory-Parakeet was the *vahana* [vehicle] of the Hindu god of love, Kama or Camdeo, cf. 'And, when thy lory spreads his em'rald wings', 'A Hymn to Camdeo' (1784), l. 73, *Sir William Jones: Selected Poetical and Prose Works*, p. 103. Batavia was the Dutch East India Company's headquarters on Java. 'Brahminy Kite, s. [...] The name is given because the bird is regarded with some reverence by the Hindus as sacred to Vishnu', *Hobson-Jobson*. Also known as the Pondicherry eagle, it was much esteemed and sometimes fed by the Brahmans, see Pierre Sonnerat, *A Voyage to the East-Indies and China*, 3 vols (Calcutta: Stuart and Cooper, 1788–89), 1: 39–40; see below n. to p. 104. The Rhinoceros bird is a large hornbill (Buceros rhinoceros), native of the East Indies; both the British Museum and Don Saltero's coffee-house possessed the head of a Rhinoceros bird; see *A Catalogue of the Rarities, to be Seen at Don Saltero's Coffee-house in Chelsea*, 36th edn. (London, [1785?]), p. 13. 'Jerry Daw's soldiers' most probably refers to the adjutant bird (Leptoptilus dubius; Hindi *hargili*), a large stork with a military gait; cf. Edward Ives, *A Voyage from England to India, in the year MDCCLIV* (London: Edward and Charles Dilly, 1773), p. 183.

73 *lawyers return rolling in wealth*: 'The attornies, who have followed the judges in search of prey, as the carrion crows do an Indian army on its march, are extremely successful in supporting the spirit of litigation among the natives', Stanhope, *Genuine Memoirs of Asiaticus*, p. 53.

douceurs: conciliatory presents or 'sweeteners'.

74 *Gentoo university at Benares*: cf. 'Benares [...] is the Gentoo University, and celebrated for its sanctity', Guthrie, *A New Geographical, Historical, and Commercial Grammar*, p. 693. In the December of 1784 Sir William Jones was studying manuscripts at Benares (Varanasi).

daughters of Paradise: this Muslim compliment compares Sophia with the *Houris*, the beautiful virgins of Muhammad's paradise, but she would have preferred a Hindu puff from 'my Bramin' (she uses this possessive reference no fewer than eleven times in the novel).

74–5 *five tribes*: for her outline of castes Gibbes draws directly upon Alexander Dow's *The History of Hindostan*, repr. in *Representing India*, 2: xxxi-xxxii. Her 'Atarri' tribe is presumably a transcription error for Dow's 'Harri cast'. Thus it would seem that Mahatma Gandhi's renaming of the untouchables or pariahs as the 'harijans' (children of Hari or Vishnu) merely adapted a former term.

75 *Revel's machine*: this represents something of a puzzle.

H. E. A. Cotton, the author of a prefatory note to the 1908 Calcutta reprint, sent a query concerning Revel's machine to *Notes and Queries* [10th series, IX (Feb. 8, 1908), 110] early in that year. It elicited no published response then, and almost a century later the mystery remains unsolved. Despite intensive research and innumerable queries to experts in the history of transport, I have failed to elucidate this matter; in fact the puzzle seems more complex. Gibbes refers to (Lord) Revel's machine in at least four of her novels, and it would seem to be some kind of some kind of carriage which might be hired and in which an invalid might fully recline. In *The Life and Adventures of Mr. Francis Clive* (1764), Lord Revel is a dissolute character, who arrives in Bath on the penultimate page of the novel, too ill and exhausted (presumably from the dissipations implied by his name) to speak, and who dies within three days: 'One morning being at the pump, their attention was engaged by the arrival of Lord Revel's Machine, out of which came with much difficulty and assistance the ignoble owner heretofore mentioned', (2: 135). In her other novel of that year, *The History of Lady Louisa Stroud, and the Honourable Miss Caroline Stretton* (1764), we read: 'I would have hired *Revel's* Machine and sent her [Letitia who is near death] down into *Warwickshire*', (2: 81). Gibbes thus appears to expect readers of this novel to recognise the conveyance of her fictional? character from *The Life and Adventures of Mr. Francis Clive*. The next appearance of the mysterious machine is in a novel of which Gibbes claimed authorship in 1804: the anonymous *The History of Miss Pittborough* (1767). Again, the context is the transportation of an invalid: 'She is visibly better, and it is hoped will soon be able to undertake a journey to the village, at least in Revell's machine', (2: 271). The final reference, here in *Hartly House, Calcutta*, presupposes that, some 25 years after her *Life and Adventures of Mr. Francis Clive*, readers would still understand the comparison she makes, which implies that she is describing some species of sedan chair or indeed sedan bed: 'the travelling palanquins are so constructed that you recline, as in Revel's machine, on a couch'. [Hickey asserts: 'Many, indeed most, men can sleep in their palankeens', *Memoirs of William Hickey*, 3: 281.] My only conclusion is a flippant one: that Gibbes doubtless had shares in the invention of this invalid carriage. The mystery of Lord Revel remains but, thanks to Gale's digitizing of the British Library's Burney Collection of Newspapers, I can at least provide a factual reference to this conveyance, confirming that it was certainly not a literary invention of Phebe Gibbes. The *Daily Advertiser* of Saturday, 20 September 1777 carried the following intelligence concerning the illness of that prominent member of the royal family, Prince William Henry, first Duke of Gloucester, in northern Italy: 'It is said that a Carriage has been built, and is now on its Way to Italy, for the Conveyance of his Royal Highness the Duke of Gloucester to England. It is an Improvement upon Revel's Machine. The Bed it contains is fitted up in a most elegant Style, and there is Room to admit of two Attendants, &c.' See my '"Hartly House, Calcutta: Allusions": A Century-Late Response', *Notes & Queries*, NS 55: 4 (December 2008), 459–61; 460.

bugeros of so large a size: cf. 'a vessel comparable to a house for both spaciousness and commodity', Ghulam Husain, *Sëir Mutaqharin*, 3: 297.

76 *she was his property*: this ferocious and tyrannical soldier provides a stark contrast with Sophia's earlier military gallants.

Malabar coast: the southwest coast of the Indian subcontinent.

76–7 *Bramins pretend [...] either delineated or carved*: this draws very heavily upon Guthrie (*A New Geographical, Historical, and Commercial Grammar*, pp. 678–9), who in turn plagiarizes Luke Scrafton, *Reflections on the Government of Indostan* (London: Strahan, Kearsley, and Cadell, 1763), pp. 3–4; see Introduction, pp. xxxviii.

Brumma: Brahma is the supreme deity of post-Vedic Hinduism. 'Brăhm is that which is supreme and without corruption', Charles Wilkins, *The Bhăgvăt-Gēētā, or Dialogues of Kreeshna and Arjoon* (1785), reprinted in *The European Discovery of India*, 1: 73. In the Hindu *trimurti* [trinity] Brahma is the Creator, Vishnu the Preserver, and Śiva the Destroyer; Brahma represents an equilibrium between the centripetal principle of Vishnu and the centrifugal principle of Śiva. Gibbes repeats Guthrie's confusion of Brahma with Manu, the mythic first man, to whom is attributed the law-code, *Mānava Dharmaśāstra*.

77 *the Vidam*: Veda [knowledge]: the four books of sacred knowledge the *Rig-veda, Yajur-veda, Sama-veda*, and *Atharva-veda*.

the Shahstah: the *śāstras* are post-Vedic compilations, treatises, or commentaries. Gibbes derives both the singularity and the spelling from Guthrie (p. 678), who found them in Scrafton: 'A comment thereon [i.e. on the Vedas], called the Shahstah', Scrafton, *Reflections*, p. 4.

Pythagorean metempsychosis: cf. 'That Pythagoras took the doctrine of the *Metempsychosis* from the *Bramins* is not disputed', John Zephaniah Holwell, *Interesting Historical Events, relative to the Provinces of Bengal, and the Empire of Indostan* (1767), repr. in *Representing India*, 1: 26. Holwell himself came to be a firm believer in the doctrine of transmigration of souls.

stupendous but disgusting: cf. 'The temples or pagodas of the Gentoos, are stupendous, but disgustful stone buildings', Guthrie, *A New Geographical, Historical, and Commercial Grammar*, p. 680. Goethe also felt such repugnance for the monstrous, many-headed gods of Hinduism depicted in the 'hideous contortions' of temple sculpture, but was completely charmed by Jones's translation of the *Śakuntalā*; see *The European Discovery of India*, 3: vii

78 *would not taste the water of their sacred rivers*: this is a strange idea as ritual ablutions in the Ganges' purifying and sacred waters involved drinking from its life-sustaining waters. It is possible that Gibbes had read of the expense of buying Ganges water for those who lived at some distance from the river, which would obviously limit its use to ritual purposes: 'the price of the holy water bears a proportion to the distance of the place where it is sold from the river', Hodges, *Travels in India*, in *European Discovery of India*, 3: 94

not to set me down for a plagiarist: see Introduction, p. xxxviii.

the religion of humanity: cf. 'The abstaining from animal food shows a greater humanity in the religion of Hindostan, than of any other known country', Henry Home, Lord Kames, *Sketches of the History of Man*, 2 vols (Edinburgh: W. Creech; London: W. Strahan, and T. Cadell, 1774), 2: 410.

79 *(Of half that live, the butcher and the tomb)*: Pope, *An Essay on Man*, l. 163, p. 41.

medicines are also rated so high: cf. the Surgeon-General's report, *Appendix to the India Courier Extraordinary*, 6 vols ([London], 1786–87), 5: 359.

ounce of bark: *Jesuits'* or *Peruvian Bark*, from various species of the Cinchona tree, contained quinine; it was ground into a powder and taken to reduce fevers.

bolus: a large pill.

blister: an ointment or plaster to raise a blister.

80 *provisions*: on the reliability of Sophia's prices, see the Introduction, p. lii.

pommelos: the pomelo, pompelmoose, or shaddock resembles an outsize grapefruit with rough, yellow skin.

horses (Arabian and Armenian): rather smaller than the Arabian, Armenian horses were famed for their strength and speed; see also p. 88.

Tigers darting: Thomson has 'The Tyger darting fierce / Impetuous on the Prey his Glance has doom'd: ('Summer", ll. 916–7), *The Seasons*, p. 90.

81 *to hunt this terrific creature*: Sophia's disapproval of a popular Mughal sport which the British adopted with some alacrity might well be influenced by Hindu respect for all living creature. A letter of 1784 to Sir William Jones from Sir John Day, the Advocate General, describes in detail an elaborate tiger hunt in which Lady Day was nearly injured when the tiger leapt on the flank of the elephant upon which she was seated; see Birmingham City Archives MS 3101/538.

Tomluek river: 'Tumlook, n.p. A town, and anciently a sea-port and seat of Buddhist learning on the west of the Hoogly near its mouth', *Hobson-Jobson*. This river is now known as the Rupnarain. *by French and English men*: in a listing of British and European residents at Calcutta, the two men described as 'cook and confectioner' were Jean Laforgue and George Meurisse; see *The East India Kalendar, or, Asiatic Register for ... 1798* (London: Debrett, 1798), pp. 84, 87.

His Majesty's Coronation: George III was crowned on 22 September 1761; presumably Sophia was writing this letter on 22 September 1784.

83 *Gentoo holidays*: Durgā *pūjā*, the festival of the goddess Durgā to celebrate the fertilizing effects of her fiery prowess, is generally celebrated during nine days of the month of Acevin, the sixth month of the Hindu Calendar, corresponding to the months of September/October. This is the key religious festival in Bengal, and during the period in which the novel is set, in addition to Hindu landowners and princes, both Muslim nawabs and the East India Company patronized the festival; see my 'Cultural Possession, Imperial Control, and Comparative Religion: The Calcutta Perspectives of Sir William Jones and Nathaniel Brassey Halhed', *Yearbook of English Studies*, 32, (2002), 1–18. See also Sukanta Chaudhuri, ed., *Calcutta, the Living City, vol. 1: The Past* (Calcutta: Oxford University Press, 1990), p. 25.

Guido: Guido Reni (1575–1642), a Bolognese painter of the Italian Baroque, though an important artist, has been criticized for a somewhat sentimental treatment of his religious subjects. Cf. Sterne's description of the Franciscan monk: 'It was one of those heads, which Guido has often painted-mild, pale-penetrating [...] as if it look'd at something beyond this world. [...] it would have suited a Bramin, and had I met it upon the plains of Indostan, I had reverenced it', Laurence Sterne, *A Sentimental Journey through France and Italy* (London: T.

Becket and P. A. De Hondt, 1768), p. 11. Sterne's two-month affair with Eliza Draper, whose husband was an official of the East India Company, ended when she was recalled to Bombay, but was immortalized into the 'Journal to Eliza' (1767), an epistolary sentimental romance in which she termed him 'her Bramin' and he addressed her as his exotic 'Bramine', This was posthumously published in 1773 as *The Letters of Yorick to Eliza*, and might well have helped inspire Sophia's relationship with 'my Bramin'. It certainly provided our heroine with one of her favourite terms—'Nabobess'.

raree-shews: spectacular displays.

plunged into the Ganges: ' On the tenth day [of Durgā *pūjā*] the statues are precipitated into the sacred river, and the verse sung at the moment of immersion is termed *Visarjona*, or the *adieu*. I subjoin a literal translation [...]: "Bear hence, bright Goddess, thy immortal charms / In amorous Śiva's thunder-darting arms: / But when the circling year again turns round / Within our peaceful walls be, Durga, found", (contributed by 'A[lexander] H[amilton]' to the editor, William Ouseley), *The Oriental Collections*, 3 vols (London: Cadell and Davies, [1797–1800]), 1: 207.

83–4 *Ganges, Kisna, and Indus [...] upon Persia*: This relies heavily upon William Macintosh, *Remarks on a Tour through the Different Countries of Europe, Asia, and Africa*, 2 vols (Dublin: J. Jones, 1786), 1: 205.

84 *better to sit than to walk*: A. L. Basham ('Sophia and the "Bramin"', in *East India Company Studies: Papers Presented to Prof. Sir Cyril Philips*, ed. Kenneth Ballhatchett and John Harrison (London: SOAS, 1987), pp. 13–30; p. 20) incorrectly thought this might be the first recorded instance of this pejorative remark; see Scrafton, *Reflections*, p. 16; and Guthrie, *A New Geographical, Historical, and Commercial Grammar*, p. 681.

eclat: with dazzling effect.

East-India stock: the information appears to have been copied from William Whitehead, *The Historian's Pocket Companion* (Newcastle: T. Angus, 1777), p. 16.

Phaetons everywhere: Sophia moralizes on the aptness—in Calcutta terms—of the myth of Phaeton, the young son of Helios, the Greek sun-god (and after whom the carriages Sophia loved to drive were named), who encountered disaster when he failed to control the chariot of the sun.

86 *taste at Calcutta in statuary*: Sophia is delighted that in Calcutta there are statues of her favourite poet Thomson, of Samuel Johnson, and 'all the literary characters to which the British empire has given birth'.

Rasselas: the eponymous hero of Johnson's moral Oriental tale, originally entitled *The Prince of Abissinia. A tale* (1759), whose search for earthly happiness leads to a degree of wisdom.

Mrs. Hartly's closet: a private secluded room.

87 *poor Marchioness of Tavistock*: a byword for marital fidelity, Elizabeth (née Keppel) inconsolably mourned her husband, Francis Russell (1739–1767), marquess of Tavistock; see Mr. Addison [pseud.], *A Collection of Interesting Anecdotes*, (London: printed for the author, 1793), pp. 186–7. Her portrait by Sir Joshua Reynolds (1732–92) may be seen at Woburn Abbey, or at: http://webapp1.dlib. indiana.edu/cushman/results/detail.do?query=tavistock&page=1&pagesize=20 &display=thumbcap&action= search&pnum=P11772

royal victim: this probably refers to the sad life of George III's sister, Princess Caroline Matilda, queen of Denmark and Norway, consort of Christian VII; see *Oxford DNB*, which also displays her portrait by Jens Juel (1745–1802). See also her autobiographical *Memoirs of an Unfortunate Queen. Interspersed with Letters* (London: J. Bew, 1776).

whole length: both Reynolds and Allan Ramsay (1713–1784) produced full-length portraits of Elizabeth Montagu whose intellect and brilliant coterie earned her the soubriquet of 'queen of the blue stockings'.

87–8 *"Whose nice discernment [...] or too much*: Duke of Buckingham, 'An Essay on Poetry', *The Works of the Earls of Rochester, Roscommon, and Dorset; the Dukes of Devonshire, Buckinghamshire*, 2 vols (London: 1731), 2: 148; the original reads 'just discernment'.

88 *Genius of Shakespear*: first published anonymously, *An Essay on the Writings and Genius of Shakespear* (1769) represented Montagu's attempt to defend the bard from the sniping of foreign critics such as Voltaire and what she saw as his inadequate treatment at the hands of Dr Johnson.

one of the first favourites of heaven: this paean to Elizabeth Montagu encouraged her to write to her sister: 'Pray who is the supposed Author of Hartley House? I cannot imagine how my name travelled to Calcutta. I dare say the Author is very good-natured, and disposed to praise even small merit', Letter of 'Sat. 21st [May?]', in *Mrs Montagu, "Queen of the Blues", Her Letters and Friendships from 1762 to 1800*, ed. Reginald Blunt, 2 vols (London: Constable, 1923), 2: 256.

the race-ground: cf. 'Every evening Pott drove Mrs. Hickey and me in his phaeton to the racecourse, where it was then the fashion for the carriages to draw up round the stand, the gentlemen and ladies passing half an hour in lively conversation', *Memoirs of William Hickey*, 3: 153.

horses are bred and attended at a great expence: race-horses in Calcutta are obviously not fed on a diet of meal; see p. 50. For a fascinating indigenous discourse on the treatment of horses; see *A Treatise on Horses, entitled Saloter*, *or, a Complete System of Indian Farriery, ... Compiled . in the Shanscrit language: translated thence into Persian, ... by Abdallah Khan Firoze Jung, ... which is now translated into English, by Joseph Earles* (Calcutta: George Gordon, 1788).

89 *John in the cloud*: someone feeling obscure or abstracted in their embarrassment.

90 *my Seapoys*: 'Sepoy, Seapoy, s. In Anglo-Indian use a native soldier, disciplined and dressed in the European style. The word is Pers. *sipahi*, from *sipah*, 'soldiery, an army', *Hobson-Jobson*. It is, however, unlikely that Sophia-unless she were a 'Nabobess'—would have a guard of sepoys; she probably means 'syces' ('Syce, s. Hind. from Ar. *saïs*. A groom', *Hobson-Jobson*).

Mongols: 'Mogul, n.p. This name should properly mean a person of the great nomad race of Mongols, called in Persia, &c., *Mughals*; but in India it has come, in connection with the nominally Mongol, though essentially rather *Turk*, family of Baber, to be applied to all foreign Mahommedans from the countries on the W. and N.W. of India, except the Pathans. In fact these people themselves make a sharp distinction between the *Mughal Irana*, of Pers. origin (who is a Shaah) [Shi'a], and the *M. Tarana* of Turk origin (who is a Sunni)', *Hobson-Jobson*.

Omar [...] Hali: Gibbes again has gleaned her information from Guthrie, *A New Geographical, Historical, and Commercial Grammar*, p. 637. Omar or 'Umar ibn al-Khattāb (c. 581–644) was the second caliph of Islam, and is regarded by most Sunnis as the brave if strict successor to Muhammad. The Shi'a Muslims regard 'Umar as usurping authority that properly belonged to 'Alī ibn Abi Tālib (c. 599–661), Muhammad's cousin and son-in-law.

English post-horse: 'A horse kept at a post-house or inn for the use of post-riders, or for hire for the conveyance of travellers', *OED*.

91 *cassemires*: fashionable cashmere shawls were made of fine soft wool of the Cashmere goat or the 'shawl goats' of Tibet, which Hastings planned to breed in Britain. The spelling 'cassimere' was widely used at the time; see, for example, Guthrie, *A New Geographical, Historical, and Commercial Grammar*, p. 691.

Doyly's behaviour: perhaps Gibbes's choice of name for Sophia's new admirer was influenced by her having read of Sir John Hadley D'Oyly (1754–1818), who held the post of the East India Company's Resident at the court of the Nawab of Bengal at Murshidabad. He was a close friend of Hastings, and Marian Hastings was godmother to his son. His wife Diana's beauty and accomplishments were much praised; see 'To Lady Doyly' [contemporary annotation in BL 1079.m.26: 'Sept. 21st: 1780'], Gilbert Ironside, *Metrical Prolusions* ([London?], [1800?]), 69–70.

93 *The ball-room at the Court-house*: Cf. 'A little farther is the court house, over which are two handsome assembly-rooms. In one of these are hung up the portraits of the king of France and of the late queen, as large as life, which were brought up by the English from *Chandernagore*, when they took that place, in the last war', Stavorinus, *Voyages to the East-Indies*, 1: 495.

Amongst the rest young Edwin [...] of love: 'Edwin and Angelina', ll. 111–12, *Select Poems by Oliver Goldsmith* (London: W. Griffin, 1775), p. 13.

Watson's Works: Lieutenant-colonel Henry Watson was chief engineer in Bengal at this time and had won a contract to construct docks and shipbuilding yards. He was interested in encouraging opium trading with China and built ships for this purpose. Although he had acted as second to Philip Francis in his duel with Hastings, his plan to establish a mathematical school for engineer officers won Hastings' support; see *Oxford DNB*.

oars beating time to the notes of the clarinets: although 'water music' had long been popular on the Thames, the British in Calcutta were to a certain extent emulating Mughal grandeur in Calcutta. Bartholomew Burges describes a 'fleet' of the Nawab of Bengal's gilded budgerows on the Ganges near Murshidabad: 'The tops of the *Budgeroes* were all covered with scarlet broad cloth and fringed with gold [...] The oars were painted red, and the *Manjies* and *Dandies* [boatmen] were all dressed in scarlet cloth coats, with narrow sleeves and long trowsers of the same, but different colured sashes and turbans, with gold fringes and borders [...] the *Manjies* and *Dandies* of the *Moor Punkies* [Morpapankhi, another variety of impressive river boats] [...] beat time to bands of music these boats were all furnished with', Burges, *A Series of Indostan Letters*, p. 73.

Music has charms: opening line of William Congreve, *The Mourning Bride*, (London: Jacob Tonson, 1697).

sensibility so oriental: this seem the greatest compliment to Doyly's sensibility, but she prefers him to have an Occidental preference for singularity in terms of wives.

94 *the Bacchanalian [...] plunge into the holy river*: the enthusiasm of the wine-soaked Western devotee of Bacchus to kiss Sophia's hand leads to Doyly's 'baptism' in Gaṅgā Mātā (Mother Ganges). 'went souse together': both men were immersed.

Quixotism: inspired, like Cervantes' Don Quixote, by lofty ideals.

95 *Mr. M.*: Doyly's appointment to a prestigious and potentially lucrative private secretaryship is presumably 'the peace-offering' of this 'Bacchanalian [...] of large fortune', whose name, we later discover, is Emson.

101 *whose worth [...] more return*: [adapted from lines six and seven of a two quatrain elegiac piece later entitled 'Anna's Urn': 'My Anna's worth, my Anna's charms / Must never more return!', John Burgoyne, *Lord of the Manor, a Comic*

Opera (London: T. Evans 1781), p. 12. The last important political act of General Burgoyne (1723–1792), who had surrendered in the American Revolutionary War at Saratoga on 17 October 1777, was to join the committee of managers of the impeachment of Warren Hastings.

102 *But love, the disturber:* this is taken from the third stanza of the much-anthologized piece entitled, 'The Cobler's End'; see *The Hive. A Collection of the Most Celebrated Songs*, 4 vols (London: J. Walthoe, 1732), 4: 89–90

alligators [...] *and their depredations*: [the Gavial or 'crocodile' of the Ganges]. 'it's no unusual thing to happen in your progress up the river to pass bodies floating down which have been dreadfully mangled by fish and birds', Madan, *Two Private Letters*, pp. 20–21. Cf. Burges's descriptions of funerary rites on the banks of the Ganges and of earlier horrific scenes in Calcutta at a slightly earlier time of famine; *A Series of Indostan Letters*, pp. 57–60; 144–5; and Fay's more contemporary remarks concerning 'the noisome exhalations which arose from these wretched objects', *Original Letters*, pp. 207–8.

the police: cf. 'The establishment by Mr Hastings of an Ordinance of Police [...] its good effects have been particularly felt and acknowledged by the British residents. Their health has been preserved, and the quarter of the city they dwell in considerably beautified and improved. The stench arising from the stagnant water of numberless tanks, and the poisonous and noxious vapours emitting from them, of course must have produced many disorders in a climate like this. We believe it has been a more deadly foe to Englishmen than all the other evils attending the burning heat of the Torrid Zone. The cause being removed by the filling up of the tanks, the effect consequently has ceased; and this moment, Calcutta may vie with any city in India for the salubrity of its air, and the longevity of its inhabitants. Instead of offensive standing pools of water in our streets, interspersed with little huts made of reeds or straw, as formerly, magnificent piles of buildings, more like palaces than the houses of private individuals, present themselves to the admiring view. In short, from the improvements, which have been and are daily making by the Commissioners on the original Plan of Police; it has been calculated by many, that fewer British subjects die now here, than, comparatively speaking, do in England, for the same number of people'; 'Some Account of the Life and Transactions of Warren Hastings, Esq.', *The Oriental Magazine; or, Calcutta Amusement*, (June, 1785), 141–42.

103 *affectionate and voluntary sacrifice*: in her largely positive opinion of the abhorrent gynophobic practice of *satī*, Sophia again reveals her Orientalist credentials, although she appears anxious to stress the strength of female courage and devotion rather than to appear the apologist. Pioneer Indologists of the stamp of Charles Wilkins and H. T. Colebrooke had erroneously concluded there was textual authority for what was, in Vedic times, purely a ceremony of final embrace or mimed copulation. The widow would then, as enjoined in the *Rig Veda* Burial Hymn: 'Rise up, woman, into the world of the living', leaving the corpse to be buried or cremated. The Orientalists were torn between an abhorrence of the practice and a fear of interfering either with Hindu 'superstitions', or Indian agency. Eventually *satī* was declared illegal by Governor-General Lord William Bentinck on 4 December 1829, and Indian scholars such as Mritunjoy Vidyalankar and Rammohun Roy powerfully condemned the practice; see Nemai Sadhan Bose, *Indian Awakening and Bengal* (Calcutta: Firma K. L. Mukhopadhay, 1976), p.199; Lata Mani, 'Contentious Traditions: The Debate on *Sati* in Colonial India', *Cultural Critique*, 7 (1987), 119–56; and my introduction to Colebrooke's *Essays on the Religion and Philosophy of the Hindus*, in *The European Discovery of India*, 6: x–xii.

hooks run through: '*charak-puja*. The Swinging Festival of the Hindus, held on the sun's entrance into Aries. The performer is suspended from a long yard, traversing round on a mast, by hooks passed through the muscle over the bladebones, and then whirled round so as to fly out centrifugally', *Hobson-Jobson*. See also *Original Letters*, p. 205.

104 *divine honours [...] the feathered race*: it is not quite clear whether the Brahman is suggesting she might prove an angel along Christian lines or whether he is thinking of Garuda, the half-bird half-human *vahana* (vehicle) of Lord Vishnu, with which the Brahmini kite is sometimes connected.

105 *Let no one judge*: dimly remembered approximation of 'He jests at scars that never felt a wound', *Romeo and Juliet*, II. ii. 1.

106 *What medicine can soften [...] banish the pain*: Aphra Behn, *The Emperor of the Moon* [1687] (London: T. Sherlock, 1777), p. 5.

107 *repine*: to complain or feel discontented.

108 *pious resignation*: the Brahman's submission to ultimate reality involves his acceptance of the 'fact' that Sophia is 'the loveliest of women'.

voluntary celibacy: The misconception that a *Brahmacharya* [student of the all-pervading self-existent power of *Brahman*] was strictly celibate is something of an over-simplification based upon the Hindu belief that sexual abstinence and other austerities can create *tapas* (spiritual heat/power).

loss of our Governor: in the face of growing metropolitan pressure for his recall, Hastings resigned and sailed from Bengal on 7 February 1785 in the *Berrington* East Indiaman. According to William Francklin, 'Hastings had the satisfaction to perceive himself followed by the universal good wishes of the princes of Hindostaun and the prayers of the natives', *The History of the Reign of Shah-*

Aulum, the present Emperor of Hindostaun (London: Cooper and Graham, 1798), p. 135.

109 *Envy will merit*: Alexander Pope, *An Essay on Criticism* (London: W. Lewis 1713), p. 41.

master of the Persian language: Hastings had drawn up a proposal, for which he enlisted the support of Samuel Johnson amongst others, for the establishment of a chair in Persian at Oxford, underling the enormous cultural value, as well as the practical benefits, of teaching and learning the Mughal language of diplomacy; see *A Proposal for Establishing a Professorship of the Persian language in the University of Oxford* ([Oxford?], [1767]).

Mrs. H-: In fact Marian Hastings' health had forced her to leave India a year earlier, in January 1784, sailing on the *Atlas* East Indiaman. Hastings paid the captain £5,000 so that his wife should have exclusive occupancy of the round-house and state cabin, and she was accompanied by the wife of Thomas Motte, free-merchant and friend of Hastings, via whom Hastings purchased diamonds.

Rochefoucault: 'Maxim CCXXXVII: In jealousy there is less love than self love', François, duc de La Rochefoucauld, *Maxims and Moral Reflections* (London: Lockyer Davis, 1775), p. 90.

Volume III

115 *Sterne*: see note to p. 83; *Guido*.

I love the precepts: 'Charming Woman can true Converts make, / We Love the Precepts for the Teachers sake. / Virtue in them appears so bright, so gay, / We hear with Transport, and with Pride obey', George Farquhar, *The Constant Couple* (1700) (London: James Knapton *et al.*, [1708?]), p. 64.

so unlike that amiable people: the contrast Gibbes draws between the two racial/religious stereotypes; the gently feminized 'Hindoo' and the aggressively masculine 'Mussulman' is remarkably common in representations of India, even those written by members of the Hastings circle, such as Nathaniel Brassey Halhed; see my 'Cultural Possession, Imperial Control, and Comparative Religion', 1–18.

sons of Omar [...] exhibit sham-fights: Gibbes is probably referring to Ashurah, on the tenth day of the Festival of Muharram, which marks the anniversary of the death of Husayn bin Ali, a grandson of Muhammad, who was killed at the Battle of Karbala. Bernart Picart refers to how Muslims 'with Colours flying, Drums beating, all in Armour [...] mimick the Battle in which *Hossein* died', *The*

Ceremonies and Religious Customs of the Various Nations, 7 vols (London: printed by William Jackson, for Claude du Bosc, 1733–39), 7: 130.

a Braminate: an interesting coinage of Gibbes.

116 *a monopoly of immortality in their own persons*: a doubly misogynistic 'explanation' of this age-old anti-Islamic slur appeared in a contemporary journal, claiming that 'it originated from motives of policy, not from principle. The Turkish women, who labour under very severe restraints, often go to the mosque under a pretence of devotion, but in reality to meet a lover. [...] their jealous husbands endeavoured to persuade their women that their construction was entirely mortal [...] and that, therefore, it was totally unnecessary to offer up prayers to God', *The Western County Magazine*, IV (Jan. 1790), 5–6.

Surajah Dowla: Siraj ud-Daula (?1729–1757), within a few months of becoming Nawab of Bengal, attempted to make the British pay higher taxes, and when they prevaricated, he attacked and captured Calcutta in June 1756. He was regarded as perpetrator of the infamous 'Black Hole' incident, the thought of which chilled Sophia (pp. 36; 130), but for which P. J. Marshall has declared that he 'seems to have been in no way responsible'; see *Oxford DNB*. Robert Clive recovered Calcutta in January 1757 and defeated Siraj ud-Daula at Plassey on 23 June 1757.

soubahs and nabobs became almost independent: Cf. 'Both Soubahs and Nabobs have named their successors, who have often succeeded with as little opposition as if they had been the heirs apparent of an hereditary dominion', Robert Orme, *A History of the Military Transactions of the British Nation in Indostan, from the year MDCCXLV* (London: Nourse, 1763), p. 37.

Rajapoots: 'Rajpoot, s. Hind. *Rajput*, from Skt. *Rajaputra*, 'King's Son.' The name of a great race in India, the hereditary profession of which is that of arms. [...] The Rajputs thus claim to be true *Kshatríyas*, or representatives of the second of the four fundamental castes, the Warriors', *Hobson-Jobson*. Robert Orme pays tribute to their sense of honour and martial prowess; see *Historical Fragments of the Mogul Empire* (London, 1782 [1783]). Gibbes derives the idea of their laying down their arms when their leader is killed from Guthrie, *A New Geographical, Historical, and Commercial Grammar*, p 680. Jemima Kindersley makes a similar allegation concerning Muslim troops; see *Letters*, pp. 206–7.

117 *Omrahs [...] Turkey*: this section is taken almost verbatim from Salmon, *A New Geographical and Historical Grammar*, pp. 451–2.

jaghires: 'Jagheer, Jaghire, s. Pers. *jagir*, lit. 'place-holding.' A hereditary assignment of land and of its rent as annuity', *Hobson-Jobson*. The question of whether *jaghires* constituted hereditary property was considered during the impeachment; see *Minutes of the Evidence taken at the Trial of Warren Hastings*, 11 vols (London: House of Lords, 1788–95), 6: 2697–9. What lies behind all this was the resilient idea that under Asiatic governments property could not be inherited; this was refuted by Abraham-Hyacinthe Anquetil-Duperron's *Législation orientale* (1778), and William Jones's *The Mahomedan Law of Succession to the Property of Intestates* (1782).

118 *Not of themselves the gay beauties [...] heart is at ease*: the chorus of 'How sweet are the flowers', *The Myrtle. Being a Favourite Collection [...] of the newest and best English and Scotch songs* (London, 1755), p. 184.

Striking effects of black and white: Sophia sentimentally develops the racial dimension to be found in Burke's differentiation between the sublime and the beautiful; see *A Philosophical Enquiry into the Origin of our Ideas of the Sublime and Beautiful* (London: R. and J. Dodsley, 1757), p. 143.

men of taste and sensibility: Sophia is much taken with the uniforms of the artillery officers; cf. Thomas Hickey (1741–1824), *Portrait of an Officer of the Bengal Artillery* (1780s); Private Collection USA; see: www.historicalportraits.com/Gallery. asp?Page=Item&ItemID=465&Desc=Bengal-Artillery-Officer-|-Thomas-Hickey

119 *'Her eye [...] my law—my oracle, her tongue'*: cf. 'Their Law, his Eye; Their Oracle, his Tongue', Epistle III, 1, 219, Pope, *An Essay on Man*, p. 49.

120 *Miss Rolle*: the surname of this 'country-born lady' might well have reminded the contemporary reader of John Rolle, eponymous anti-hero of the opposition satire *Rolliad*; although its principal targets were Pitt and Henry Dundas, Hastings featured prominently.

the only one in Calcutta: a Mrs Hodges opened a boarding school 'for young Ladies and children near the Armenian Church' in 1780; see *Bengal Gazette*, 1: 27, cited in Tarun Kumar Mukhopadhyay, *Hicky's Bengal Gazette* (Calcutta: Subarnarekha, 1988), p. 11.

121 *a birth-night*: 'The evening of a royal birthday; the court-festival held thereon', *OED*.

the present Governor: John Macpherson (*c*.1745–1821) was cousin of James 'Ossian' Macpherson. 'As no new governor-general was immediately appointed, Macpherson succeeded to the chair. [...] After a short nineteen months of struggle and controversy, he lost his position to Earl Cornwallis on 18 September 1786. However, to soften the blow the government arranged his creation as a baronet on 10 June 1786', *Oxford DNB*.

122 *Lionel and Clarissa*: Isaac Bickerstaff, *Lionel and Clarissa. A Comic Opera* (London: Griffin, 1768).

127 tradrille: *'tredrille, tredille: A card-game played by three persons, usually with thirty cards'*, OED.

129 *sons of Esculapius*: Aesculapius was the Greek god of medicine; physicians, like lawyers, and even clergymen, prove a trifle expensive in Calcutta.

The Conscious Lovers: Sir Richard Steele, *The Conscious Lovers. A Comedy* (London: Tonson, 1723); see p. 134.

130 *natives of Bengal have no dirty customs like the Europeans*: even in their avoidance of snuff Indians prove superior.

131 *tide of the Ganges*: 'The great *Bore*, or head wave, of the tide begins about seventy miles lower, at *Hoogly* point, where the river first contracts its channel, and it is perceptible above town. At Calcutta, this head rises instantaneously to the height of five feet', Thomas Pennant, *The View of Hindoostan*, 4 vols (London: Henry Hughs, 1798–1800), 2: 297.

pendant for pilots: 'pendant, n. *Naut.* A sharply tapering flag used for signalling', *OED*. Hugli pilots were widely respected for their skills; see *Country Trade East-India Pilot for the Navigation of the East-Indies and Oriental Seas* (London: Laurie & Whittle, 1799).

this machine: I can discover no source for this 'juggernaut'-like conveyance for prisoners, so, like Revel's, this machine must remain something of a mystery for the present.

132 *a linguist [...] who is a Baronet*: somewhat surprisingly, Sophia fails to mention Sir William Jones by name. A Crown rather than a Company employee, his 'liberal gratuity' was his Supreme Court salary of £6,000 p.a.

Into the heaven of heavens &c. &c.: *Paradise Lost*, VII: 12–14.

133 *like another Alexander*: an amusingly apposite simile for Sophia's tedium, both in respect of Alexander's conquests in Hindustan and his apocryphal meeting with an Indian ascetic who asked him why he was attempting to conquer the world when he had not first conquered himself.

Mrs. Southgate's beautiful lawns: I have discovered information concerning the elegant gardener of Chertsey. *The Morning Herald and Daily Advertiser* of Wednesday, 22 October 1783 announced: 'By the death of Mrs. Southgate, Lord Petre's income receives an increase of four thousand per annum. The seat of the above-mentioned lady near Weybridge, is considered one of the best in the farm-like stile in England, and the garden is the very first which was laid out on that principle'. This mention of Robert Edward, ninth Baron Petre (1742–1801), a prime mover in Roman Catholic emancipation, enabled me to identify 'Mrs Southgate' as Bridget Southcote (d. 14 October 1783, aged 85), the daughter of Sir Francis Andrews, and widow of Philip Southcote. Her husband, who had died in 1758, was the celebrated landscape gardener, the son of Edward Southcote, the friend of Pope, and of a prominent Catholic family, linked by marriage to the Petres. Philip Southcote occupies an important place in the history of landscape gardening, acknowledged by Joseph Spence and George Mason as the inventor of the garden farm or 'ferme ornée', in which tastefully planted ornamental walks wound through a working farm. Thus the 'villa' of 'Mrs Southgate' was 'sweet Southcote's' or Woburn (occasionally Wooburn) Farm, long a fashionable resort of the intellectual and leisured classes. See '"Hartly House, Calcutta": Allusions', 461. '[P]arterres' are ornamental arrangements of flower beds.

bricks: before 1772 the Company had a contract which supplied eleven inch bricks at 6s. 8d. a thousand, but the entrepreneurial Henry Watson (see p. 93) suggested that he might be awarded the contract as he intended to make bricks with the clay excavated in his construction of the dockyards; see Charles Caraccioli, *The Life of Robert Lord Clive, Baron Plassey*, 4 vols (London: T. Bell, 1775–77), 4: 470–81.

134 *Moorshedabad [...] near this city is the Gentoo university I have already mentioned*: Sophia is a little confused here. At p. 74 she had referred to 'the Gentoo university at Benares', which is (according to Rennell, *Description of the Roads in Bengal and Bahar*, p. 86) some 366 miles from Murshidabad. She must here be referring to another centre of Sanskritic learning, Nadia or Nabadwip, an ancient capital of Bengal, approximately 57 miles from Murshidabad. It was at the University of Nadia that Sir William Jones learned Sanskrit with the help of Pandit Ramlochan; see *Letters*, 2: 680–86, 754.

mal-à-propos: inappropriate.

Beville: 'Bevil' is the usual spelling for the young male lead in Steele's *The Conscious Lovers*.

135 *the Madeiras*: this was a usual port of call for East Indiamen; Gibbes relies here again on Guthrie, *A New Geographical, Historical, and Commercial Grammar*, pp. 751–2. Jones arrived here on 1 May 1783, and was entertained 'at the house of the Consul Mr. Murray'; *Letters*, 2: 618.

136 *St. Johanne [...] Dukes and Marquisses*: Sophia mentions that the large casks or 'pipes' of Madeira often arrived in England 'having twice doubled the Cape'. Johanna (Anjouan) belongs to the Comoros islands on the eastern coast of Africa. Jones arrived here on 28 July 1783 and, in his 'Remarks on the Island of Hinzuan or Johanna', noted: 'some (of the natives) appeared vain of the titles which our countrymen had given them in play, according to their supposed stations: we had *Lords, Dukes,* and *Princes* on board', *Asiatick Researches,* 2 (1790), repr. in *Representing India,* 8: 77–107; 78.

St. Helena: this island had been in the possession of the East India Company since 1600, and was maintained for the re-provisioning of East Indiamen (generally on their homeward voyage), but it is in the South Atlantic on the west coast of Africa.

Balagant: Balaghat; cf. 'the mountains of Balagate, which run almost the whole length of India from north to south, they are so high that they stop the western monsoon', Guthrie, *A New Geographical, Historical, and Commercial Grammar,* p. 690.

136–7 *Madras [...] spoiling their cloaths*: cf. William Hodges' experience of landing at Madras in a: 'Massoolah boat: a work of curious construction [...] they are formed without a keel, flat bottomed, with the sides raised high, and sewed together with the fibres of the cocoa-nut tree, and caulked with the same material: they are remarkably light, and managed with great dexterity by the natives: they are usually attended by two kattamarans (rafts) paddled by one man each, the intention of which is, that, should the boat be overset by the violence of the surf, the persons in it may be preserved', Hodges, *Travels in India,* repr. in *The European Discovery of India,* 3: 4. Neither Hodges, nor any other sources I can find, mentions the idea of capital punishment for the boatmen in the event of a European drowning.

137 *White and Black Towns*: cf. Charles Theodore Middleton, *A New and Complete System of Geography,* 2 vols (London: J. Cooke, 1778–79), 1: 157. Gibbes appears unaware that Calcutta was similarly segregated.

Table Bay: back to the Cape; again the geographical ordering of Sophia's voyage is awry. Cf. Thomson's note on fire-flies, *The Seasons,* p. 87.

The Line: on 'crossing the Line', i.e. the equator; see Sir George Staunton, *An Authentic Account of an Embassy from the King of Great Britain to the Emperor of China,* 2 vols (London: G. Nicol, 1797), 1: 142ff.

138 *nem. con.*: (*nemine contradicente*) no one speaking against.

life is a chequered scene: cf. Hugh Blair, *Sermons,* 7th edn. (W. Strahan, T. Cadell, and W. Creech, 1779), p. 430.

139 *we rise or sink with our company*: Philip Dormer Stanhope, Earl of Chesterfield, *Maxims* (Ludlow: T. Knott; and London: Champante and Whitrow, 1799), p. 30.

poor monk's box: despite her aversion to snuff, Sophia compares her romantic memento with the exchange of snuff boxes in Laurence Sterne's *A Sentimental Journey through France and Italy,* 2 vols (London: T. Becket and P. A. De Hondt,

1768), 1: 56–7. Cf. the exchange of a snuff-box and a betel box in Bernardin de Saint Pierre, *The Indian Cottage*, pp. 84–5.

140 *Rosamond at Woodstock*: this celebrated affair had been recently dramatized at Covent Garden; see Thomas Hull, *Henry the Second; or, the Fall of Rosamond: a Tragedy*, 4th edn. (London: Bell, 1774).

141 *revolution in the ornamentals of gardens*: Sophia's Indian revolution in garden design will rival that of Sir William Chambers' Chinese emphasis in his influential *Dissertation on Oriental Gardening* (1772).

142 *miserable with a good grace*: cf. 'they [princesses] ought to resolve to be miserable with a good grace', Laurent Angliviel, M. de La Beaumelle, *Memoirs for the History of Madame de Maintenon*, 3 vols (Dublin: Bradley, 1758), 2: 17.

Belate Be Bee-the English lady: 'Billattee': Europe; 'beebee' [or 'bibi']: lady; see George Hadley, *A Compendious Grammar of [...] the Jargon of Hindostan, (commonly called Moors)*, 4th edn. (London: Sewell, 1796), pp. 177; 224.

Sab: 'Sahib, s. The title by which, all over India, European gentlemen, and it may be said Europeans generally, are addressed, and spoken of, when no disrespect is intended, by natives', *Hobson-Jobson*.

143 *When my Bramin was alive*: having reacted with great emotional *mobilité* to the new 'danger at Calcutta', i.e. 'Beville', whom she is courting vicariously for Arabella, it is interesting that her self-psychologizing now associates 'my Bramin' with the 'strange wild desire to outshine all my female acquaintances'.

Zara: Aaron Hill, *The Tragedy of Zara* (1736), an adaptation of Voltaire's *Zaire* (1732). Hill had written *A Full and Just Account of the Present State of the Ottoman Empire* (1709), after spending three years at Constantinople with Lord Paget, his relative and the English ambassador; see *Oxford DNB*. This is a significant choice of play for Sophia to watch at this stage in the novel, concerned as it is with interfaith relationships, sexual jealousy, virtue, and accusations of infidelity.

145 *For as the twig is bent, the tree's inclin'd*: Alexander Pope, *An Epistle to the Right Honourable Richard Lord Visct. Cobham* (London: Lawton Gilliver, 1733 [1734]), l. 102; p. 6.

148 *petits soupers*: light suppers for a few intimate acquaintances.

149 *Oh talk not to me of the wealth she possesses*: Isaac Bickerstaff, *Lionel and Clarissa. A Comic Opera* (London: Griffin, 1768), II. i; p. 27.

Lord Cornwallis: Charles, Marquess Cornwallis (1738–1805) was appointed governor-general under the terms of William Pitt's East India Act (1784) with a brief to eradicate corruption. He was also appointed commander-in-chief in India: see *Oxford DNB*.

Hereditary advantages [...] self-ennobled individual: Gibbes uses this opportunity to supply a further compliment to Hastings, and a characterization of India as a 'land of commerce and plain understanding'.

150 *sons of Omar*: See nn. to pp. 90 and 115 above.

151 *nolens volens*: willy-nilly, willing or unwilling.

153 *My shepherd is kind and my heart is at ease*: Moses Mendez, *The Chaplet. A Musical Entertainment*. (London: M. Cowper, 1749), p. 22.

154 *French leave*: to depart without notice or permission.

155 *Lord C— is arrived*: he arrived in Calcutta on 10 September 1786, not October as *Oxford DNB* has it.

baise-mains: kisses of the hand, compliments.

large assortments of Eastern manufactures: captains and officers of East Indiamen were allocated space for their own 'investment' cargoes.

simplex munditiis: '[L., lit. 'simple in your adornments' (Horace *Odes* I. v. 5).] Unostentatiously beautiful; elegantly simple', *OED*.

so well have I instructed him: the Brahman's tenets live on, suitably sentimentalized in Sophia's tender teaching of Doyly, who finds it as difficult to swat a mosquito as his instructress does to contemplate 'a fishing party'. It was said of Hastings that he tried to avoid stepping upon ants when in his garden at Daylesford.

156 *libations to Neptune*: drinking toasts to the Graeco-Roman god of the sea for her safe voyage.

give such an Irishism your passport: permit such an apparent self-contradiction.

157 *wives are now chosen [...] from among these India-born ladies*: Sophia makes clear that 'men of nice feeling' choose 'country-born' wives in preference to 'fishing-fleet' adventurers. See also p. 15. One of the 'readers' who consults Gibbes's 'Benevolent Society' is Lavinia whose mother, desirous that her daughter should be a lady, is determined to give 'her daughter an opportunity of captivating a nabob'. She laments: 'What kind of soul must that girl possess, who is capable of submitting to have applications made in her name to the East India Company for credentials, to ensure her some degree of estimation in a country to which she voluntarily and declaredly transports herself for the purpose of obtaining a husband?' In a typically practical manner, the next month sees Mrs Brereton, a member of the Society, determined to settle a small annuity upon Lavinia and take her as a 'worthy companion', *The London Magazine, or Gentleman's Intelligencer*, 38 (June 1769), 304–5; (July 69), 367.

Hymen: the Graeco-Roman god of marriage.

158 *to have been a Nabobess*: all Sophia's former reservations concerning Islam dissolve in the magnificence of the procession of Mubarak ud-Daula.

taken umbrage: have resented. The etymology of 'umbrage' (L. *umbra*, a shadow), together with her use of the word 'reflection', emphasises Sophia's assertion that such Asiatic splendour puts 'London sights' in the shade.

158–9 *Seven elephants [...] master to alight*: this section was plagiarized as news in the Principal Occurrences section of *The New Annual Register, or General Repository of History, Politics, and Literature, for the Year 1790*, 1791, 21–22. Three paragraphs of description are taken verbatim from Gibbes, and content from two others is slightly rearranged, excluding only Sophia's enthusiasm for the 'fine-looking' black guards, her thrill at becoming the object of the Nabob's attention, and her desire to have an elephant at her command; see Introduction, pp. xix–xx.

sumpter-horses: pack-horses.

159 *instead of verandas, fine glass plates*: the use of 'verandahs' is an error for Venetian blinds (cf. her description of a palanquin on p. 8), possibly caused by the printer's difficulty in reading Gibbes's hand-writing. As for the reference to glass plate, apart from the fact that glass was extremely expensive [see p. 13] (which wouldn't trouble the Nawab), Gibbes herself had pointed out that palanquins have blinds rather than glass, and this for the obvious reason that they would prove much cooler. Although I have failed to find any description of a palanquin with glass windows, I am reluctant to conclude that this is a piece of Gibbesian embroidery as, in the palace of the Maharajah of Benares at Ramnagar, there is an elegant state howdah [canopied seat borne on the back of an elephant] which is fully glazed for use in the monsoon season.

half-reasoning elephant: cf. 'half reas'ning elephant', Pope, *An Essay on Man*, l. 214; p. 17.

bomb-shells: '*The Calcutta Gazette* of November 30, 1786, records that when the Nabob of Moorshedabad visited the Fort in company with the Governor-General "on this occasion the great guns were exercised and several shells thrown, at which His Excellency the Nabob expressed much satisfaction."'; see *Hartly House, Calcutta; A Novel of the Days of Warren Hastings*, p. 367. On Saturday, 17 March 1787, Cornwallis was given a display of artillery firing at Dum-Dum Camp, four miles north-east of Calcutta: 'Colonel Pearse clearly showed that shells, carcasses, and smoak balls can be thrown with as much facility and certainty from guns and howitzers as from mortars', *Calcutta Gazette*, 22 March 1787, *Selections from Calcutta Gazettes of the Years 1784, 1785, 1786, 1787, and 1788*, ed. W.S. Seton-Karr (Calcutta: Military Orphan Press, 1864), pp. 199–200.

aid-de-camp: Cornwallis's aides-de-camp at this time were Captain Charles William Madan [see n. to p. 48 above], and Captain Harry Haldane.

160 *Lady Wortley Montagu*: Having described the splendid retinue of 'his *Sublimity*', she continues: 'The Sultan appeared to us a handsome man of about forty, with something, however, severe in his countenance, and his eyes very full and black. He happened to stop under the window where we stood, and (I suppose being told who we were) looked upon us very attentively, so that we had full leisure to consider him'; see Lady Mary Wortley Montagu, *Letters written during her travels in Europe, Asia and Africa*, 3 vols (London: Becket and De Hondt, 1763), 2: 22.

ship [...] of three decks: 'The *Marquis Cornwallis* was a three-masted, square-rigged ship, the standard for the vast majority of ocean-going ships of the time. With three decks and weighing 586 tons, it had a length of 121 feet and a breadth of 36 feet. The ship, named for Lord Cornwallis, then Governor-General, was built in Calcutta in 1789, and in 1793, Hogan & Co., its owners, commissioned Solvyns to paint the "*The Marquis Cornwallis*, An East Indiaman"', Robert L. Hardgrave, *Boats of Bengal: Eighteenth-Century Portraits by Balthasar Solvyns* (New Delhi: Manohar, 2001), pl. I. 8. It is possible, however, that Gibbes is referring to an earlier ship named *Cornwallis*. *The Calcutta Monthly Register* carried an account of the loss of the *Cornwallis* in a storm on 27 December 1789 in the Madras roads, describing it as 'one of the finest ships that had ever been built at Pegue' [in what is now lower Burma], (1790), 31–32.

162 *bright regions of eternity*: cf. 'the ineffable Pleasures of the bright Regions of Eternity!', Jane Barker, *A Patch-work Screen for the Ladies; or, Love and Virtue Recommended* (London: E. Curll; and T. Payne, 1723), p. 119.

Sentimental sorrow: 'The poor and the busy have no leisure for sentimental sorrow', *The Beauties of Samuel Johnson, LL.D.* (London: G. Kearsley, 1787), p. xxvii.

condign: deserved, appropriate. 'Johnson 1755 says, 'It is always used of something deserved by crimes', *OED*. It is instructive to consider Sir William Jones's remarks to the Supreme Court Jury about a murder committed by soldiers in Patna: 'The woman, who will repeat her sad story to you, actually saw her husband, a native peasant, stabbed by one soldier, while two held him; (and how highly it imports the honour of our government, that the natives be protected from the outrages of our soldiery, must be obvious to all) but the night was too dark for her to distinguish their faces', 'Charge to the Grand Jury, at Calcutta, June 10, 1787', *Works*, 7: 22–31; 23.

an officer in the army: the appalling crime of the rape of a native girl and the murder of her father, together with Gibbes's comment that such outrages are 'much oftener perpetrated than detected', provide a sobering reflection for both Sophia Doyly and the reader concerning the realities of colonial violence.

Select bibliography

Books by Phebe Gibbes

The Life and Adventures of Mr Francis Clive, 2 vols (London: Lowndes, 1764).

The History of Lady Louisa Stroud, and the Honourable Miss Caroline Stretton, 2 vols (London: printed for, and sold by, F. Noble and J. Noble, 1764).

The Woman of Fashion: or, the History of Lady Diana Dormer, 2 vols (London: printed for J. Wilkie, 1767).

The History of Miss Pittborough. In a series of letters. By a Lady, 2 vols (London: printed for A. Millar, and T. Cadell; and J. Johnson and Co., 1767).

The Fruitless Repentance; or the History of Miss Kitty Le Fever, , 2 vols (London: Newbery, 1769).

The History of Miss Eliza Musgrove, 2 vols (London: Johnston, 1769).

The History of Miss Sommerville, Written by a Lady, 2 vols (London: Newbery and Carman, 1769).

Modern Seduction, or Innocence Betrayed: Consisting of Several Histories of the Principal Magdalens, Received into that Charity since its Establishment. Very Proper to be Read by All Young Persons; as they Exhibit a Faithful Picture of those Arts most Fatal to Youth and Innocence; and of those Miseries that are the Never-Failing Consequences of a Departure from Virtue. By the author of Lady Louisa Stroud, 2 vols (London: Printed for F. Noble, near Middle-Row, Holbourne; and J. Noble, in St. Martin's Court, near Leicester-Square, 1777).

Friendship in a Nunnery; or, The American Fugitive. Containing a Full Description of the Mode of Education and Living in Convent Schools, both on the Low and High Pension: the Manners and Characters of the Nuns; the Arts Practised on Young Minds: and their Baneful Effects on Society at Large. By a Lady, 2 vols (London: J. Bew, 1778).

Elfrida; or, Paternal Ambition. A Novel. By a Lady, 3 vols (London: J. Johnson, 1786).

Zoriada: or, Village Annals. A Novel, 3 vols (London: T. Axtell, 1786).

The Niece; or, The History of Sukey Thornby. A Novel, 3 vols. By Mrs. P. Gibbes.

Author of The History of Lady Louisa Stroud (London: Printed for F. Noble, at his Circulating Library, No. 324, Holborn, 1788).

Hartly House, Calcutta, 3 vols (London: J. Dodsley, 1789).

Jemima. A Novel (London: Printed for William Lane, at the Minerva-Press, Leadenhall-Street, 1795).

Heaven's Best Gift. A Novel, 4 vols. *By Mrs Lucius Phillips, a Near Relation to Major General Phillips* (London: printed for the Author, and Sold by W. Miller, n.d. [1798]).

Letters

BL MSS: Royal Literary Fund 2: 74

Biographical, bibliographical, and critical studies

Aravamudan, Srinivas, *Enlightenment Orientalism: Resisting the Rise of the Novel* (Chicago and London: University of Chicago Press, 2012).

Basham, A. L., 'Sophia and the "Bramin"', in *East India Company Studies: Papers Presented to Prof. Sir Cyril Philips*, Kenneth Ballhatchett and John Harrison, eds (London: SOAS, 1987), pp. 13–30.

Batchelor, Jennie, *Women's Work: Labour, Gender, Authorship, 1750–1830* (Manchester: Manchester University Press, 2010).

Blain, Virginia, Patricia Clements, and Isobel Grundy, eds, *The Feminist Companion to Literature in English: Women Writers from the Middle Ages to the Present* (London: Batsford, 1990).

Buettner, Elizabeth, 'Problematic Spaces, Problematic Races: defining "Europeans" in late Colonial India', *Women's History Review*, 9: 2 (2000), 277–98.

Couturier, Maurice, *Textual Communication, A Print-based Theory of the Novel* (London: Routledge, 1991).

Crane, Ralph J. and Radhika Mohanram, *Imperialism as Diaspora: Race, Sexuality, and History in Anglo-India* (Liverpool: Liverpool University Press, 2013).

Dyson, Ketaki Kushari, *A Various Universe: A Study of the Journals and Memoirs of British Men and Women in the Indian Subcontinent, 1765–1856* (Delhi: Oxford University Press, 1978).

Foster, William, 'Who Wrote Hartly House?', *Bengal Past and Present*, 15 pt. 2, no. 30 (1917), 28–29.

Franklin, Caroline, 'The Novel of Sensibility in the 1780s', in *The Oxford History of the Novel in English, vol. 2: English and British Fiction 1750–1820*, ed. Peter Garside and Karen O'Brien (Oxford: Oxford University Press, 2015), pp. 164–81.

Franklin, Michael J., '"Hartly House, Calcutta: Allusions": A Century-Late Response', *Notes & Queries*, NS 55: 4 (December 2008), 459–61.

Franklin, Michael J. 'Radically Feminizing India: Phebe Gibbes's *Hartly House, Calcutta* (1789) and Sydney Owenson's *The Missionary: An Indian Tale* (1811), in *Romantic Representations of British India*, Michael J. Franklin, ed. (London: Routledge, 2006), pp. 154–79.

Freeman, Kathryn S., '"She had eyes and chose me": Ambivalence and Miscegenation in Phebe Gibbes's *Hartly House, Calcutta* (1789)', *European Romantic Review*, 22: 1, (2011), 35–47.

Freeman, Kathryn S., 'Confronting Sacrifice, Resisting the Sentimental: Phebe Gibbes, Sydney Owenson, and the Anglo-Indian Novel', in *British Women Writers and the Asiatic Society of Bengal, 1785–1835* (Farnham: Ashgate, 2014), pp. 63–94.

Ghose, Indira, *Women Travellers in Colonial India: The Power of the Female Gaze* (Delhi: Oxford University Press, 1998).

Green, Katherine Sobba, *The Courtship Novel 1740–1820: A Feminized Genre* (Lexington: University Press of Kentucky, 1991).

Grundy, Isobel, '"The barbarous character we give them": White Women Travellers Report on Other Races', *Studies in Eighteenth-Century Culture*, 22 (1992), pp. 73–86.

Grundy, Isobel, '(Re)discovering women's texts', in *Women and Literature in Britain, 1700–1800*, Vivien Jones, ed. (Cambridge: Cambridge University Press, 2000), pp. 179–96.

Grundy, Isobel, with Patricia Clements (Director), Sharon Balasz, Susan Brown, Rebecca Cameron, Kathryn Carter, Renee Elio, and Dave Gomboc, 'Delivering Childbirth', 'Orlando Project Encoding', www.ualberta.ca/ORLANDO/Child birth.htm

Grundy, Isobel, Corrinne Harol, and Susan Brown, *Orlando: Women's Writing in the British Isles from the Beginnings to the Present* http://orlando.cambridge. org/public/svPeople?person_id=gibbph

Joseph, Betty, *Reading the East India Company, 1720–1840: Colonial Currencies of Gender* (Chicago and London: University of Chicago Press, 2004).

Khan, Maryam Wasif, 'Enlightenment Orientalism to Modern Orientalism: the Archive of Forster's A Passage to India', *Modern Fiction Studies*, 62: 2, (Summer 2016), 217–35.

London, April, *Women and Property in the Eighteenth-Century English Novel* (Cambridge: Cambridge University Press, 1999).

Malhotra, Ashok, *Making British Indian Fictions 1772–1823* (Basingstoke: Palgrave, 2012).

Messenger, Ann, *His and Hers, Essays in Restoration and Eighteenth-Century Literature* (Lexington: University Press of Kentucky, 1986).

Nussbaum, Felicity A., *Torrid Zones: Maternity, Sexuality, and Empire in Eighteenth-Century English Narratives* (Baltimore and London: John Hopkins University Press, 1995).

Nussbaum Felicity, A. '"An affectionate and Voluntary Sacrifice": Sati, Rape, and Marriage in British Narratives of the East', *Nineteenth-Century Contexts*, 19: 4 (1996), 347–71.

Pratt, Mary Louise, *Imperial Eyes: Travel Writing and Transculturation* (London: Routledge, 1992).

Rajan, Balachandra, 'Feminizing the Feminine: Early Women Writers on India', in *Romanticism, Race and Imperial Culture, 1780–1834*, Sonia Hofkosh and Alan Richardson, eds (Bloomington and Indianapolis: Indiana University Press, 1996), pp. 49–72.

Rajan, Balachandra, *Under Western Eyes: India from Milton to Macaulay* (Durham, NC, and London: Duke University Press, 1999).

Rangarajan, Padma, *Imperial Babel: Translation, Exoticism, and the Long Nineteenth Century* (New York: Fordham University Press, 2014).

Raven, James, 'The Anonymous Novel in Britain and Ireland, 1750–1830', in *The Faces of Anonymity: Anonymous and Pseudonymous Publication from the Sixteenth to the Twentieth Century*, Robert J. Griffin, ed. (London: Palgrave, 2003).

Raven, James, and Antonia Forster, eds. Volume I: 1770–1799 of *The English Novel, 1770–1829: a Bibliographical Survey of Prose Fiction Published in the British Isles*, 2 vols, Peter Garside, James Raven, and Rainer Schöwerling (general eds) (Oxford: Oxford University Press, 2000).

Regan, Marguerite, 'Feminism, Vegetarianism and Colonial Resistance in Eighteenth-Century British Novels', *Studies in the Novel*, 46: 3 (Fall 2014), 275–92.

Reynolds, Nicole, 'Phebe Gibbes, Edmund Burke, and the Trials of Empire', *Eighteenth-Century Fiction*, 20: 2 (Winter 2007–8), 151–76.

Shah, Priya J., '"Orientalised at all points": Sensibility and Consumption in *Hartly House, Calcutta*', *South Asian Review*, 30: 2 (2009), 98–118.

Sharpe, Jenny, *Allegories of Empire: The Figure of Woman in the Colonial Text* (Minneapolis: University of Minnesota Press, 1993).

Teltscher, Kate, *India Inscribed: European and British Writing on India 1600–1800* (Delhi: Oxford University Press, 1995).

Tierney, James E., ed., *The Correspondence of Robert Dodsley: 1733–64* (Cambridge: Cambridge University Press, 2004).

Todd, Janet, ed., *A Dictionary of British and American Women Writers 1660–1800* (Totowa, NJ, Rowman and Littlefield, 1987).

Tompkins, J.M.S., *The Popular Novel in England: 1770–1800* (Lincoln, Nebraska: University of Nebraska Press, 1961).

Turner, Cheryl, *Living by the Pen: Women Writers in the Eighteenth Century* (London: Routledge, 1992).

White, Daniel E., *From Little London to Little Bengal: Religion, Print, and Modernity in Early British India, 1793–1835* (Baltimore: The Johns Hopkins University Press, 2012).

Printed in the USA
CPSIA information can be obtained
at www.ICGtesting.com
LVHW041420230424
778203LV00002B/241